Enlightened Martyrdom

Enlightened Martyrdom
The Hidden Side of Falun Gong

Edited by
James R. Lewis and Huang Chao

SHEFFIELD UK   BRISTOL CT

Published by Equinox Publishing Ltd.

UK: Office 415, The Workstation, 15 Paternoster Row, Sheffield, South Yorkshire, S1 2BX
USA: ISD, 70 Enterprise Drive, Bristol, CT 06010

www.equinoxpub.com

First published 2019

© James R. Lewis, Huang Chao and contributors 2019

All rights reserved. No part of this publication may be reproduced or transmitted in any form or by any means, electronic or mechanical, including photocopying, recording or any information storage or retrieval system, without prior permission in writing from the publishers.

British Library Cataloguing-in-Publication Data
A catalogue record for this book is available from the British Library.

ISBN-13 978 1 78179 498 2 (hardback)
         978 1 78179 499 9 (paperback)
         978 1 78179 804 1 (ePDF)

Library of Congress Cataloging-in-Publication Data
Names: Lewis, James R., editor. | Chao, Huang, editor.
Title: Enlightened martyrdom : the hidden side of Falun Gong / edited by James R. Lewis and Huang Chao.
Description: Sheffield, UK ; Bristol, CT : Equinox Publishing Ltd, 2019. | Includes bibliographical references and index.
Identifiers: LCCN 2018021712 (print) | LCCN 2018035441 (ebook) | ISBN 9781781798041 (ePDF) | ISBN 9781781794982 (hb) | ISBN 9781781794999 (pb)
Subjects: LCSH: Falun Gong (Organization)
Classification: LCC BP605.F36 (ebook) | LCC BP605.F36 E55 2018 (print) | DDC 299/.51—dc23
LC record available at https://lccn.loc.gov/2018021712

Typeset by S.J.I. Services, New Delhi

Contents

	Introduction *James R. Lewis and Huang Chao*	1
1.	The Religion and Politics of Falun Gong *Junpeng Li*	10
2.	The Doctrine of Li Hongzhi: Falun Gong – Between Sectarianism and Universal Salvation *David A. Palmer*	35
3.	From Spiritual Healing to Protest: Falun Gong's Emerging Culture of Martyrdom *Susan J. Palmer*	60
4.	Burning Faith: Interpreting the 1.23 Incident *James R. Lewis*	85
5.	Devil Killing and the Essence of Falun Gong *Fang Yong*	110
6.	The Self-contradictions in Li Hongzhi's Statements about Illness *Cao Yan*	125
7.	Scientific or Anti-scientific: A Critical Analysis of "Science" Discourses in Falun Gong *Wang Chengjun*	134
8.	"You Don't Want to Have That Kind of Thought in Your Mind": Li Hongzhi, Aliens, and Science *Stefano Bigliardi*	160

9. Falun Gong's Attack on Academic Freedom 195
    Helen Farley

10. Friendly Fire: How Falun Gong Mistook Me for
    an Enemy 213
    Heather Kavan

11. The Falun Gong Political Narrative: Creating the
    Illusion of So-called "Forced Organ Harvesting" 230
    Campbell Fraser

12. "Clarifying the Truth": Falun Gong's Media Strategies 244
    James R. Lewis

Index 260

Introduction

James R. Lewis and Huang Chao

> Falun Gong adepts are fearless of persecution and even seem, by their provocative acts, to deliberately seek it: persecution validates their doctrine and brings them closer to the salvation promised by Li Hongzhi. (Palmer 2001)

When it became evident that the People's Republic of China (PRC) was on the verge of banning the Falun Gong movement, Li Hongzhi, the movement's founder, and his family escaped China, relocating permanently in the United States. Subsequently, the dramatic crackdown on Falun Gong in 1999 made international headlines. From the safety of his new home, Master Li encouraged his followers left behind in the PRC to vigorously demonstrate against the Chinese government, even if it meant imprisonment or martyrdom. Alternately, he could, of course, have instructed his followers to just lie low and continue the practice secretly. Instead, he held this kind of cautious approach up for ridicule, e.g., "There are also many new practitioners who practice in hiding at home, afraid of being discovered by others. Just think: what type of heart is that?" (Li Hongzhi, cited in Palmer 2007, 253).

At a gathering in Canada in 2001 that was attended by the sociologist of religion Susan Palmer (not to be confused with the sinologist David Palmer), Li Hongzhi "congratulated the martyrs of Tiananmen Square who 'consummated their own majestic positions' and presumably earned posthumous enlightenment, or a crown of martyrdom: 'Whether they are imprisoned or lose their human lives for persevering in Dafa cultivation, they achieve Consummation'" (Susan Palmer 2003, 356). Palmer discusses the philosophy of karma and martyrdom behind these protests, and rightly notes that, "While

Western politicians, journalists and human rights groups respond to social justice arguments, for the practitioners themselves, it is spiritual and apocalyptic expectations that fuel their civil disobedience" (ibid., 349).

Further, Master Li actively discourages his followers from telling outsiders about his esoteric teachings; rather, he explicitly directs them to say that Falun Gong is just a peaceful spiritual exercise group being persecuted by the PRC. A quick internet search for "Falun Gong" reveals that they have succeeded in propagating their side of the story at the expense of the People's Republic of China. Another little-known fact about Falun Gong is that the group will vigorously protest any news story that disagrees with their point of view. Thus, for example, in response to an Associated Press (AP) piece in 2005, "Chinese Show off Repentant Falun Gong," practitioners staged a mass protest at AP headquarters in New York City, demanding that the report be withdrawn. In more recent years, Falun Gong has attempted to silence critical scholars, including three of the contributors to the present volume.

The present collection provides a comprehensive overview of Falun Gong: the movement's background, history, beliefs, and practices. But whereas previous treatments have generally tended to downplay Falun Gong's "dark side," in the following pages we have made an effort to include treatments of the less-palatable aspects of this movement. *Enlightened Martyrdom* will, in other words, provide a recap of what has been discussed in earlier scholarship, but will move forward to cover Falun Gong's subsequent conflicts, as well as the movement's strident efforts to muzzle critical analyses of its ideas and its struggle.

The lead chapter in the book, Junpeng Li's "The Religion and Politics of Falun Gong," applies the conflict-amplification model to the development of Falun Gong. Falun Gong emerged in the early 1990s as a health-enhancing practice and part of the state-sanctioned *qigong* movement in China. Faced with increasing state suspicion of *qigong* and fierce competition from other groups, it metamorphosed into a new religious movement in the mid-1990s. State efforts to keep Falun Gong out of the political realm had the effect of releasing the group's political potential and led to its campaign of "truth clarification," which further alerted the state to its ideological challenge and capacity to mobilize. Through a process of mutual feedback, the antagonism between the two parties culminated in religious violence and in Falun Gong's transformation into a political movement.

The second chapter, David A. Palmer's "The Doctrine of Li Hongzhi: Falun Gong – Between Sectarianism and Universal Salvation," proposes a brief analysis of the doctrine of Li Hongzhi (LHZ), the founder of Falun Gong. Four main themes dominate LHZ's writings: (1) an *apocalyptic theme*, stressing the moral decadence of humanity and the omnipresence of the forces of evil. In particular, extraterrestrials are infiltrating themselves in the body of humanity through modern science, the great enemy of virtue; the Buddhist prophecy of the imminent destruction of the world and inauguration of a new universal cycle is close to being fulfilled. (2) An exhortation to *rigorous spiritual discipline*, calling on followers to purify their hearts of all attachment to the things of this world. The gods have abandoned the orthodox religions of the past, which have already completely lost the spirit of the true Dharma. (3) A *messianic theme*: Li Hongzhi is the omniscient and omnipotent savior of the entire universe. He has revealed, for the first time in history, the fundamental Law of the universe, which is the only protection against the apocalypse. (4) A *sectarian practice:* Li Hongzhi's disciples must concentrate exclusively on Falun Gong; it is forbidden to read or even think about any other religion, philosophy, or school of thought or of *qigong*. They must devote themselves heart and soul to Falun Gong's psycho-physiological discipline; the perceptions and visions triggered by this practice are attributed to Li Hongzhi's supernatural power.

Susan J. Palmer's "From Spiritual Healing to Protest: Falun Gong's Emerging Culture of Martyrdom" explores Falun Gong's emerging resistance movement and the escalation of Master Li's apocalyptic ideology in response to the PRC's draconian measures of social control; factors which have stimulated a culture of martyrdom among his disciples. On the basis of field research and interviews with practitioners, this study proposes a four-phase model of conversion, culminating in an activist's commitment to the Master's call to serve in the protest demonstrations against the People's Republic of China's persecution of Falun Gong. Since Falun Gong's civil disobedience led to the death of over 343 practitioners in 2003 (and estimated deaths in the tens of thousands by 2016), it is important to analyze the process of conversion/commitment to the cause and the practitioners' own spiritual understanding of their activist efforts in a two-tiered resistance movement that is concerned both with global human rights and also with a cosmic battle between gods and demons, an apocalyptic process called *fa*-rectification.

On January 23, 2001, a small group of Falun Gong practitioners set themselves on fire in Tiananmen Square. One practitioner died in the square and four were seriously burnt (the youngest burn victim subsequently died in a hospital). The government quickly held up the incident as an act of "cult violence," while the Falun Gong movement just as quickly accused PRC authorities of having staged the incident in order to discredit Falun Gong. In "Burning Faith: Interpreting the 1.23 Incident" James R. Lewis sets out to assess the plausibility of these conflicting interpretations. Naturally, the two major parties to the controversy which forms the background for this incident dismiss each other's perspectives as self-evidently false. Specifically, PRC authorities consider that FLG's defenders have been duped by Falun Gong propaganda, while FLG supporters summarily dismiss everyone who gives serious consideration to the Chinese position as being either on Beijing's payroll or mindless zombies, and every single piece of accusation against them as Beijing-backed propaganda. Lewis restricts his analysis to discussing the strong points made by each side of this controversy regarding the details of the 1.23 Incident, and then puts forward evidence to support an alternative interpretation of the event.

Falun Gong practitioners claim that their most important task is to return human beings to their real (spiritual) home. As such, they consider Falun Gong's opponents to be devils, who are challenging the laws of the universe. In Falun Gong, it is believed that devils reside amongst the common people, posing a threat to Dafa (Dharma). As Fang Yong argues in "Devil Killing and the Essence of Falun Gong," some practitioners conclude that it is necessary to eliminate these devils, an interpretation which has led to the deaths of ordinary people. A clear distinction is made by Falun Gong practitioners between themselves and ordinary people. Part of the Falun Gong doctrine includes the idea that the common people should be thankful to Falun Gong for seeking to eliminate devils. The idea that devils reside in society leads to the real-life practice of "devil killing." This practice tells us not only that Falun Gong is intolerant of those who oppose its views; in essence, the organization is also operating in a way that threatens human safety.

Li Hongzhi, the leader of Falun Gong, asserts that medicine does not touch the source of illness, which is karma. All that medicine achieves is to drive bad karma back into the body, thus delaying the maturation of the "bitter fruits" of disease. With this in mind, Li recommends that his disciples relinquish medical therapy and simply bear the suffering of illness. Li also insists that alternative practices like *qigong* cannot be used to eliminate illness and bad karma; it is only Li himself who has the divine power to rid his disciples of their ailments. Additionally, Li indicates that he has the power to reintroduce bad karma to his disciples' bodies if they do not properly follow his doctrine. In "The Self-contradictions in Li Hongzhi's Statements about Illness" Cao Yan asks, how can the contradictions in Li's claims be resolved? Can he uphold his contention that he can totally eliminate bad karma if he also asserts that he can cause it to return to people? Such a statement implies that this karma was never completely removed in the first place; if it has ceased to exist, then surely it cannot be returned. It is argued here that Li's words are more than mere statements about illness; they are also used as a tool to facilitate control over his followers, as revealed in these contradictions.

As many researchers have argued, the use of science to justify beliefs has long been a popular "legitimation strategy" in new religions. In contrast with other new religions that have adopted science as a source of legitimation, however, Falun Gong's use of "science" discourse is confusing and inconsistent. While it is sometimes claimed by Falun Gong that its doctrines, creeds, and beliefs can be well explained by modern science, at other times its teachings are positioned as transcending the realm of natural science. Li Hongzhi has even gone as far as to suggest that science is responsible for many different types of modern social "disease" (including social and environmental problems). In "Scientific or Anti-scientific: A Critical Analysis of 'Science' Discourses in Falun Gong," Wang Chengjun offers critical reflections on the science-related discourses present in Falun Gong. First, he analyzes such science-related discourses, arguing that they fall into three different categories. Second, he traces these discourses back to their origins in order to suggest that, even if science-based legitimation of the faith is effective in persuading its practitioners, it is by no means successful in a wider sense. Finally, he concludes with some more specific remarks on the ways in which "science" discourses have been used by Falun Gong.

One of the most unusual claims made by Li Hongzhi is that technology and science were introduced to Earth by sinister aliens. Such aliens manipulate human beings, keeping them in a state of discord and corruption and planning eventually to take over the whole planet. Some of these aliens already live on Earth, disguised as human beings. Such teachings emerged initially in Falun Gong's literature, but were made visible to the public in a 1999 interview for *Time* magazine. These ideas have also been reiterated by Master Li at various conferences and in later texts. Master Li's "alien theory" or "alien theology" can be studied from a number of different perspectives. In "'You Don't Want to Have That Kind of Thought in Your Mind': Li Hongzhi, Aliens, and Science," Stefano Bigliardi focuses on alien-related claims made by Li Hongzhi in order to try to reconstruct their role within his teachings as a whole, looking in particular at his conceptualization of science.

In a progressive Western democracy such as Australia, academic freedom is something usually taken for granted. With impunity, academics can critique government policy, make a stand with or against matters considered important to society, or bring to light those things that may be unknown to members of the general public. In this environment, as an academic in the discipline of studies in religion at a major Australian university, Helen Farley wrote a number of book chapters about the then little-known Chinese movement Falun Gong. As a consequence, she attracted the attention of a member of that movement, who took exception to what she wrote. In "Falun Gong's Attack on Academic Freedom," Farley describes the systematic attempt made by that individual to discredit her as an academic and to have her dismissed from her employment. It describes her employer's responses to the event, and the responses of other academics, societies, and publications in the field. Upon further investigation, she discovered that she was not the first academic to have received this sort of treatment from aggrieved Falun Gong practitioners. Her chapter looks at how Falun Gong practitioners justify their persecution of academics who are seen to have presented Falun Gong in an unfavorable light.

In "Friendly Fire: How Falun Gong Mistook Me for an Enemy," Heather Kavan describes how Falun Gong members in Western countries have forged an identity for their spiritual path as a group subjected to human rights violations for simply doing breathing exercises. The new narrative re-cast their apocalyptic leader Li Hongzhi as a hero akin to Gandhi, who has mobilized millions of followers to nonviolently resist an oppressive regime. In accord with this story, practitioners have staged headline-generating events, dispatched thousands of press releases, and protested against any portrayal that is not in accord with their new image. But Li's writings to members tell a different narrative to the one told in the Western media. Drawing on her ethnographic research, Kavan discusses the differences between the group's public and private communications. Although practitioners revised their publicly proclaimed ideology to appeal to Western moral ideals of amelioration of suffering and personal freedom, these ideals were not part of their in-group communications. Rather, sacrifice, martyrdom, and exclusivity were intrinsic to members' beliefs and life choices. The chapter closes with an outline of the responses to her study. Kavan discusses the internet passages about her that resulted in several Falun Gong authors being banned from Wikipedia, and the lingering shadowy harassment of her. This harassment was an expression of Li Hongzhi's "stepping forward" ideology, in which practitioners must defend his version of the *fa* to compete for entry into heaven, only allowed for limited numbers.

The Falun Gong (FLG) organization has for the last several years placed stories of so-called forced organ harvesting as central to its sustained and concerted effort to undermine the Chinese government, and specifically the Communist Party of China. These claims have been comprehensively investigated by a team of internationally renowned experts in human organ transplantation, and have been dismissed as fabrications. Despite the fact that this expert group reached this conclusion, based on several trips to China, the FLG continues to lobby governments and international organizations with what it claims is evidence of ongoing mass murder of its members in China. There is a clear reason for this; the FLG has invested so much time and effort into promoting so-called forced organ harvesting as its central battleground theme, it must find ways to perpetuate these rumors, fearing loss of face in the international community. The FLG has been careful to position its members as victims, and has used this mentality throughout in order to present its case as an underdog against the might of China. In "The Falun Gong Political Narrative: Creating the Illusion of So-called 'Forced Organ Harvesting,'" Campbell Fraser explores the manifestations of this victim mentality, through an analysis of the FLG organization and its supporters.

The Falun Gong organization has been mostly successful at promoting itself to the world outside of mainland China as a peaceful spiritual exercise group that is being unfairly persecuted by the Chinese government. This is partly the result of denying or downplaying the aspects of Li Hongzhi's teachings that are vengeful, belligerent, and violent. However, as James R. Lewis argues in "'Clarifying the Truth': Falun Gong's Media Strategies," this is also the result of a conscious media strategy which involves, on the one hand, creating its own media outlets that focus on persecution and human rights themes and, on the other hand, deploying a sophisticated media strategy that takes advantage of anti-PRC sentiments in Western media.

References

Palmer, David A. 2001. "Falun Gong: Between Sectarianism and Universal Salvation," *China Perspectives*, 35, 14–24.

Palmer, David A. 2007. *Qigong Fever: Body, Science, and Utopia in China*. New York: Columbia University Press.

Palmer, Susan J. 2003. "Healing to Protest: Conversion Patterns Among the Practitioners of Falun Gong," *Nova Religio: The Journal of Alternative and Emergent Religions*, 6:2, 348–6.

James R. Lewis is a much-published researcher in the field of new religious movements, and is Professor of Philosophy at the School of Philosophy, Wuhan University, China. At present, he edits or co-edits four academic book series, and is the general editor for the *Alternative Spirituality and Religion Review*, and Associate Editor of the *Journal of Religion and Violence*. Recent publications include *New Age in Norway* (Equinox, 2017), *Cambridge Companion to Religion and Terrorism* (Cambridge University Press, 2017), and *Oxford Handbook of New Religious Movements* (Oxford University Press, 2016).

Huang Chao is an Associate Professor in the School of Philosophy, and Executive Director of the Research Center for International New Religions and Cults, at Wuhan University, China.

1. The Religion and Politics of Falun Gong[1]

Junpeng Li

This chapter investigates the escalation of the conflict between Falun Gong and the Chinese state, and argues that politics and religion are two interwoven elements in understanding the historical trajectory of the Falun Gong movement. By documenting the evolution of Falun Gong from a health-enhancing practice to a spiritual group, and eventually to a political organization aimed at overthrowing the communist regime, it shows how the interaction between Falun Gong's spiritual teaching and China's political ecology led to the politicization of the movement. In other words, the rather vague definitions of the "religious" and the "political" gradually highlighted the spiritual nature of Falun Gong, thereby releasing its political potential and resulting in its political confrontation with the communist state. Taking a chronological approach, this chapter begins with Falun Gong's rise as a *qigong* practice in the early 1990s. It then moves on to Falun Gong's metamorphosis into a spiritual group in the mid-1990s and transformation into a political movement in the late 1990s. To make sense of the state's campaign against Falun Gong and Falun Gong's confrontation with the state, I argue that we must examine both China's state–religion relations and Falun Gong's spiritual teaching.

---

1. This chapter draws on materials in Junpeng Li (2014).

Healing Practice

Falun Gong emerged as a member of the state-sanctioned *qigong* movement. Routinely taught by a charismatic leader and transmitted via a master/student lineage, *qigong* is a holistic health-enhancing technique that combines controlled breathing, meditation, and physical movement. *Qi* refers to the vital energy of the body, whereas *gong* denotes power or practice.

While *qigong* was not a completely new phenomenon, it was not until the late 1940s and the early 1950s that it emerged as a single category and was then able to spread to the wider society (Palmer 2007, 8). With the exception of the ten years of the Cultural Revolution, the state not only tolerated *qigong*, but also consciously promoted it. The national enthusiasm for paranormal abilities in the late 1970s and the early 1980s provided a further opportunity for *qigong*'s rise in popularity. Aware of the state's definition of religion and its hostility toward religious sects, the *qigong* circle downplayed its spiritual dimension, and actively sought recognition from the scientific community by labeling itself as a "somatic science." By the mid-1980s, there were between 60 million and 200 million *qigong* practitioners, and more than 2000 *qigong* groups, nationwide (Ownby 2003, 233–4).

Li Hongzhi was born into an ordinary family in northeast China in the early 1950s. In 1992, having worked as a security guard for many years, Li founded the Falun Gong Research Society (FGRS), and began to offer classes and give lectures. From May 1992 to December 1994, he taught 56 classes with a total of approximately 60,000 attendees (Clearwisdom.net 2004a). Lasting 7 to 10 days, and aimed at helping the participants practice Falun Gong and maintain their physical health, the classes usually started with Li treating the participants' physical diseases and clearing their meridians, and then proceeded with him installing an invisible Law Wheel in their lower abdomens and in other parts of the body (Zhang Weiqing and Qiao Gong 1999, 61). During this period, Li consistently distinguished Falun Gong from religion by promoting its health benefits.

In 1993, Li moved to Beijing and embarked on a national tour. Falun Gong still appeared to be nothing more than a *qigong* practice. In his lectures, Li not only avoided political issues, but also advised practitioners to preserve social stability and respect the law; he even appeared to be nationalistic (Ownby 2005, 208). As he himself acknowledged, "In the beginning, we spread the practice by teaching the *Fa* in the form of a low-level *qigong* that was for healing and keeping fit. That was because we needed to allow everyone a period of time to get to know it" (Li Hongzhi 2005b, 1).[2]

Li's strategy proved very effective, and a great number of practitioners found Falun Gong appealing solely for its health benefits. Indeed, it was not until the crackdown that most of the practitioners were shocked to learn that their daily practice was anything more than another traditional health-enhancing technique. Even today, many overseas practitioners come to Falun Gong for health reasons alone.

Li appeared to be well aware of the importance of being legitimized by the state. In 1993, the FGRS became a direct-affiliate branch of the state-sponsored *Qigong* Science Research Society of China (QSRAC), an official recognition enjoyed by only eleven *qigong* groups. In addition, Falun Gong donated to state-sponsored charities and spent lavishly to entertain state officials and others it deemed significant (Ye Hao 1999). Li offered free disease treatments to high-ranking state officials, as well as to persons decorated by the state. In turn, Falun Gong and its health benefits were recognized by the state. The official newspaper of the Ministry of Public Security (MPS) reported that most who received Li's treatment "saw remarkable improvements," and Li received a letter of thanks from a state-sponsored foundation (Clearwisdom.net 2004a). In 1992 and 1993, Falun Gong participated in the annual Oriental Health Exposition and created a sensation (Zhang Weiqing and Qiao Gong 1999, 76–8). Falun Gong even received approval and support from the top of China's power ladder (Fang 1999, 46).

2. The citation dates used in the text are those of the most recent publications. The original dates of speeches or writings are given in brackets in the References at the end of the chapter.

A Spiritual Group

Despite the state's efforts to confine *qigong* to the category of physical fitness techniques, as well as the *qigong* community's conscious self-promotion as a somatic science, the line between *qigong*'s healing attributes and its spiritual ingredients had never been impermeable. While on the surface the practice of *qi* merely appears to be controlled breathing, it can also refer to a certain type of mentality or state of consciousness. Moreover, throughout Chinese history *gong* in various forms has often contained more or less spiritual elements associated with Buddhism, Daoism, Confucianism, popular religion, and mysticism; many *gong*s cultivated the vital energy of the body with the ultimate goal of spiritual attainment. As Palmer (2007, 284–5) maintains, "[*Q*]*igong* leads inevitably to chains of belief; its organization builds itself outside of medical institutions to take on an increasingly religious form." Yang (2012, 113) goes further by claiming that "most *qigong* groups and practices are a form of implicit religion."

Although Li and his practitioners repeatedly claimed that Falun Gong was not a religion,[3] in the mid-1990s it underwent a dramatic transformation into a spiritual group. Li started criticizing other *qigong* masters and distancing Falun Gong from the *qigong* community. While spirituality had never been completely lacking, in the early stage it had fallen into the gray zone of morality and character; now it became the central message of Li's teaching. By the mid-1990s China had developed a dynamic religious market, and Falun Gong had to compete with approximately twenty major *qigong* groups. As Li's statement in the preceding section shows, Falun Gong's differentiation from the other popular *qigong* groups by reference to its spiritual components was a conscious strategic move.

On the one hand, ever since China's market-oriented economic reforms took off in 1978, laments for the loss of morality had

3. Falun Gong appears to have softened its stance and now acknowledges that it can be considered a religion in the Western context (Clearwisdom.net 2004b).

permeated people's daily conversations. In the 1990s, out of the shadow of Maoism and the 1989 Tiananmen incident, the demand for religion was rapidly growing. On the other hand, because of the state's tight control of the official religions and its suppression of the unofficial ones, seekers attempted to meet their spiritual needs with alternatives that fell between the sanctioned and the unsanctioned. The demand–supply imbalance propelled the formation of a huge gray market for quasi-religious products (Yang 2012, 85–158). Li did not shy away from condemning the perceived moral slide and Falun Gong was particularly appealing to the many Chinese who viewed the present social order as anomic.

However, spirituality had always been an integral part of Li's teaching. While Li initially spoke of Falun Gong as a type of *qigong* and repeatedly stated that it was not a religion, in *Falun Gong*, first published in 1993, he explicitly required its practitioners to "make cultivation of character their top priority and regard character as the key to developing *gong*" and stated that character "contains much more than virtue" (Li 2006a, 28). More important, the change took place in the context of increasing state suspicion and scrutiny of the *qigong* community. The state's unease with *qigong* began as early as the 1980s, but for a long time its policy toward it was "no promoting, no criticizing, no disputing." When Falun Gong emerged in the early 1990s, the state began to enforce control by appointing several former high-ranking CCP (Chinese Communist Party) officials to the leadership of the QSRAC. It was decreed that *qigong* groups had to register with the authorities, and CCP branches were established within these groups to distinguish "false" *qigong* from "scientific" *qigong* (Ownby 2008, 166; Yang 2012, 116–17).

Falun Gong's spiritual transformation can be analyzed in terms of eight aspects. First, Li consciously differentiated Falun Gong from the rest of the *qigong* community. During this period, he more than once accused other *qigong* groups of charlatanism and chided them for their obsession with *qi* to the neglect of the higher cosmic power, represented by *gong* and *fa*: "Falun Dafa disciples aren't allowed to do [healing]. … When it comes to true higher things, among the masses of *qigong* cultivators nobody really has a clue, no clue at

The Religion and Politics of Falun Gong 15

all. Starting today, what we're going to explain are all Laws of high levels" (Li Hongzhi 2003a, 43–4, 4).

Second, Li explicitly stated that Falun Gong was not a *qigong*, and changed its formal name to Falun Dafa, the Great Way of the Law Wheel, in an effort to emphasize that the practice went far beyond physical exercises by increasing spiritual awareness. Moreover, Falun Gong formally seceded from the *qigong* movement by withdrawing from the QSRAC.[4] Li ceased to teach in person in China in 1994 and overseas in 1995, in order to spread his spiritual messages at a higher level (Ye Hao 1999).

Third, Li sanctified *Zhuan Falun* as the primary scripture:

> [N]o matter how many more scriptures we publish, they are merely supplementary materials to *Zhuan Falun*. Only *Zhuan Falun* can truly guide your cultivation. It contains inner meanings that go from the level of ordinary people to incomparable heights. (Li Hongzhi 2002b)

> [I] have left man a ladder to heaven – *Zhuan Falun*. (Li 1999a)

As previously mentioned, the content of *Zhuan Falun* was not completely new in relation to Li's previous teaching. It takes no

---

4. Falun Gong and the state have issued conflicting statements regarding FGRS's withdrawal from the QSRAC. The state maintains that the QSRAC expelled FGRS in November 1996 because of Li's fraudulent conduct (Zhang Weiqing and Qiao Gong 1999, 104–6), whereas Falun Gong insists that it voluntarily severed its affiliation with the QSRAC in March 1996 on the grounds that Li had stopped offering classes and intended to devote himself exclusively to the *fa*, and that he was dissatisfied with the QSRAC's manner of operation (Ye Hao 1999). My comparison of a number of accounts indicates that Li did announce many times (as early as September 1994) that Falun Gong was no longer affiliated with *qigong* before the QSRAC officially revoked its registration. In addition, a statement from the QSRAC in September 1996 indicated that Falun Gong had "withdrawn of its own accord from" the QSRAC (Zhang Weiqing and Qiao Gong 1999, 111). Furthermore, the two accounts are not completely irreconcilable. Whichever side of the story one chooses to believe does not affect the point I am making here.

close reading to discern that the book's religious overtones are much stronger than Li's earlier lectures and the teachings of the other *qigong* masters. It was largely the sanctification of *Zhuan Falun* that led to Falun Gong's rupture with the *qigong* milieu. After 1994, the "reading, rereading, and eventual absorption of Li's teachings through his written materials ... constituted the core of Falun Gong practice" (Ownby 2005, 205). Most practitioners read *Zhuan Falun* every day, and many could recite it flawlessly. During the 1999 Tianjin and Zhongnanhai demonstrations, almost every sit-in protestor had a copy of *Zhuan Falun* at hand to read during the entire day, sometimes aloud. Moreover, Li (2005a, 176) forbade the practitioners to make any marks on his books, and especially not on sentences written by Li himself, claiming that his words are "beaming with golden light, and ... every character is a Law Body of [his]." My conversations with Falun Gong practitioners confirmed that they all followed this commandment literally, and many insisted that they could see the golden light in Li's words.

Fourth, Li developed a theological system in *Zhuan Falun*. Drawing largely on spiritual elements from Buddhism and *qigong*, Falun Gong also blended ingredients from Daoism and other popular religions. Its central tenet was the cultivation of one's character guided by *Zhen* (Truthfulness), *Shan* (Compassion), *Ren* (Forbearance), the fundamental components of the universe. Character included "the transformation of virtue ... and karma ..., the abandonment of ordinary human desires and attachments, and the capacity to endure the toughest hardships of all" (Li 2006b, 3). Li held that "when someone dies, ... only the ... layer of the largest molecules [of the dimension of his is] shed, while his bodies in other dimensions aren't destroyed" (Li Hongzhi 2003a, 15). Li incorporated apocalyptic themes by asserting that "there have been 81 times when mankind lay in total ruin" and that another cycle of destruction and renewal was imminent (ibid., 11, 58).

Fifth, salvation became the central message of Li's teaching; he claimed that Falun Gong was "saving all sentient beings" (ibid., 36). To the practitioners, Li was the way and the truth: "If I can't save you nobody can" (ibid., 161).

Sixth, Li's status was elevated to that of a messiah-like figure. As Wallis (1977, 248–50) observes, authority based on extraordinariness is contestable and therefore highly insecure. To convert extraordinariness into charisma and accord his authority a transcendental legitimation, Li penetrated the realm of the supernatural by transforming his status from a magician to a mystagogue (Weber 1993, 46–59), and eventually to a god. In the early 1990s, Li identified himself as an ordinary human teacher who had received guidance from more than twenty mysterious masters (Zhang Weiqing and Qiao Gong 1999, 33–44). Li's status quietly changed in *Zhuan Falun*, however, wherein he claimed that he had achieved the highest level of cultivation. According to government records, Li was born on July 27, 1952, but he has insisted that his real date of birth is May 13, 1951, which in the lunar calendar is the Buddha's birthday. Falun Gong also widely distributed photographs in which Li is seen dressed in a Buddhist saffron robe and sitting in the lotus position. In 1998, he further proclaimed, "No matter how vast this Dafa is, I am not within it, while all of you beings are within it" (Li Hongzhi 2004).

Li's self-deification appeared to peak in 1999 in an interview with *Time Asia*:

> *Time*: Are you a human being?
> Li: You can think of me as a human being.
> *Time*: Are you from earth?
> Li: I don't wish to talk about myself at a higher level. People wouldn't understand it. (Dowell 1999)

Indeed, many Falun Gong practitioners regarded Li as a true god and therefore above all other gods. Minghui.org includes numerous personal testimonies of Li's magic power. A practitioner told me that he survived a car accident because of Li's blessing.

Seventh, Li's authority was monopolized (Lu 2005, 181–2). Seemingly cautious about the danger of schism and subversion for spiritual groups, Li forbade the teaching of Falun Gong in another person's name, disapproved of other master–disciple relationships, and insisted that spiritual connections could only exist between the practitioners and him.

Eighth, Falun Gong established a pyramidal organizational structure. At the center was the FGRS in Beijing with Li as president. In the mid-1990s, Falun Gong established 39 principal assistance centers and tens of thousands of minor assistance centers in cities, counties, and villages, all with heads and assistants. The FGRS managed all relevant affairs and appointed the main leaders of the assistance centers, accompanied by a series of written rules and regulations.

Within a few years, Falun Gong rose to become arguably the largest *qigong* group in China (Palmer 2007, 219) and attracted more than 100 million practitioners worldwide, according to Falun Gong's own figures. Although the accuracy of this figure is questionable,[5] considering that it had been in existence for less than a decade, Falun Gong's success was indisputable. Li's first public lecture in Changchun in May 1992 was attended by merely 180 students. The number increased to 1,500 in his class in Beijing only five months later (Clearwisdom.net 2004a). By September 1994 Li was confident that there existed hundreds of thousands of practitioners nationwide (Li Hongzhi 2002a, 22). In 1996 alone, *Zhuan Falun* sold hundreds of thousands of copies, and became a bestseller in China. By 1999, it had been translated into nine languages. A comparison of the "questions and answers" sections of Li's pre- and post-*Zhuan Falun* lectures reveals that the practitioners were

---

5. The number of Falun Gong practitioners is disputed. Unlike many other religions, Falun Gong has no formal ritual of initiation or withdrawal from its community of practitioners (Porter 2003, 126–8). Falun Gong estimates that in 1999, at the outset of the crackdown, it had 100 million practitioners in more than 30 countries, and more than 70 million in China alone (Falun Dafa Information Center 2009). Since February 2001, the state has claimed a starkly different figure of 2 million Falun Gong practitioners, but Falun Gong sources insist that the state's internal estimate at the end of 1998 placed the figure at 70 to 100 million (Amnesty International 2000). I believe that Falun Gong's own claim is grossly exaggerated, whereas the state's estimate of 2 million is a serious underestimate. Palmer (2007, 259–61) compares and analyzes the conflicting estimates, with the conclusion that 10 million is a more reasonable number.

initially preoccupied with health enhancement, and that salvation had subsequently become their major concern.

A Political Movement

Falun Gong's success as a spiritual group foreshadowed the end of its honeymoon with the state and was the prelude to the crackdown. Although superficially harmless, Falun Gong's spiritual teaching posed a great challenge to the symbolic order of the authoritarian regime. What set it apart from many other potential subversives was its challenge to all three of the aforementioned bases of state legitimacy. In particular, Li disdained the utilitarian ideology and instrumental rationality promoted by the state in the 1990s, and more than once castigated the perversion of moral standards he associated with materialist consumerism. Falun Gong's cosmology went far beyond the prevailing narrow nationalism and ethnocentrism, and Li repeatedly asked practitioners to abandon all earthly attachments – let alone national and ethnic pride. While the state's high mobilization capacity enabled it to react swiftly to overt political subversives and crush nascent challenges, the perceptible, yet intangible, threat posed by a quasi-religious *qigong* practice was much more difficult for the state to quell in the name of social stability. Even though Li was careful not to condemn the political authorities prior to the crackdown, he was unwilling to take part in the symbolic order of the authoritarian apparatus (e.g., Falun Gong's withdrawal from the QSRAC).

The state's first measures against Falun Gong took place in 1994. In October, the Ministry of Civil Affairs (MCA) and the MPS disbanded the International Federation of Qigong Sciences, and arrested its founder. In December, the CCP called for the authorities to "unremittingly and lawfully fight" against "pseudoscience." The state-controlled media quickly responded and started a campaign in early 1995. Many stories were published about Falun Gong practitioners' psychosis, and parallels were drawn between *qigong* and Aum Shinrikyo, a doomsday sect that had recently carried out the sarin gas attack in Japan. He Zuoxiu, a prestigious physicist, and Sima Nan, a well-known journalist, who had both criticized *qigong* as pseudoscience, escalated their attacks on *qigong* and its supporters within the political establishment (Palmer 2007, 170–4). Later that year, the municipal authorities of Hangzhou, a major city in southeast China, for the first time banned the teaching of Falun Gong (Zhang Weiqing and Qiao Gong 1999, 105). An examination of Li's lectures during this period, however, shows that he appeared to be self-possessed and opposed to any aggressive response by Falun Gong practitioners. When asked about the appropriate action a practitioner should take in response to attacks, Li replied plainly, "Just ignore them. There is no need to argue or fight with them" (2005a, 146). In addition, he explicitly forbade practitioners to participate in demonstrations and other political activities: "[The practitioners] can't meddle in a country's politics and laws, and they shouldn't interfere with everyday people's affairs. … Aren't [actions such as marching] attachments that a cultivator should get rid of?" (2002a, 29).

Indeed, *Zhuan Falun* offered systematic theological explanations for hardship. First, a person's suffering resulted from the misdeeds of a previous life, and was therefore cosmic justice: "[The tribulations are] all caused by your own karmic debts … So from here on out, when you run into a conflict you shouldn't think that it's just by chance" (Li Hongzhi 2003a, 75–6).

Second, forbearance heralded the nonviolent gestures of Falun Gong: "To be a practitioner you should … be able to 'not hit back when attacked, not talk back when insulted.' You have to endure" (ibid., 190).

Third, when adverse circumstances arise, forbearance would bring virtue to a practitioner and get rid of his or her karma: "The worse [a persecutor smears] you, … the more virtue he loses, and that virtue is all given to you. … [Y]our own karma will get transformed … and it [will all turn] into virtue" (ibid., 78).

The political storm erupted in 1996. In June, the *Guangming Daily*, an influential national newspaper controlled by the CCP, published a pseudonymous commentary accusing *Zhuan Falun* of being a pseudoscientific book that spread feudal superstition. It was later disclosed that Pan Guoyan, a high-ranking official of the General Administration of Press and Publication, under the administration's authorization, had written the commentary (Duan Qiming 2006). More than twenty major newspapers quickly followed suit. This wave of attacks proved fatal, because Falun Gong and the whole *qigong* movement had gained official sanction and popular support largely under the guise of somatic science. With this identity in question, and in particular its estrangement from the scientific establishment, Falun Gong lost its legitimacy and protection. In July, the state promulgated an order banning the distribution of major Falun Gong publications. In September, the QSRAC issued a statement accusing Li of "wantonly deifying himself, wantonly spreading feudal superstition, and wantonly fabricating political rumors" (Zhang Weiqing and Qiao Gong 1999, 108), and in November it announced its revocation of Falun Gong's registration. Since October, Li had spent a substantial amount of time in the United States, and he eventually emigrated to the USA and was granted permanent resident status in 1998. In 1997 and 1998, the MPS twice ordered investigations into Falun Gong's activities.

Li was clearly aware of the unfavorable situation. In August 1996, he said, "From the incident with the *Guangming Daily* until now, ... some [disciples] have ... circulated rumors without any concern for Dafa's stability, worsening factors that undermine the Fa" (Li Hongzhi 2001a, 31). However, he still showed restraint: "I have repeatedly stressed that we have nothing to do with politics, that we are absolutely not meddling in politics, that we are absolutely not involved in politics. If Li Hongzhi were engaged in politics, what I am spreading today would be an evil practice" (Li Hongzhi 2007a). Deprived of the protection of the QSRAC and the scientific establishment, Falun Gong decided to seek legitimacy through other channels. Between April 1996 and late 1997, Falun Gong successively applied to the Ethnic Affairs Committee of the National People's Congress, the Buddhist Association of China, and the United Front Work Department of the CCP Central Committee, for registration as a "nonreligious Falun Gong academic mass

22   *Enlightened Martyrdom*

association," a "nonreligious Buddhist cultural group," and a "nonreligious Falun Gong academic association," respectively. Each application was rejected (Ye Hao 1999). Faced with an adversarial climate, Falun Gong began to loosen its organizational structure (Tong 2002, 641–2).

However, from the outset, Falun Gong practitioners had reacted to the attacks in a swift and serious manner. Immediately after the *Guangming Daily* incident, Falun Gong launched a letter-writing campaign that flooded the newspaper with thousands of letters in protest. The campaign received Li's endorsement in August, praising those who "wrote without reservation to the authorities for the sake of Dafa's reputation" and who "spoke out against the injustice done by the irresponsible report." More important, Li started to frame the political turbulence as a test of a practitioner's character (Li Hongzhi 2001a, 31–2). The most significant activity within Falun Gong's repertoire of contention, however, was demonstrations. Between June 1996 and April 1999, the practitioners mounted more than 300 peaceful demonstrations against the perceived media bias, demanding that "erroneous" information about Falun Gong be corrected (Ownby 2008, 169). However, up until May 1998, all demonstrations were limited to small gatherings. While praising those practitioners engaged in activism, Li (2001a, 31) also spoke highly of those who "were determined to steadfastly cultivate" and stayed at home.

The first major demonstration was staged in 1998 in response to He Zuoxiu's claim in an interview on Beijing Television (BTV) on May 24 that a doctoral student from his institute suffered from psychosis induced by Falun Gong. In the ensuing eight days, thousands of Falun Gong practitioners visited or wrote letters to BTV demanding "clarification." While insisting that "Dafa absolutely should not get involved in politics," Li changed his tone and framed the Beijing practitioners' protest as helping "the media understand [the] actual situation and learn about [Falun Gong] positively so that [the media] would not drag [the practitioners] into politics" (2001b, 49). Moreover, he began to reprimand those who stayed home: "What do you mean by [steadfast cultivation]? ... Do you mean that you didn't participate in it, and that you 'steadfastly did actual cultivation'? It sounds like you're trying to find excuses and justifications for missing an opportunity to reach Consummation. You're being crafty even with me" (Li Hongzhi 2004). At this point, Li began referring to the activism as "guarding the Law," which is indicative of how protest had become an essential aspect of cultivation (Palmer 2007, 253).

While Falun Gong was not the only *qigong* group to publicly protest against perceived media misrepresentation, the persistence and visibility of its activism was readily apparent. It should also be noted that during this period, Falun Gong's protests more often than not achieved their goals. For example, after the eight-day demonstration, the director of BTV apologized in private, fired the journalist who interviewed He Zuoxiu, and promised to air a positive report on Falun Gong (Zhang Weiqing and Qiao Gong 1999, 201). A number of newspapers which had criticized Falun Gong later issued statements of apology. A reflection of Falun Gong's tremendous social influence, these temporary and modest achievements in turn fed into Falun Gong's more aggressive activism. Between April 1998 and July 1999, Falun Gong launched at least twenty large demonstrations, each with more than 1,000 participants (Palmer 2007, 254–5).

This period of heightened activism reached its apogee in response to the publication of an essay by He Zuoxiu on April 11, 1999, entitled "I Do Not Approve of Teenagers Practicing *Qigong*" in a popular science magazine run by Tianjin Normal University. In the period April 18–24, more than 10,000 practitioners went to the university and other government agencies to "clarify the truth," with approximately 6,300 practitioners present at the climax. He Zuoxiu was inundated by telephone calls from practitioners demanding a "debate." On April 24, 45 practitioners were arrested and the police reportedly beat some up. When requesting the release of their detained fellows, the practitioners were told by the local police that they required approval from Beijing. On April 25, an estimated 10,000 to 30,000 practitioners assembled outside the CCP headquarters compound at Zhongnanhai in Beijing, and staged a 13-hour silent sit-in protest demanding the right to practice Falun

Gong and an end to police harassment. It was the largest demonstration in China since the Tiananmen Square protests of 1989 and had significant political repercussions.

Remarkably, from 1994 to the summer of 1999, most of the activists believed that the state was just misinformed, and their sole purpose was simply to inform the state that "Falun Dafa was good." They first sought out local governments, and upon learning that the local officials were only carrying out the state's orders, decided to seek justice from the center. Ironically, a direct but unintended consequence of these protests was the consolidation of the state's vigilance over Falun Gong's mobilization capacity and potential to mount an ideological challenge, in particular as displayed in the protest of April 25. As distinct from most other challengers, Falun Gong's mobilization was both cross-sectional and cross-regional, because it was able to recruit practitioners from different regions and social strata; this swiftly conjured up images of other religiously inspired uprisings of the past two centuries, such as the White Lotus and the Taiping Rebellion. Regarding the ideological challenge, the "siege" of the CCP headquarters inevitably "projected the image of a powerful alternative order ... not afraid of the [CCP]" (Palmer 2007, 295). While the practitioners boasted that "tens of thousands [of them] were [in Zhongnanhai] for one whole day and left no trash; not even a small piece of paper" (Xia Yun 2010), the perfectly peaceful and orderly nature of the collective action demonstrated that it was carefully calculated and had specific goals. In this sense, state repression did not come completely unexpected.

Three months later, the state officially outlawed Falun Gong. Labeling Falun Gong an "evil cult," the state escalated its campaign and mobilized its entire bureaucratic machinery to arrest the protestors, purge the practitioners, and crush the resistance. Falun Gong books, audiotapes, videotapes, and other paraphernalia were confiscated and destroyed. The propaganda apparatus was mobilized to denounce Falun Gong, alongside other quasi-religious groups and "fraudulent" *qigong* masters. Between July 22 and October 30, the police detained 35,000 Falun Gong practitioners in Beijing alone and sent approximately 2,000 practitioners to labor camps (Pomfret

1999).⁶ The crackdown marked the collapse of the entire *qigong* sector.

Notably, even immediately before and after the crackdown, Falun Gong took every opportunity to try to convince the state of its "apolitical" nature. In June 1999, a month prior to the ban, Li (2005c, 2) claimed, "[B]y no means do I want to get involved in ordinary human affairs, much less do I desire someone's political power." Li's statement (1999b) on July 22, two days after the ban, still conveyed the same message, even at the cost of contradicting his previous statements with respect to Falun Gong's relationship with *qigong*: "Falun Gong is simply a popular *qigong* activity. ... We are not against the government now, nor will we be in the future."

As the crackdown was underway, Li began to take an activist stance and responded more directly. The major task of practitioners changed from cultivation to "clarifying and spreading the truth" (Rahn 2002, 54): "[I]f the evil hadn't persecuted us, we wouldn't need to explain the truth to people whatsoever ... . When being treated unfairly, people should be allowed to speak – this is a human being's most basic right" (Li Hongzhi 2002c, 4).

In June 2000, Li began to directly criticize the CCP and Jiang Zemin, then China's highest political leader, who was widely believed to be directly responsible for launching the crackdown. Portraying the CCP as "evil wretches" (Li Hongzhi 2005d, 20) and Jiang as the "King of Terror" prophesied by Nostradamus (Li Hongzhi 2005e), Li started calling on practitioners to rectify the Great Law (Li Hongzhi 2005f), and castigated the bystanders:

> I feel sorry for those people who aren't able to step forward ... . There are also some people who say, "Why doesn't Master finish this sooner?" ... These people aren't even ashamed to say this! ... While Dafa encounters persecution, while disciples are being arrested, persecuted, and beaten to death ... , what are they doing? While their Master is being slandered, what are they doing? ... No matter how he "persists in studying the

---

6. The state insisted that it only arrested approximately 150 Falun Gong practitioners, including those being sought (Schoof 1999).

Fa and doing the exercises" at home, he is being controlled by demons and is "enlightening" along an evil path. (Li Hongzhi 2000)

In 2001, Li began to call on the practitioners to overthrow the communist regime:

> As long as the evil isn't completely eliminated …, we still need to keep doing even better. We must expose and eliminate the evil. Chinese people have been the biggest victims amidst the evil's damage. All the methods employed by the evil political gang of scoundrels in the Chinese government are the most despicable, the most evil, and unknown to history – they have reached the extreme, they couldn't possibly be worse. (Li Hongzhi 2002d, 15)

Li's speech in 2003 was virtually a fully fledged anti-communist manifesto:

> [I] don't want to defeat you, Communist Party, you're not worth it. It's you … [who] has caused your collapse while you have persecuted the people and the masses … . How wicked – could this regime still be allowed to exist? … [F]or those of you who haven't done well or who stepped forward late, … you must seize the final chance … . (Li Hongzhi 2003b)

By the early 2000s, Falun Gong had indeed evolved into a high-profile anti-CCP political movement. By asking the practitioners to let go of their "last attachments" (Li 2005d), Li began to lead Falun Gong's struggle along a revolutionary course. At this stage, political activism had become a necessary path to salvation, and Li's teaching had a huge influence on the practitioners' defiance of the state. As Johnson (2001) notes, "[I]nterviews with Falun Gong members in recent months reveal [a] more subtle source of pressure: the demands of … Li. [Li's recent writings have] stressed unwavering activism and opposition to the state … . While few complain, they say they can meet Mr. Li's requirements only by sacrificing everything, in a desperate … bid to force the government to lift its ban."

The practitioners had found in Li's teaching the "mytho-logics" which structured their emancipatory and anti-communist discourse. In other words, religion had become an effective tool for political mobilization against persecution, and politics and religion could not be separated any longer. Li (2007b) acknowledged the political nature of Falun Gong by then: "If people can be saved through politics, ... then we can make use of that form – what would be wrong with that?"

Discussion: Politics and Religion

This chapter highlights the blurry boundaries of politics and religion and their fatal interpenetration. After the founding of the People's Republic, the Chinese state's policies toward religion and civic organizations created a unique niche for *qigong*. In the early 1990s, after *qigong* successfully opened up a space in the gray zone between state and society, Falun Gong adopted a strategy of accommodation and emerged as a naturalistic, "scientific" *qigong* practice eschewing explicit spiritual teaching. In the mid-1990s, faced with increasing state suspicion of *qigong* and fierce competition from thousands of *qigong* groups, Falun Gong brought its spiritual dimension to the fore. This proved a huge success, as it met the needs of spiritual seekers in the gray market. Unsettled by Falun Gong's ideological challenge, the state began to take measures to keep the group out of the political realm. However, the minor irritations that ensued convinced the practitioners that the state was merely misinformed. To convince the state of its "apolitical" nature, Falun Gong launched a persistent "truth clarification" campaign, but the small-scale demonstrations further warned the state of Falun Gong's defiance of its symbolic order. The linkage and clustering of the events eventually exploded into the massive Zhongnanhai protest of 1999. Shocked by Falun Gong's mobilization capacity and ideological challenge, the state officially banned the group and has since harshly purged its practitioners. But the crackdown only served to fully release Falun Gong's political potential. While Li previously only vaguely referred to evil, the crackdown polarized and intensified Falun Gong's apocalyptic message, which now unequivocally views the CCP as a nefarious force. Falun Gong in exile has become a major anti-CCP force that has launched waves of political activities aimed at the overthrow of the CCP.

The conflict between Falun Gong and the state brings us to the question of what is political under authoritarian rule, as the escalation of the level of conflict can be seen as a result of conflicting interpretations of what counts as "political" and "religious." In communist China, the political (and similarly the religious) is never a separate sphere in society, but always intersects with other social phenomena; politicization is not an event, but a process in flux (Kipnis 2008, 139–56). This case also reveals the importance of interpretations of social reality and the significance of the institutionalization of a certain interpretation. As Weller (1994) maintains, authoritarianism does not preclude independent interpretations; moreover, official interpretations are ultimately thin and feeble. The politicization of Falun Gong was a direct consequence of the state's effort to control the interpretive community. Falun Gong grew explosively under interpretive ambiguity. The confrontation was triggered by the state's imposition of official interpretations of Falun Gong's religious and political nature, which culminated in the latter's complete metamorphosis into a political movement. An authoritarian regime is characterized by a fluid line between political and cultural resistance, with political resistance having clear cultural roots, and cultural resistance having the potential of developing into a political movement. Thus, any attempt by the authorities to institutionalize and monopolize a new interpretation can be a catalyst for political resistance.

In retrospect, the story of Falun Gong is one of unintended consequences. First, to a certain extent, the state's sanctioning and promotion (in the early stage) of *qigong* sowed the seeds of disaster for itself, although the *qigong* groups, including Falun Gong, did not intend to challenge the state prior to the crackdown. Second, Falun Gong's spiritual transformation had much to do with the state's growing unease with *qigong*'s tendency toward "superstition" and "pseudoscience," an inevitable development because of *qigong*'s borderline status between state and society, and between science and religion. Third, while Falun Gong was celebrating its popularity as a spiritual group, the state sensed open defiance and a potential threat, and began to curb its activities. Fourth, Falun Gong's political militancy was directly triggered by the state's policies of preventing civic associations from being religious and *qigong* and other quasi-religious groups from being political. Fifth, before the crackdown, the intention of Falun Gong demonstrations was merely to "clarify the truth," given that the state was the sole arbiter of legitimacy. However, in the authoritarian context of China, the persistent civil disobedience only worsened the situation. Sixth, it appeared that the more desperately Falun Gong tried to persuade the state that it was "apolitical," the more likely it was that the state would perceive it as "political"; and the more efforts Falun Gong practitioners made to appear nonviolent, the more they alarmed the state. Seventh, the state's suppression became the driving force of the open confrontations between Falun Gong and the state, for the practitioners regarded opposition as a test of their inner nature and as a means of enhancing one's virtue. Eighth, the crackdown in 1999 led to the metamorphosis of Falun Gong into a major political movement. Religion provided a system of shared meanings and symbols that Falun Gong has used to legitimize its resort to contentious tactics. Deeply entrapped in the interactive loops of recrimination and antagonism, Falun Gong and the state were inexorably moving toward political militancy, until the conflict spiraled out of control and culminated in violence.

References

Amnesty International. 2000. *The Crackdown on Falun Gong and Other So-called "Heretical Organizations."* March 23. http://www.amnesty.org/en/library/asset/ASA17/011/2000/en/77562be8-df70-11dd-acaa-7d9091d4638f/asa170112000en.pdf (accessed May 17, 2012).

Clearwisdom.net. 2004a. "A Chronicle of Major Historic Events during the Introduction of Falun Dafa to the Public." October 8.
http://en.minghui.org/emh/articles/2004/10/8/53286p.html
(accessed May 9, 2013).

Clearwisdom.net. 2004b. "Answers to Commonly Asked Questions about Falun Gong." September 1.
http://en.minghui.org/emh/articles/2004/9/1/52070.html (accessed May 17, 2012).

Dowell, William. 1999. "Interview with Li Hongzhi." *Time Asia*, 10 May.
http://www.time.com/time/world/article/0,8599,2053761,00.html
(accessed May 28, 2012).

Duan Qiming. 2006. "Pan Guoyan: daxiang meiti jiepi Li Hongzhi diyiqiang" [Pan Guoyan: first shot of the media's exposure and criticism of Li Hongzhi]. November 27.
http://www.kaiwind.com/redian/fxds/200706/t39265.htm
(accessed May 17, 2012).

Falun Dafa Information Center. 2009. "Key Statistics Related to Falun Gong." September 27. http://faluninfo.net/article/909/?cid=162 (accessed May 17, 2012).

Fang, Bay. 1999. "An Opiate of the Masses?" *U.S. News & World Reports*, 22 February, 45–6.

Johnson, Ian. 2001. "Burden of Belief." *Wall Street Journal*, 27 March.

Kipnis, Andrew B. 2001. "The Flourishing of Religion in Post-Mao China and the Anthropological Category of Religion." *Australian Journal of Anthropology*, 12 (April): 32–46.
https://doi.org/10.1111/j.1835-9310.2001.tb00061.x

Li Hongzhi. 1999a. "Lecture in Sydney."
http://www.falundafa.org/book/eng/lectures/1996L.html
[1996] (accessed May 17, 2012).

Li Hongzhi. 1999b. "A Brief Statement of Mine."
http://en.minghui.org/emh/download/publications/peacereport_statement.html (accessed May 17, 2012).

Li Hongzhi. 2000. "Serious Teachings."
http://en.minghui.org/emh/special_column/cultivation/serious-teachings-000928.doc (accessed May 17, 2012).

Li Hongzhi. 2001a [1996]. "Huge Exposure." In *Falun Dafa Essentials for Further Advancement*, pp. 31–2.
http://www.falundafa.org/book/eng/pdf/jjyz_en.pdf (accessed May 17, 2012).

Li Hongzhi. 2001b [1998]. "Digging Out the Roots." In *Falun Dafa Essentials for Further Advancement*, pp. 48–50.
http://www.falundafa.org/book/eng/pdf/jjyz_en.pdf (accessed May 17, 2012).

Li Hongzhi. 2002a [1994]. "Explaining the Fa for Falun Dafa Assistants in Changchun." In *Explaining the Content of Falun Dafa*, pp. 6–43.
http://www.falundafa.org/book/eng/pdf/yj_en.pdf (accessed May 10, 2013).

Li Hongzhi. 2002b [1995]. "Comments for Republication." In *Explaining the Content of Falun Dafa*, p. 3.
http://www.falundafa.org/book/eng/pdf/yj_en.pdf (accessed May 17, 2012).

Li Hongzhi. 2002c [2000]. "Teaching the *Fa* at the Western U.S. *Fa* Conference." In *Guiding the Voyage*, pp. 1–5.
http://www.falundafa.org/book/eng/pdf/daohang.pdf (accessed May 17, 2012).

Li Hongzhi. 2002d [2001]. "Teaching the *Fa* at the 2001 Canada *Fa* Conference." In *Guiding the Voyage*, pp. 15–18.
http://www.falundafa.org/book/eng/pdf/daohang.pdf (accessed May 17, 2012).

Li Hongzhi. 2003a [1994]. *Zhuan Falun*.
http://www.falundafa.org/book/eng/pdf/zfl_new.pdf (accessed May 25, 2012).

Li Hongzhi. 2003b. "Teaching the *Fa* at the 2003 Midwest-U.S. *Fa* Conference." http://www.falundafa.org/book/eng/lectures/20030622L.html (accessed May 17, 2012).

Li Hongzhi. 2004 [1998]. "Teaching the *Fa* at the Assistants' *Fa* Conference in Changchun."
http://www.falundafa.org/book/eng/lectures/19980726L.html (accessed May 17, 2012).

Li Hongzhi. 2005a [1994]. "Teaching the *Fa* and Answering Questions in Guangzhou." In *Zhuan Falun Fajie*, pp. 134–89.
http://www.falundafa.org/book/eng/pdf/zfl_fajie.pdf (accessed May 17, 2012).

Li Hongzhi. 2005b [1995]. "Teaching the *Fa* in Beijing at the *Zhuan Falun* Publication Ceremony." In *Zhuan Falun Fajie*. 1–45.
http://www.falundafa.org/book/eng/pdf/zfl_fajie.pdf (accessed May 17, 2012).

Li Hongzhi. 2005c [1999]. "Some Thoughts of Mine." In *Essentials for Further Advancement II*. 2–4.
http://www.falundafa.org/book/eng/pdf/jjyz2.pdf (accessed May 17, 2012).

Li Hongzhi. 2005d [2000]. "Eliminate Your Last Attachment(s)." In *Essentials for Further Advancement II*. 20–2.
http://www.falundafa.org/book/eng/pdf/jjyz2.pdf (accessed May 17, 2012).

Li Hongzhi. 2005e [2000]. "In Reference to a Prophecy." In *Essentials for Further Advancement II*. 14.
http://www.falundafa.org/book/eng/pdf/jjyz2.pdf (accessed May 17, 2012).

Li Hongzhi. 2005f [2001]. "Fa-Rectification and Cultivation." In *Essentials for Further Advancement II*. 48.
http://www.falundafa.org/book/eng/pdf/jjyz2.pdf (accessed May 17, 2012).

Li Hongzhi. 2006a [1993]. *Falun Gong*.
http://www.falundafa.org/book/eng/pdf/flg_2006.pdf (accessed May 19, 2012).

Li Hongzhi. 2006b [1997]. *The Great Way of Spiritual Perfection*.
http://www.falundafa.org/book/eng/pdf/dymf_2006.pdf (accessed May 19, 2012).

Li Hongzhi. 2007a [1996]. "Teaching the *Fa* at the International Experience-Sharing Conference in Beijing."
http://www.falundafa.org/book/eng/lectures/19961111L.html (accessed May 17, 2012).

Li Hongzhi. 2007b. "*Fa* Teaching at the 2007 New York *Fa* Conference."
http://www.falundafa.org/book/eng/lectures/20070407L.html (accessed May 17, 2012).

Li, Junpeng. 2014. "The Religion of the Nonreligious and the Politics of the Apolitical: The Transformation of Falun Gong from Healing Practice to Political Movement." *Politics and Religion* 7(1):177–208.
https://doi.org/10.1017/S1755048313000576

Lu, Yunfeng. 2005. "Entrepreneurial Logics and the Evolution of Falun Gong." *Journal for the Scientific Study of Religion*, 44 (June): 173–85.
https://doi.org/10.1111/j.1468-5906.2005.00274.x

Ownby, David. 2003. "A History for Falun Gong: Popular Religion and the Chinese State since the Ming Dynasty," *Nova Religio*, 6 (April): 223–43. https://doi.org/10.1525/nr.2003.6.2.223

Ownby, David. 2005. "The Falun Gong." In James R. Lewis and Jesper Aagaard Petersen (eds.), *Controversial New Religions*. New York: Oxford University Press, pp. 195–214.
Ownby, David. 2008. *Falun Gong and the Future of China*. New York: Oxford University Press.
Palmer, David A. 2007. *Qigong Fever*. New York: Columbia University Press.
Pomfret, John. 1999. "China Said to Detain 35,000 in Sect," *Washington Post*, November 30.
Porter, Noah. 2003. *Falun Gong in the United States: An Ethnographic Study*. Dissertation.com.
Rahn, Patsy. 2002. "The Chemistry of a Conflict: The Chinese Government and the Falun Gong," *Terrorism and Political Violence*, 14 (Winter): 41–65. https://doi.org/10.1080/714005633
Schoof, Renee. 1999. "China Denies Detaining More Than 35,000 Falun Gong Activists." December 2. http://www.lexisnexis.com.ezproxy.cul.columbia.edu/hottopics/lnacademic/?verb=sr&csi=7911 (accessed May 6, 2012).
Tong, James. 2002. "An Organizational Analysis of the Falun Gong: Structure, Communications, Financing," *China Quarterly*, 171: 636–60. https://doi.org/10.1017/S0009443902000402
Wallis, Roy. 1977. *The Road to Total Freedom*. New York: Columbia University Press.
Weber, Max. 1993. *The Sociology of Religion*. Boston: Beacon. (First published 1922.)
Weller, Robert P. 1994. *Resistance, Chaos and Control in China: Taiping Rebels, Taiwanese Ghosts and Tiananmen*. Seattle: University of Washington Press. https://doi.org/10.1007/978-1-349-13203-4
Xia Yun. 2010. "Stories from the April 25 Appeal." April 25. http://en.minghui.org/html/articles/2010/4/28/116508.html (accessed May 18, 2012).
Yang, Fenggang. 2012. *Religion in China*. New York: Oxford University Press.
Ye Hao. 1999. "Youguan Falun Gong shifou you zuzhi de zhenxiang" [Truth about the Organizational Nature of Falun Gong]. July 31. http://home.netvigator.com/~falunhk/zhenxiang2_gb.htm (accessed May 18, 2012).
Zhang Weiqing and Qiao Gong. 1999. *Falun Gong chuangshi ren Li Hongzhi pingzhuan* [Li Hongzhi: A Critical Biography of the Founder of Falun Gong]. Carle Place, NY: Mingjing.

Junpeng Li is a professor in the School of Sociology at the Central China Normal University and a China Public Policy Postdoctoral Fellow at the Harvard Kennedy School. He is also the editor of the *International Sociology Reviews* and book review editor of *Studies of Transition States and Societies*. His work has appeared in such journals as *Contemporary Politics* and the *Chinese Journal for Sociology*, and he has received awards from the International Sociological Association and the Society for the Study of Social Problems.

2. The Doctrine of Li Hongzhi
Falun Gong – Between Sectarianism and Universal Salvation

David A. Palmer[1]

Ever since the Zhongnanhai demonstration of 25 April 1999 and the Chinese state's anti-Falun Gong campaign launched three months later, Li Hongzhi and his millions of followers have never ceased to puzzle observers of Chinese society and politics. The first surprise was Falun Gong's ability to organize over 10,000 protesters around the Party's nerve center, catching security forces completely off guard. This led to the astounding discovery that after only seven years of existence, Falun Gong had managed to recruit tens of millions of followers.[2] Moreover, the movement's tenacious resistance,

1. An earlier version of this paper appeared in *China Perspectives*, 35, May–June 2001, pp. 14–24 and is reprinted here with permission. The author's agreement was given without being fully informed of other contributions to this volume, and should not be taken to imply his endorsement of the views or claims therein. The text has been slightly updated. Although the data in the chapter remain limited to Falun Gong prior to its repression in 1999, bibliographic references have been enriched to direct readers to scholarship on Falun Gong that has been published since 2001. Research was funded by a doctoral fellowship of the Social Sciences and Humanities Research Council of Canada.

2. In 1997, Li Hongzhi claimed to have 100 million followers, most certainly an exaggerated figure, including 20 million regular practitioners (Li 1997b, 122). The Chinese official media speak of 2 million practitioners, probably an underestimate. For a demographic analysis and critical discussion on estimations of the number of followers, see Palmer (2007, 259–61). It is impossible to estimate the number of disciples in China since the crackdown on the movement.

in spite of two decades of systematic repression, continues to disconcert Chinese authorities.

For a time, Falun Gong seemed to represent one of the greatest threats the Chinese Communist Party had ever encountered since its accession to power in 1949; more serious, according to some, than the 1989 student movement. Indeed, Falun Gong disciples have a coherent ideological system, an unconditional loyalty to their Savior, Li Hongzhi, an inner discipline forged through rigorous practice, and a flexible underground network organization.

Is Falun Gong a religion? A cult? A political movement? What is its ideology? Chinese propaganda labels Falun Gong as an "anti-scientific, anti-social and anti-human evil cult." It is often described in Western media as a "mystical movement," a "Buddhist- and Taoist-inspired organization," etc. Such terms tell little about Li Hongzhi's true doctrine, and reveal the difficulty in pinpointing Falun Gong's distinctive ideology. What belief system inspires its disciples to such courage in the face of repression?

In order to help the reader to answer these questions, this chapter proposes a brief analysis of the doctrine of Li Hongzhi, founder of Falun Gong, as elaborated in his writings, which are considered by disciples as sacred scriptures (*jing*), and the reading of which constitutes an essential component of daily practice. The writings are for the most part edited transcriptions of Li Hongzhi's preachings during "Dharma assemblies" (*fahui*), held during tours around China in 1994 and in Western countries from 1996 on, and of the Master's answers to disciples' questions during these assemblies. One of the first of these works, *Zhuan Falun* ("Turning the Dharma-Wheel"), is considered by many disciples as the "Bible" of Falun Gong, containing the Law of the universe in its entirety, and in relation to which the other writings bring merely clarifications and explanations.

This study considers only the texts that were published prior to the 1999 crackdown, which were distributed by mainland Chinese and Hong Kong publishers (such as the China Television and Broadcasting Press, the Qinghai People's Press and the Inner Mongolia Culture Press), as well as on the internet, and which were widely circulated among Falun Gong practitioners in China. Following the repression, Li Hongzhi has continued to produce voluminous writings that have been published online; however, these are not considered here. Owing to the radically different context of Falun Gong after 1999 – in which a growing mass movement centred in China was transformed into a transnational network deeply preoccupied with responding to the repression and consisting of both diasporic communities and underground practitioners in China – there have been changes in the content and emphasis of Li's teachings.³ This chapter focuses on the teachings of Li Hongzhi as they were available to practitioners in China in the years immediately preceding the 1999 crackdown.⁴ I focus on textual sources and do not address how or to what extent these texts were understood and put into practice by practitioners.⁵

Four main themes dominate the master's writings from this period: (1) an *apocalyptic theme*, stressing the moral decadence of humanity and the omnipresence of the forces of evil. Extraterrestrials are infiltrating themselves into the body of humanity through modern science, the great enemy of virtue; the Buddhist prophecy of the imminent destruction of the world and inauguration of a new universal cycle, is close to being fulfilled. (2) An exhortation to *rigorous*

3. For an in-depth study of this issue from the angle of the sociology of social movements, see Juncker (2019); for an anthropological approach, see Dalby (2017).
4. Li Hongzhi's writings have been published in multiple editions and can now be found online in several languages on the Falun Dafa website: www.falundafa.org. Quotations in this chapter are based on editions available prior to the 1999 crackdown; the translations are my own. For a discussion of the corpus of Li Hongzhi's writings, see Penny (2012, 93–103); on Falun Gong's presence in cyberspace, see Ownby (2008a, 200–11).
5. Unfortunately, there are no in-depth, field research-based academic studies of Falun Gong practitioners in mainland China. On practitioners in the North American diaspora, see Ownby (2008a, 125–60; 2008b), Porter (2003), Susan Palmer (2003), Burgdoff (2003), Chan (2013), and Dalby (2017).

spiritual discipline, calling on followers to purify their hearts of all attachment to the things of this world. The gods have abandoned the orthodox religions of the past, which have already completely lost the spirit of the true Dharma. (3) A *messianic theme*: Li Hongzhi is the omniscient and omnipotent savior of the entire universe. He has revealed, for the first time in history, the fundamental Law of the universe, which is the only protection against the apocalypse. (4) A *sectarian practice:* Li Hongzhi's disciples must concentrate exclusively on Falun Gong; it is forbidden to read or even think about any other religion, philosophy, or school of thought or *qigong*. They must devote themselves heart and soul to Falun Gong's psycho-physiological discipline; the perceptions and visions triggered by this practice are attributed to Li Hongzhi's supernatural power.

Antecedents in the *Qigong* Milieu

Falun Gong's scriptural canon sets it apart from other movements in the *qigong* milieu, of which it is an outgrowth. At the same time, it crystallizes many ideas that had been circulating in popular *qigong* networks since the 1980s. Indeed, in the first years following its foundation in 1992, Falun Gong appeared little different from the thousands of other *qigong* methods being taught in China: a set of traditional gymnastic and meditation exercises. *Qigong* had appeared in 1949 as an attempt by the new communist regime to extract traditional breathing arts from their "feudal" and "religious" settings. This new "*qigong*" was at the time little more than a series of hygienic and therapeutic techniques propagated by the new regime's medical institutions as a cheap and efficient way to improve the health of the Chinese people.[6]

After the end of the Cultural Revolution, traditional and sectarian masters emerged from obscurity and began to transmit their

---

6. For a detailed study of the history of *qigong* in post-1949 China, see Palmer (2007); for a summary, see David Palmer (2003).

lineages under the guise of *qigong*. A plethora of *qigong* movements were founded, each teaching a set of techniques and concepts often derived from traditional Chinese religion. In the 1980s, intellectuals in *qigong* circles tried to reformulate these concepts in scientific language, with the aim of creating a new super-science of *qigong*. Their project aimed to reconcile ancient techniques and concepts with Marxism and scientism, so that it would become possible to train and develop the "exceptional functions of the human body" (telepathy, photokinesis, clairvoyance, etc.) within a legitimate and respectable scientific setting, and putting China in the lead of a new worldwide scientific revolution. From a simple method of disease prevention and therapy, *qigong* had come to be seen as a scientific means of acquiring and exploiting paranormal powers.

But "*Qigong* Science", unable to produce replicable proofs of its claims, mired itself in quackery and ridicule. The first years of Falun Gong coincide with a period of disappointment and confusion in the *qigong* world, which had become the target of a fierce polemic against its "pseudo-science" in the Chinese media. In this context, Li Hongzhi distanced himself from the *qigong* milieu and redefined the purpose of *qigong* practice: in Falun Gong, the ultimate goal is neither physical health nor the acquisition of psychic powers, but the purification of the heart and spiritual salvation.

The *qigong* milieu was already rife with religious concepts and behavior, but these were rarely explicitly or systematically articulated. In Falun Gong, however, *qigong* exercises are merely the physical adjunct to a religious movement of universal salvation with its own clearly elaborated doctrine. Although other *qigong* masters had also enjoyed playing the role of savior, preaching to assemblies of disciples, none had, like Li Hongzhi, gone beyond the stage of personal charisma to publish "sacred writings," the study of which was to become more important than the original body exercises of *qigong*.[7]

---

7. Note that Li Hongzhi categorically denies founding a religion "... I do not engage in religion, and our Falun Dafa is absolutely not a religion" (Li 1999a, 41).

Moral Corruption and the Apocalypse

Li Hongzhi bases his apocalyptic doctrine on the Buddhist eschatology of the *kalpas* or universal cycles, in a manner comparable to the tradition of Chinese salvationist and sectarian movements. For over a thousand years, a constellation of sects have pointed to social chaos and corruption as foretelling the end of the present *kalpa* inaugurated by the Sakyamuni Buddha, and have preached paths to salvation and preparation for ushering in the new *kalpa*. The first mention of this doctrine in China appears to date from the Tang dynasty (Overmyer 1976, 83; Ownby 2008a, 23–44).[8] Some of these sects were involved in rebellions against the imperial State, such as the revolts of Xu Hongru (1622), Wang Lun (at the end of the eighteenth century) and the Eight Trigrams (1813); consequently, popular sects have often been the targets of harsh repression campaigns.

Li Hongzhi's doctrine echoes this sectarian eschatology, proclaiming that we have now reached the "age of the end of the Dharma" prophesied by Sakyamuni Buddha – a period that would

---

8. Note, however, that Li Hongzhi condemns many beliefs linked to popular sectarianism: asked about the Inborn Mother (*wusheng laomu*), the principal divinity of many popular sects, he answers: "What Inborn Mother? There is simply no such divinity" (Li 1997a, 189). Asked about Maitreya, the promised future Buddha awaited by several sects, he answers that "… Maitreya doesn't have a Dharma-Gate, these are but the inventions of heretical and demonic dharmas" (ibid., 192). As for Yiguandao, a movement which spread in the early twentieth century preaching the unity of the five great religions (Buddhism, Daoism, Confucianism, Christianity, and Islam), Li Hongzhi states that "it's an evil cult; from the moment of its appearance the Qing Emperor killed them (*sic*). At the beginning of the republican period, the Nationalist Party killed them, executing them in groups. Since Liberation by the Communist Party, [the Party] has been repressing the 'Yiguandao'… it's not ordinary people who are killing them, but it's the will of Heaven. Up there, they want [Yiguandao] to be killed, its existence is not allowed. To speak of the 'Five Teachings in the Same Hall' (*wujiao tongtang*) is a serious case of seditious teachings. It's a sign of demonic activity among ordinary people" (Li 1995, 87–8).

be marked by unprecedented moral degeneration. "At present, the universe is undergoing momentous transformation. Each time this transformation occurs, all life in the universe finds itself in a state of extinction. ... all characteristics and matter that existed in the universe explode, and most are exterminated. ... A new universe is then created by the Great Awakened Ones of an extremely high level ..." (Li 1998, 165). These extinctions are a cyclical phenomenon, which occurs each time civilization's scientific development outstrips its moral attainment. Hundreds of thousands and even millions of years ago, civilizations existed which had reached extremely high levels of material, technological, and artistic progress. It was these civilizations that built the moon and the Pyramids, which had nothing to do with Egypt. But they had abandoned their morals, and so the Awakened Ones exterminated them (Li 1996, 23). "In fact, these prehistoric civilizations sank to the bottom of the sea. Later, many changes occurred on Earth, and [the Pyramids] rose back to the surface" (Li 1995, 13–14). During the apocalypse, all science and technology disappears, and the handful of survivors has to start again at the Stone Age (ibid., 38–40).[9] Earth has already undergone eighty-one such mass exterminations.

A small number of living beings, including humans and others, were nonetheless saved from the apocalypse and sent to other planets. These extraterrestrials now want to return to Earth (1999b, 70–1). Their weapon: modern science, which they use as a tool to infiltrate themselves in the minds of humans. "I tell you, the development of present-day society is entirely produced and controlled by aliens" (1999a, 4). Science is actually a religion with its own clergy of Bachelors, Masters, Doctors, Research Fellows, and Professors. However, contrary to the divinely transmitted religions, aliens spread science in order to control humans (1999b, 28). The aliens, in order to conduct experiments on humans, abduct them and use them as pets on their planet. They have discovered that humans have a perfect body, and want to take possession of it. By using science to

9. To simplify the following section, all citations are to the works of Li Hongzhi in the reference list. Thus, only the dates and page numbers are given in parentheses.

infiltrate themselves in human bodies, they aim to substitute themselves for men. They inject their "things" into human molecules and cells, turning them into slaves of computers and machines, until they can be replaced by the aliens. "Why are computers developing so rapidly? Why is the human brain suddenly so active? This is the result of the manipulation of the human mind by extraterrestrials. They have assigned a serial number to each human capable of using a computer" (ibid., 70–1).

Modern science is the greatest enemy of morality. "As soon as we speak of morals and of the distinction between good and evil, such non-scientific subjects are seen as superstitions. But isn't that using the bludgeon of science to beat away at the essential dimension of man – human virtues?" (1996, 21). For science cannot confirm the existence of gods or of virtue; it is ignorant of the moral retribution of karmic causality (1999b, 29).

The tyranny of amoral science is symptomatic of the moral decline of contemporary society and of the end of the universal cycle. In ancient China, those who pursued a spiritual calling were admired by others. But today such persons are objects of derision. "In mainland China, the 'Cultural Revolution' has eliminated people's so-called old ideas, forbidding them from believing in the sayings of Confucius. People no longer have self-mastery, they have no norms, and they no longer believe in religion. They no longer believe that they will be punished for their evil deeds" (1995, 123–4). Since the opening-up and reform policy, the economy has livened up, but negative things are also penetrating the country (1998, 310). Although the older generation continues to cherish its values, ensuring the preservation of the social order, Chinese youth does not have the slightest inkling of morality (1997a, 3). "Today, when people study [the story of] Lei Feng[10] they say that he was crazy. However, in the fifties and sixties, who would have said that he was crazy? The moral level of humanity is sliding deeper and deeper. People's sole ambition is personal profit; they hurt others for their

10. A People's Liberation Army soldier in the 1960s, Lei Feng was elevated to the status of national hero and role-model by state propaganda for his self-sacrifice and devotion to serving the people.

own interest, they struggle and scheme against each other without an afterthought" (1998, 13).

"Today," says Li Hongzhi, "beauty is valued less than ugliness, goodness less than evil, and a well-groomed appearance less than shabby attire" (1995, 126–7). In the past, singers were trained in the art of music; today any ugly and uncouth good-for-nothing can climb onto the stage, cry out at the top of his voice, and become an instant celebrity. Elegant halls are filled with the noise of "Disco" and "Rock." In the past, art sought after beauty; today, it erupts with demonic tendencies – a consequence of the sexual promiscuity of artists. Prostitution, fashion, and football riots are all signs of demonic power (ibid., 126; 1997a, 89–90). "As for the toys sold in stores, in the past, dolls were a pleasure to look at. Nowadays, the uglier they are, the better they sell. Skulls, monsters, there are even toys shaped like feces: more horrible means higher sales!" (1995, 129). "People recognize only money and not people. There is no feeling, human relationships have become monetarized." People don't hesitate to offend the cosmic order for money: products, magazines and films promoting sexual license are everywhere to be seen; drugs are manufactured and sold; drug addicts don't hesitate to cheat and rob others to pay for their fix; things have reached the point where "people practice intergenerational incest"; "the abomination of homosexuality reflects the hideous psychological perversion and loss of wisdom of our era." Underground criminal organizations have infiltrated all sectors of society; their leaders have become the idols of the youth, who scramble to be their followers (1995, 141–2). If society continues to change this way, in what state can we expect to end up (ibid., 131)?

"Men wear long hair and women cut theirs short: *yin* is asserting itself while *yang* is weakened, the roles of *yin* and *yang* have been inverted" (ibid., 139). For Li Hongzhi, women's liberation destabilizes the cosmic balance. In the natural order, woman should be *yin* and soft, while man should be *yang* and hard. In the past, men knew how to love and protect their wives, and women knew how to take care of their husbands. But since women's liberation, we see only divorce, conflicts, and abandoned children (1997a, 104–5).

The world is saturated with the black karmic matter produced by the evil deeds of men. Even stones, bricks, plants, trees, and animals are full of impure karmic matter – so much so that medicines can no longer cure diseases, and ever stranger new illnesses keep appearing (1998, 257; 1995, 45–6). The "creditors" of our karmic debts are coming back to us with misfortune (1998, 195).

Li Hongzhi describes a world full of demons and possessed bodies. Animals, anxious to escape the apocalypse, have begun to engage in spiritual disciplines. But, lacking human qualities, they can only progress to the level of demon, from which they try to possess human bodies (ibid., 102). These animal demons have already possessed the bodies of Taiwanese monks, of Indian gurus, of Japanese cult leaders, of *qigong* masters and disciples (1995, 131–2, 138; 1997a, 118, 218, 245; 1998, 183–96, 250). Even the tablets on altars for ancestor worship are low-level demons (1997a, 238). Buddhist icons in temples are possessed by the evil spirits of foxes, snakes, and yellow weasels. If you have an impure desire, for example, to get rich, the statue will grant your wish, but only in exchange for possessing your body without your knowing it (1995, 121–2). Therefore, Li Hongzhi concludes: "The Earth is the trash can of the universe ... the evil men of the universe fall downwards, until they reach its centre: Earth" (ibid., 43–5).

Spiritual Discipline

"He who wishes to heal his illnesses, cast off misfortune, and eliminate bad karma, must practice spiritual discipline (*xiulian*), and return to his authentic root," to his benevolent human nature. "... Such is the true purpose of being human," says Li Hongzhi. "What should we do? We must purify the body [of the disciple], and make him capable of exercising himself until he reaches a higher level. He must purify his mind of all evil ideas, of the karmic field around his body, and of the factors harming bodily health" (1998, 4–5).

In this process of purification through spiritual discipline, the substance of the body, down to its tiniest particles, is gradually replaced by an energetic matter one hundred million times more dense than a molecule of water (ibid., 6, 66). But in order to achieve this, one must look inwards, purify one's heart, abandon one's desires, passions, and sentiments, cultivate the virtues of patience, understanding, and detachment, and conform to the fundamental qualities of the universe, which are Truth, Benevolence, and Forbearance (*zhen shan ren*) (ibid., 25–6).

Virtue or Merit (*de*), according to Li Hongzhi, is a form of white matter that enters our body each time we do a good deed or are victimized by others. Bad karma, on the other hand, is a kind of black matter that penetrates us when we commit an evil deed. Thus, if someone insults you, the aggressor's white matter will pass from his body into yours, while your black matter will be absorbed by his body. Therefore, even though you may appear humiliated, the real loser is the aggressor, because he took your black matter and gave you his white matter (ibid., 28).

There is a reason for all the ills that afflict society: people must repay the karmic debts they have contracted through their evil deeds in past lives. But, at the same time, it is our suffering which propels us to seek a way out and to rise to a higher level. If life were pleasant and painless, would there be any reason to strive for anything better (ibid., 62)? The misfortunes of life put our attachments to the test and give us an opportunity to increase our heart's degree of purity. The transformation of "black matter" into "white matter" is an extremely painful process (ibid., 129).

If one's spiritual discipline is successful, one may realize one's Buddha-nature, attain to illumination, and enter paradise. If one fails, on the other hand, the merit accumulated by our efforts will only allow us rebirth as a rich or powerful person (1997a, 72). The essence of successful spiritual discipline is to recognize that all the benefits of one's discipline come from the master, not from oneself: "practice comes from the disciple, while Power comes from the Master" (1998, 29). Indeed, spiritual discipline is a complex process by which the body is transformed in multiple spaces. "Can you achieve that alone? No, you can't. These things are arranged by the Master ..." (ibid., 48).

The Messianic Theme

Li Hongzhi is different from the thousands of *qigong* masters who were active in China in the 1980s and 1990s. According to an early hagiography (Li Hongzhi 1999d), Li Hongzhi was initiated into the Great Buddha-Law at the age of four by the Master of Complete Enlightenment; by the age of eight, he already possessed immense supernatural powers. During his adolescence, he learned Daoist martial arts from the True Man of the Eight Extremes, as well as from the Master of the True Way, who planted esoteric teachings into his mind while he was sleeping. Later came a female Buddhist master, followed by a succession of over twenty Masters, who made him undergo unimaginable trials.

As his capacities increased, Li Hongzhi gained a deeper understanding of the state of humanity. "Mankind should live in superb conditions, but his spiritual confusion leads him into a state in which the soul and body are gnawed away and tortured ... Conscious of his duty, [Li Hongzhi] was determined to do everything he could to bring health back to the people and to build a paradise for noble souls. To this end, he decided to create a method of the Great Dharma which could be practiced by common people, based on his own Great Dharma which had been transmitted to him alone, and which he had been practicing secretly for many years." All of his masters aided him in this task, so that "Falun Gong assimilated not only the distinctive qualities of Li Hongzhi, or merely the best of one, two, or several schools, but indeed, it integrates all types of prodigious powers of the universe, that is to say its essence, which is now crystallized in Li Hongzhi alone."

"I only appear to be a man," says the Master (1999a, 45). "The difference between you and me is that my brain is completely open, but not yours" (1996, 20). Li Hongzhi has uncountable "Dharma bodies" (*fashen*) which accompany his disciples, protect them, and heal them (1997a, 61; 1998, 111) on the condition that they keep their hearts pure of any selfish desire to be cured (1998, 114–15). The true disciple is indeed he who practices spiritual discipline with an absolutely pure and devoted heart. If he has the slightest personal desire, he is not a true disciple and Li Hongzhi will do nothing for him, even if he practices all the external forms of Falun Gong. The "Dharma bodies" of Li Hongzhi know all that goes through the minds of his followers (ibid., 148–9).

He has already exorcised the demons and impurities from the bodies of his true disciples, as well as an enormous quantity of their bad karma. But he hasn't eliminated all of it, in order that they may undergo the trials and suffering which must result from their karmic debts. These trials are indeed necessary for spiritual progress (ibid., 113, 131–2).

In a single training workshop, Li Hongzhi claims to eliminate the illnesses of 80 to 90 per cent of the participants and to give them paranormal powers that a whole lifetime of spiritual practice would be unable to achieve (ibid., 221). Indeed, Falun Gong allows one to surpass in a short period of time the level of spiritual accomplishment of cave hermits who have been practicing spiritual refinement for centuries (1997a, 110). For it is not the disciple who cultivates himself through his practice, but the Dharma-Wheel (Buddhist swastika) planted by Li Hongzhi in the lower abdomen of each follower, which refines him and increases his psychic powers. The swastika never stops turning and releasing powers, even while the disciple is not practicing the Falun Gong exercises (1998, 270).

Li Hongzhi has appeared not only to save humanity, but also to "rectify" all forms of life and matter in the universe. "[I have already] essentially rectified the universe. All that remains is humanity, that most superficial layer of matter, but this is also on the verge of being accomplished. My Power (*gong*) is entirely capable of stopping this material layer from breaking up, exploding, or whatever, entirely capable of stopping it (*applause*). Thus these phenomena which were prophesied in history will simply not occur" (1999a, 46). Before Li Hongzhi accomplished his mission, the universe had no future. Indeed, after speaking in 1994 of the imminent explosion of the universe, he declared in 1997 that he had already prevented its destruction (ibid., 94).

Li Hongzhi's Power is transmitted through his "omnipotent" (ibid., 122) book, *Zhuan Falun*, every single word of which contains a multitude of Buddhas, Daos, Gods, and Dharma bodies, which bring enlightenment to the reader. Each time the disciple reads the book, his level of understanding rises to a superior level, and he discovers truths that he had missed the previous time (1996, 10) – insights which yet are only a small fraction of the Master's wisdom (1997a, 106). The book explains mysteries never before revealed to humanity (1996, 4). "*Zhuan Falun* has strongly shaken the world scientific community!" (1999b, 18–19). The highest gods say: "you have given men a ladder to heaven – *Zhuan Falun*" (ibid., 16).

Zhuan Falun explains the Great Law of the universe, which Li Hongzhi has revealed to humanity for the first time in the history of our civilization (it was, however, transmitted on a large scale in a previous universal cycle, hundreds of millions of years ago) (1998, 33). This Dharma goes beyond anything that any religion or philosophy has ever taught to humanity. All religious teachings and forms of spiritual practice of the past are but low-level forms of this Great Dharma (1999a, 7). The teachings of Laozi and Sakyamuni, founders of Daoism and Buddhism, apply only to the Milky Way, while Falun Gong applies to the whole universe (1998, 35). "The doctrines of the Buddhist religion cover only the tiniest part of the Buddha-Dharma" (1995, 146). As for Christianity, to compare it with Falun Gong would be like comparing a ramshackle hut with a magnificent palace (1999b, 57).

Orthodox religions, i.e. Daoism and Buddhism (for Li Hongzhi, Christianity is a form of Buddhism; 1998, 159) have long been in decline, and today practice only external forms. They are now incapable of bringing salvation to humanity. Buddhas and gods no longer pay attention to these religions (1999b, 31); rather, they are now studying Falun Gong by the myriads (1997a, 37). For Buddhas and gods only recognize people's hearts and not external religious forms (1999a, 59). This is why religious devotees' prayers are never answered nowadays (1996, 17). Li Hongzhi thus rejects most ritualized forms: to become his disciple, it is not necessary to kowtow before the master; one should merely have a pure heart.

> Presently, I am the only one in the whole world who is teaching the orthodox Dharma (*zhengfa*). What I am doing has never been done before. I have opened a great gate in this period of the end of the Dharma. In fact, this doesn't happen once in a thousand or even ten thousand years ... (1998, 90).

To become a Falun Gong disciple is an opportunity one should not pass by: Li Hongzhi will stop his teaching in the near future. "I say, time is running out ... I am not only saving humans. When you will have reached enlightenment, I will have other things to do; I won't be able to teach you anymore. I will not be transmitting the Dharma among humans for long ... There will be a day when spiritual practice will come to an end. Everything will stop in a flash, then it won't be easy to practice spiritual discipline ... " (1999a, 92). At that moment, all traces of Falun Gong will disappear. The ink will vanish from Li Hongzhi's books, which will turn into mere blank pages (ibid., 131).

A Sectarian Practice

How does one become a Falun Gong disciple? One must keep a pure heart, and commit oneself to a path of mental and bodily discipline. This implies the regular study of *Zhuan Falun*, which one should first read from cover to cover in a single shot (1999a, 19), then reread regularly (1995, 155) as often as possible (1997b, 154). Some disciples go so far as to commit the entire book to memory. One must also practice five daily series of slow-motion gymnastic and meditation exercises. Falun Gong gymnastic forms are simpler and easier to learn than many other *qigong* methods (1998, 38–9), but they must be followed rigorously: even children must not be lax in practicing the body postures exactly as prescribed by Li Hongzhi (1997a, 87). One must practice as much as possible, even five hours a day if one has the time, but always remembering to give the highest priority to studying Li Hongzhi's writings (1999c, 72). Falun Gong must be practiced within society: although some disciples practice spiritual discipline to the exclusion of all other activities, Li Hongzhi does not encourage monasticism. One must undergo the trials of this degenerate world in order to progress along the path.

A cardinal rule of Falun Gong is that practice must be exclusive. Nobody is forced to practice Falun Gong, but whoever chooses to follow Li Hongzhi's Law must devote himself exclusively to it. Li Hongzhi does not stop anybody from choosing another path than Falun Gong – but "today, nobody else can, like me, truly raise (the practitioner) to a superior level" (1998, 40).

The notion of exclusive practice is common in meditational traditions, which emphasize concentration and the avoidance of mental dispersion. Following this logic, Falun Gong disciples must focus exclusively on Li Hongzhi's exercises and writings (ibid., 88–9). But this rule is carried to the extreme: even though he draws heavily on the concepts of various Buddhist, Daoist, and Christian traditions, Li Hongzhi claims that the mixing of traditions is the worst problem in this age of the end of the Dharma (1995, 56). "It is forbidden to mix even the slightest thought of another *qigong* method" to Falun Gong practice (1998, 90). To think of another method could lead to deforming the rotating swastika planted by Li Hongzhi in the disciple's lower abdomen, which could have dangerous consequences (ibid., 108). One should not read, nor even glance at, the books of other *qigong* masters, for they are filled with the spirits of snakes, foxes, and weasels. "A small thought appears in your brain: oh yes, this sentence makes sense. As soon as this thought lights up, the possessor demons [in the book] will come out" (ibid., 150; 1997a, 279). Li Hongzhi even suggests burning such books, which prevent his Dharma bodies from protecting his disciples (1998, 215). Most *qigong* masters are swindlers, who are hundreds of times more numerous than authentic masters (1997a, 204), "and you are unable to distinguish them" (1998, 107). Likewise, it is "absolutely forbidden" (1997a, 125) to read religious and medical classics such as the *Daoist Canon*, the *Inner Book of the Yellow Emperor*, the *Book of*

Mountains and Seas, the *Book of Changes* or Buddhist sutras (1998, 217). "What do you want to read these books for? These books do not deal with practicing the Great Dharma, what good is there in reading them? What can you get from them?" (1997a, 82).

The practice of *Taijiquan* is forbidden (ibid., 161), as are martial arts that include a practice of inner discipline (ibid., 324). Also forbidden are massage (ibid., 198), talismans sold in temples (ibid., 175), the recitation of incantations (ibid., 85), donating money for the construction of temples (ibid., 234), ancestor worship (ibid., 270), and even raising pets, for these could become demons after coming into contact with the spiritual energies of the disciple (ibid., 117–18). On the other hand, Li Hongzhi discourages, but does not oppose, some disciples' practice of burning incense or making offerings of fruit before his portrait (ibid., 89; 1999a, 115).

Li Hongzhi's obsession with purity applies to human races as well. "Mixing the races of the world is not allowed. Now that the races are mixed, this has created an extremely grave problem." For each race has its own celestial world: the white race has its Heaven, which occupies a tiny part of the universe; the yellow race has its Buddha-world and Dao-world, which fill up almost the whole universe. Children born of mixed marriages are not linked to any celestial world, "they have lost their root" (1996, 110–11). Cosmic law forbids cultural and racial mixing – this is why, claims Li Hongzhi, Jesus did not allow his disciples to teach their faith in the Orient. It is also why East and West were originally separated by impassable deserts, a barrier that has been destroyed by modern technology. "As a result of racial mixing ... the body and intelligence of the child are unhealthy. ... Modern science knows well that each generation is inferior to the preceding one..." (ibid., 112–13).

The true disciple of Li Hongzhi must not take medicines in case of illness. Therapeutic care only changes the outward form of illness (1998, 63), which actually grows out of a subtle body in a deep space that is untouched by treatment (ibid., 251). Illness is a means of repaying one's karmic debt: one must thus let it follow its natural course, unless Li Hongzhi intervenes personally to eradicate it. While common people may take medicines, the spiritual practitioner must abstain if he wishes to eliminate his bad karma (1997b, 17).[11]

It is also forbidden to give therapy to others with Falun Gong. This rule sets Falun Gong apart from other *qigong* schools, which teach their disciples how to heal the sick by emitting subtle energies (*qi*). According to Li Hongzhi, the practitioner who treats others by *qigong* merely absorbs the morbid energies of the patient into his own body (1998, 74). Thus, the bodies of those who attempt to heal others are possessed (ibid., 250).

Teaching Falun Gong is a "duty" of the disciple. "You must speak of the Dharma and propagate it," even though this obligation is not forced (ibid., 294; 1999a, 72, 85). But the dissemination of Falun Gong must follow certain rules which aim to preserve the purity of the Master's teachings: (1) teaching must be free; one must not collect fees at training sessions the way Li Hongzhi did in the first years of Falun Gong; (2) one must not insert personal ideas into teaching: one should only quote the Master's literal words and share one's personal experiences and feelings about practice; (3) disciples must not give lectures, but must rather meet in small groups to read Li Hongzhi's writings or listen to his tapes; (4) one must not recruit followers by healing the sick (1998, 120–3). Following the spread of Falun Gong, humanity will have a better future:

> [I]f everybody practices the inner spiritual discipline, if all turned to their own hearts, ... if they thought of others in their

---

11. This aspect of Falun Gong teachings has been the subject of much controversy. For a thorough discussion of Li Hongzhi's teachings on taking medicine, and how such teachings are put into practice by practitioners in America, see Porter (2003, 155–77). Porter observes that practitioners have a range of attitudes, but in general initially they try to abstain from medical care. However, if illness persists or becomes unbearable they do tend to resort to conventional treatments. He concludes that "the accusation that Li Hongzhi forbids the use of medicine is untrue, but there does seem to be credible evidence that critics ... are correct in stating that Falun Gong creates an environment that encourages practitioners not to use medical care" (ibid., 172).

deeds, human society would then become good, morals would rise, spiritual civilization would change for the better, public safety would be ensured, there might not even be policemen. People wouldn't have to deal with it, each would care for himself, looking within his own heart – wouldn't that be wonderful? (ibid., 329–30)

Conclusion

Falun Gong doctrine contains the basic structural elements of a religion of universal salvation. It reminds humanity of its spiritual essence and points to a path of transcendence, leading to the abandonment of selfish desires and attachments in order to "return to one's original nature." Stressing the moral corruption of the contemporary world, it advocates detachment from common social norms based on money and competition, replacing them with a transcendent ideal of conformity to the universal principles of "Truth, Benevolence and Forbearance." It gives meaning to suffering, which it explains as both the consequence of our own sins and a trial that is necessary for our spiritual progress. It situates the present state of humanity within a cyclical context, explaining the origin, the development, and the decadence of humanity in each cosmic cycle. Moreover, it traces a clear and simple path for liberation from the sufferings of this world: a single master, a single book, a single practice.

That such a large number of Chinese adhered to such a doctrine in such a short span of time, that its propagation was so spontaneous, and that a core of disciples remains so steadfast in the face of repression, seems to indicate that Falun Gong resonates with a deep and unquenched thirst for meaning, community, and faith in a country whose traditional religious structures have for the most part been destroyed in the past century (Goossaert 2000, 98–103, 204–6). The substitute cults of the State, of Science, and of Money have left a spiritual vacuum that manifests itself in the corruption, the fraud, and the moral disarray into which China seems to be mired. Even the material and social advantages promised by those idols of the twentieth century remain inaccessible to large sections of the population – seniors, laid-off workers, petty intellectuals – who have been pauperized and marginalized by the new market economy.

Many observers may yet wonder how the irrational and sectarian aspects of Falun Gong doctrine could have been so readily accepted by such a large number of people, including many professionals in science and technology.[12] Though it is true that Falun Gong took root in a fertile social milieu, one should not neglect the dynamics of its propagation, which followed a Chinese religious model whereby the adoption of concrete practices that are perceived as useful precedes adherence to a doctrine or community. Falun Gong is not a Christian-style dogma that one must first accept before being admitted to participation in community life. Li Hongzhi's *doctrine* cannot be separated from Falun Gong mind-and-body *techniques*. Its gymnastic and meditation exercises can be practiced by anyone, regardless of intention to become a follower of the movement or not, and can produce immediate and perceptible effects. Daily practice of Falun Gong gymnastics improves the disciple's state of health and feeling of well-being. The visions and perceptions experienced during meditation produce altered states of consciousness that become an intimate and subjectively felt "proof" of the existence of spiritual dimensions outside of everyday reality. These experiences facilitate the disciple's detachment from the ordinary world and increase his desire to further explore the inner worlds penetrated during meditation. At the same time, however, by projecting the practitioner outside of ordinary reality, meditation makes him vulnerable: he now needs new bearings, a new interpretive framework, which are provided by the Master and the doctrine. These link the immediate and intimate experience of the disciple to the cosmology, the eschatology, and social ideology of the Master, thus uniting the individual subjectivities of each disciple around a common belief

---

12. According to surveys conducted in various Chinese cities in the late 1990s, Falun Gong practitioners were disproportionately female and aged over 50, but they also included a higher proportion of college graduates than in the local population (see Palmer 2007, 256–60).

system. Adherence to Falun Gong doctrine is the result of a process that begins with a concrete, physical, and individual experience, and ends in an abstract, spiritualist, and universalist ideology.

All along this process, Li Hongzhi stressed the capital importance of virtue and purity of heart. He went against the grain of post-Maoist cynicism, which, forsaking communist ideals, considered the profit motive as the sole mover of men, and of the Hollywood-inspired hedonism of Chinese pop culture incarnated by TV and music stars. Falun Gong's attractiveness proves that morality still strikes a powerful chord in China, a country which, in past eras, made Virtue the pillar of its civilization. Falun Gong morality, however, was perceived by its followers as of an entirely different nature from the empty and hypocritical moralistic discourse of state propaganda. The free teaching of the method, the warm and supportive atmosphere of the practice and sharing sessions, the discipline of the volunteer trainers, were perceived as signs of an authentic virtue that was hard to find in an increasingly competitive and materialist society. Whereas the simple, honest, and virtuous person is often ridiculed and abused by his co-workers in today's China, Falun Gong raises his suffering to the level of a heroic spiritual struggle in which he must resign himself and bear the blows, each insult and each wound being a gift of "white matter" which will help him to move a step higher toward celestial perfection (Li 1998, 135–6, 317–18).

Falun Gong's ideology and moralism helped draw into its fold masses of disoriented *qigong* practitioners in the years 1994 to 1999. With so many quacks and swindlers posing as "*qigong* masters," practitioners didn't know whom to believe in. Opponents of *qigong* were waging a harsh polemic in the press, and it had become difficult to answer back in the name of "*qigong* science." *Qigong* schools and lineages had multiplied, but the milieu still lacked a satisfactory conceptual system that could give meaning to the practice, the phenomena, and the abuses linked to *qigong*. At such a juncture, Li Hongzhi's doctrine was able not only to give explanations, but also to lead *qigong* practitioners to a new level that transcended the old scientific and ethical problems of *qigong*: that of a religion of salvation.

Moreover, the repression of Falun Gong a few years later only confirmed the Master's claims: the isolation, the harassment, and the cruelty suffered by followers in mainland China are seen as evidence of the demonic forces of society rising up against the Great Law, and as salutary trials along the disciple's quest for "Merit." In such a context, it becomes easier to understand why many Falun Gong disciples are fearless of persecution and may even seem, by their provocative acts, to deliberately seek it: persecution validates their doctrine and brings them closer to the salvation promised by Li Hongzhi.

Falun Gong's sectarianism reinforces this antagonistic dynamic, confirming the vision of a world divided between the "saved" disciples of Li Hongzhi and the rest of the world possessed by demons. Falun Gong fundamentalism, which calls for the mutual exclusion of beliefs, practices, and races, and which forbids the absorption of ideas, techniques, or substances (medicines) exogenous to the Master's system, goes against a certain Chinese syncretic tradition which always seeks to harmoniously integrate the best elements of the cosmos. Animosity flared early on between Li Hongzhi and other figures in the *qigong* milieu; Falun Gong was expelled from the semi-official China *Qigong* Science Research Society in 1996. This event sealed the rupture between the *qigong* milieu and Falun Gong, and reinforced the latter's sectarian attitude. The deaths of disciples who had refused medical treatment for illness drew media criticism, adding to the sect's persecution complex. Additionally, the repeated protests by followers, both before and after the official crackdown, at newspaper offices, around Zhongnanhai, on Tiananmen Square – which could only lead to a hardening of the State's entirely predictable response within the logic of the Chinese political system – seemed calculated to draw official power into a moral battle, pitting the demonic oppressor against heroic martyrs.

Though Falun Gong is certain to endure, its influence as a mass movement seems to have subsided. However, the aspirations which it had incarnated remain unappeased: China continues to search for its religion. Falun Gong is the latest in a series of millenarian movements that have gripped China in the past 150 years. The country was torn by the Taiping rebellion of the mid-nineteenth century, with its promised advent of the "Heavenly Kingdom of the Supreme Peace." At the end of the Qing dynasty and during the republican period (1911–1949), it witnessed a wave of salvationist movements that promised to redeem China from its moral corruption (Goossaert and Palmer 2011, 91–108; Palmer 2011). It was carried away by the communist utopianism and Maoist messianism of "New China." It was mesmerized by "*Qigong* fever" and its hope of transforming humanity with the psychic powers of mind over matter; and it was then shaken by the Falun Gong tragedy. Each of these movements rejected traditional religious forms and promised the collective redemption of China or even of all humanity. Succeeding each other in waves, they attracted massive followings. The Falun Gong episode shows that Chinese millenarianism is not dead: what will be its next incarnation?

References

Burgdoff, Craig A. 2003. "How Falun Gong Practice Undermines Li Hongzhi's Totalistic Rhetoric," *Nova Religio*, 6 (2), 332–47. https://doi.org/10.1525/nr.2003.6.2.332

Chan, Cheris. 2013. "Doing Ideology amid a Crisis: Collective Actions and Discourses of the Chinese Falun Gong Movement," *Social Psychology Quarterly*, 76 (1), 1–24. https://doi.org/10.1177/0190272512467653

Dalby, Scott. 2017. "Disciples of the Buddha Law: The Incorporation of Practitioners in Falun Gong Cultivation and Movement Formations in New York and Hong Kong." Ph.D. dissertation, University of Amsterdam.

Goossaert, Vincent. 2000. *Dans les Temples de la Chine: Histoire des cultes, vie des communautés*. Paris: Albin Michel, pp. 98–103, 204–6.

Goossaert, Vincent and David A. Palmer. 2011. *The Religious Question in Modern China*. Chicago: University of Chicago Press. https://doi.org/10.7208/chicago/9780226304182.001.0001

Juncker, Andrew. 2019. *Making Activists in Global China: Transnational Mobilization in the Falun Gong and the Chinese Democracy Movement*. Cambridge: Cambridge University Press.

Li Hongzhi. 1995. *Zhuan Falun, Juan er* [Turning the Dharma-Wheel, Part Two]. Beijing: Zhongguo shijieyu chubanshe.

Li Hongzhi. 1996. *Falun Fofa (Zai xini jiangfa)* (The Buddha-Law of the Dharma-Wheel [Dharma-Talks in Sydney]). Publisher unknown.

Li Hongzhi. 1997a. *Zhuan Falun fajie* [Explanations to "Turning the Dharma-Wheel"]. Hong Kong: Falun Fofa Chubanshe.

Li Hongzhi. 1997b. *Falun Fofa: zai meiguo jiangfa* [The Buddha-Law of the Dharma-Wheel: Dharma Talks in America]. Hong Kong: Falun Fofa Chubanshe.

Li Hongzhi. 1998. *Zhuan Falun* [Turning the Dharma-Wheel], in *Falun Dafa* [The Great Law of the Dharma-Wheel]. Hailaer: Neimenggu Wenhua Chubanshe.

Li Hongzhi. 1999a. *Falun Fofa – zai beimei shoujie fahui shang jiangfa* [The Buddha Law of the Dharma-Wheel – Dharma Talks at the First North American Dharma Assembly]. Xining: Qinghai Renmin Chubanshe, p. 41.

Li Hongzhi. 1999b. *Falun Fofa – zai Ouzhou fahui shang jiangfa* (The Buddha-Law of the Dharma-Wheel – Dharma Talks at the European Dharma Assembly). Xining: Qinghai Renmin Chubanshe.

Li Hongzhi. 1999c. *Falun Fofa (zai xinjiapo fahui shang jiangfa)* (The Buddha-Law of the Dharma-Wheel [Dharma Talks at the Singapore Dharma Assembly]). Hong Kong: Falun Dafa Chubanshe, p. 72.

Li Hongzhi. 1999d. "Brief Biography of Li Hongzhi, Founder of Falungong and President of the Falungong Research Society," *Chinese Law & Government*, 32(6): 14–23 [translation of "Zhongguo Falungong chuangshiren, Falungong yanjiuhui huizhang Li Hongzhi xiansheng xiaozhuan," in Li Hongzhi, *Zhongguo Falungong* [China's Falun Gong]. Beijing: Zhongguo guangbo dianshi chuban gongsi, 1994].

Overmyer, Daniel. 1976. *Folk Buddhist Religion: Dissenting Sects in Late Traditional China*. Cambridge, MA: Harvard University Press. https://doi.org/10.4159/harvard.9780674183179

Ownby, David. 2008a. *Falun Gong and the Future of China*. New York: Oxford University Press. https://doi.org/10.1093/acprof:oso/9780195329056.001.0001

Ownby, David. 2008b. "In Search of Charisma: The Falun Gong Diaspora," *Nova Religio*, 12 (2), 106–20. https://doi.org/10.1525/nr.2008.12.2.106

Palmer, David A. 2003. "Modernity and Millennialism in China: *Qigong* and the Birth of Falun Gong," *Asian Anthropology*, 2(1), 79–109. https://doi.org/10.1080/1683478X.2003.10552531

Palmer, David A. 2007. *Qigong Fever: Body, Science and Utopia in China*. New York: Columbia University Press.

Palmer, David A. 2011. "Chinese Redemptive Societies and Salvationist Religion: Historical Phenomenon or Sociological Category?" *Journal of Chinese Ritual, Theatre and Folklore*, 172, 21–72.

Palmer, Susan. 2003. "From Healing to Protest: Conversion Patterns Among the Practitioners of Falun Gong," *Nova Religio*, 6 (2), 348–64. https://doi.org/10.1525/nr.2003.6.2.348

Penny, Benjamin. 2012. *The Religion of Falun Gong*. Chicago: University of Chicago Press. https://doi.org/10.7208/chicago/9780226655024.001.0001

Porter, Noah. 2003. "Falun Gong in the United States: An Ethnographic Study." MA thesis, University of South Florida.

David A. Palmer is an Associate Professor at the Institute for the Humanities and Social Sciences and the department of Sociology of the University of Hong Kong. After completing his PhD in the Anthropology of Religion at the École Pratique des Hautes Études in Paris, he was the Eileen Barker Fellow in Religion and Contemporary Society at the London School of Economics and Political Science. He is the author of the award-winning *Qigong Fever: Body, Science and Utopia in China* (Columbia University Press, 2007), co-author with Vincent Goossaert of *The Religious Question in Modern China* (University of Chicago Press, 2011; awarded the Levenson Book Prize of the Association for Asian Studies), and co-author with Elijah Siegler of *Dream Trippers: Global Daoism and the Predicament of Modern Spirituality* (University of Chicago Press, 2017).

3. From Spiritual Healing to Protest
Falun Gong's Emerging Culture of Martyrdom[1]

Susan J. Palmer

On May 19, 2001, an Experience Sharing Conference was held at the Westin Hotel in Ottawa, organized by the Falun Gong. I was present in the role of a researcher working with David Ownby, Professor of History at the University of Montreal.[2]

Suddenly, we beheld Master Li. He appeared at noon, unannounced, at the Ottawa Congress Centre, where a thousand-odd Falun Gong practitioners – overwhelmingly Chinese – sat in silk suits for the day of testimonials that is the essence of all their Experience Sharing Conferences.

Li Hongzhi, who had disappeared from public view shortly after the People's Republic of China (PRC) government's crackdown[3] on Falun Gong began in July 1999, had surfaced only twice since to deliver short speeches. But now he was standing at the podium,

---

1. An early version of this chapter appeared as "From Healing to Protest: Conversion Patterns Among the Practitioners of Falun Gong," in *Nova Religio: The Journal of Alternative and Emergent Religions*, Vol. 6, No. 2 (April 2003), pp. 348–64.

2. David Ownby has since published *Falun Gong and the Future of China*. New York: Oxford University Press, 2008.

3. "Crackdown" is the term used by the media to denote the social control methods (arrests, beatings, imprisonment) utilized by the PRC government; it is also used in the Falun Gong movement.

almost as tall as his eight-foot photograph, dressed in a business suit, his black hair combed neatly to one side. He spoke in Chinese, his tone of voice authoritative but sensitive, for twenty minutes – then saluted his disciples and left through a door behind the podium, ushered out by bodyguards.

I was wearing headphones, but the translator was so excited she kept correcting herself, so it was hard to follow. I grabbed another set of headphones, but that translator was sobbing with emotion. Later, David Ownby (who speaks Chinese fluently) told me Master Li had announced that we were living in a unique period of history, so it was important to "eliminate the evil." At the end of the day his videotaped appearance was replayed, accompanied by a good translation. His speech appeared on the Internet within three days (Li Hongzhi 2001a). What Master Li had to say was fascinating.

Master Li's message was unabashedly apocalyptic. He made statements that clearly demonstrated how Falun Gong's catastrophic beliefs have intensified under the influence of the draconian social control measures of the Chinese government – what Falun Gong members consider as "persecution." First, he said the aim of "cultivation" should no longer be associated with *individual* "improvement" or even spiritual enlightenment (referred to as "consummation"). Second, he reminded his students they were living in the "*fa*-rectification" period (when the *fa*, or Universal Law, triumphs over the force of evil in a vast cosmic struggle). Third, he insisted that the appropriate action for all disciples is to engage in the *collective* work of activist protest against Jiang Zemin's "persecution of Falun Gong." He proclaimed that "we Dafa disciples ... have been entrusted with a great historic mission ... to safeguard the Fa ... and to expose the evil ..."

During the May 2000 conference in Ottawa, there were many events scheduled to raise the public's awareness of the plight of Falun Gong practitioners in the PRC. Photographs of dead victims lined the path to the House of Commons, where the disciples, dressed in conspicuous red and orange tracksuits, were performing *qigong*. Professor Zhang Kunlun, whose experience of incarceration and torture is documented by Williams and Wu (2004), then gave a speech.⁴ These events supported the theme of Master Li's speech, which encouraged continued civil disobedience despite overwhelming reprisals. But Master Li, at the end of his speech, offered a "way out" through magical techniques of self-defence. He introduced a new ritual to his students, instructing them to hold their hands in the *Jieyin* position and "think about eliminating evil in the Three Realms." At the end of the day, we watched the videotape of Master Li's speech, and then a contact person from Toronto stood up and walked us through this freshly minted ritual, urging us to "help Master Li suffocate the evil."

As I joined in, participating in the ritual, I was reflecting on this new Chinese resistance movement that showed signs of making a cultural impact as significant as Gandhi's *satyagraha* ("force of truth" or "holding on to truth"), a nonviolent resistance movement against British rule in India. But unlike Gandhi's movement, beneath Falun Gong's familiar rhetoric of religious liberty and human rights, one finds a rapidly evolving apocalyptic theology. While Western politicians, journalists, and human rights groups respond to the social justice arguments of Falun Gong's spokesperson, as far as the practitioners themselves are concerned, their civil disobedience is fueled by spiritual ideas and apocalyptic expectations. The Master's message at the Ottawa conference underscored a dramatic strategic shift in his movement. Falun Gong's ongoing protest demonstrations in Tiananmen Square and the cruel reprisals of the PRC government have been well documented in the international news media – but the esoteric philosophy that fuels their civil disobedience has been virtually ignored. The Falun Dafa online newsletter of May 2001, *Minghui*, described the profound effect of Master Li's appearance in reinforcing a sacrificial, militant activism among his disciples:

> Practitioners were overwhelmed with joy when our great Teacher made an appearance later in the morning session.

---

4. Williams and Wu (2004) claim that the Canadian professor, Zhang Kunlun, was tortured with electric shocks at an eastern Shandong *laogai* camp in 2000 as part of the PRC's crackdown on the Falun Gong.

> They listened intently as Teacher addressed the audience for about 20 minutes. Practitioners resolved to strive forward to eliminate their personal attachments and the evil within the three realms, spread the truth to the people of the world who are affected by the vicious propaganda initiated by Jiang Zemin, and use the firm, righteous thoughts of Dafa cultivators to aid in eliminating the evil factors in other dimensions that interfere with Fa rectification. (Minghui 2001)

This chapter will focus on the early process whereby Chinese practitioners in the West gradually came to embrace an apocalyptic worldview that demands extraordinary sacrifice and intense commitment to the cause – often at the cost of jeopardizing their own families and hard-won careers. I will trace the various stages of conversion and the commitment route whereby practitioners arrive at this point and will explore their understandings of the apocalyptic ideology that drives Falun Gong's resistance to the PRC.

Many of my informants had faced the threat of prison, torture, even death. They all knew fellow practitioners who had been killed or imprisoned. And yet, in most individuals' lives, it had all started out as a quest for healing and power, for the mysterious force latent in ancient "cultivation practices" – what we in the West might refer to as "traditional Chinese folk medicine."

Research Methodology

My initial research was undertaken with David Ownby, Professor of History at the CETASE institute of l'Université de Montreal.[5] This involved field research at Experience Sharing Conferences in Montreal in February 2000 and Ottawa in May 2001. We distributed two "membership" questionnaires in Chinese and in English

---

5. Since David Ownby speaks fluent Mandarin, I found my interviews were constantly being interrupted because our Chinese informants would flock excitedly around this American in cowboy boots and hat to watch him converse effortlessly in their own language.

64 *Enlightened Martyrdom*

(see Palmer and Ownby 2000). (It should be noted that Falun Gong practitioners strongly object to being called "members," since they do not pay membership fees, nor keep membership lists. In the face of the opposition to their movement in the PRC, they seem to find it expedient to downplay the organized features of their movement.) I interviewed English-speaking practitioners in Toronto's old, well-established Chinese community over the weekend of January 28–29, 2000, and returned for the May 13, 2000 World Falun Dafa Day of public demonstrations, while Ownby conducted his interviews in Chinese. I also interviewed Falun Gong practitioners in New York City and in Waco and Dallas, Texas, setting up these interviews by using the simple technique of writing to contact persons in different cities inviting them to meet me at the baggage carousel at the airport while I was waiting for a connecting flight on my way to an academic conference. Each time I would see a group of Asians in business suits and carrying briefcases coming towards me. Altogether I have notes from around sixty in-depth interviews and thirty brief or partial interviews. I have tended to limit my research to Chinese practitioners, since Western disciples are a minority in the movement and tend to fit the idiosyncratic portrait of spiritual seekers.

The conversion stories of nearly all my informants fit very nicely into the seven-step model of conversion presented by Lofland and Stark (1965), beginning with "tension" (usually a health crisis) and culminating in the seventh-stage commitment of being a "deployable agent." After I had attended three Experience Sharing conferences, however, it became evident that the style and content of many of my informants' supposedly spontaneous conversion tales were shaped by the standard model of a ritual testimonial that has evolved in the movement. These ritual narrations can be deconstructed by a few judicious questions, so as to fill in the missing data and flesh out the complexities in their personal lives. From these data, it is possible to construct a tentative model of a four-phase process of conversion and commitment to Falun Gong/Falun Dafa.

Four Phases of Conversion

Falun Gong practitioners typically describe four aspects of their own conversion process. These can be identified as the healing phase, the moral reform phase, the spiritual phase, and the more activist apocalyptic phase.

By "phases," I do not mean to suggest a precise chronological sequence in each individual's life. Moreover, different practitioners will emphasize different aspects and benefits of the teaching. Nevertheless, I observed a general shift in the focus of the movement between early 2000, when healing and moral reform were the main topics, and the spring of 2001, when spiritual/apocalyptic ideas and the collective struggle for human rights were the main issues.

Falun Gong's initial attraction, for most of my informants, lay in the healing potential – not only of the *qigong* exercises, but of what they refer to as "The Book", *Zhuan Falun* (Li Hongzhi 1999). Once healing is accomplished, the practitioner's goal shifts. The next concern is for moral reform, with a focus on cultivating *xinxing* (translated in Falun Gong pamphlets as "moral qualities"). These are worked on through self-observation and a self-conscious handling of discordant relationships at home or at work. Many described a sudden detachment from materialistic concerns, and a renewed compassion for troublesome relatives.

For the mature practitioner, both the healing and the moral upgrading are later understood as early stages in a process of purification, seen as the "letting go of attachments" and a liberation from karma, propelling the individual towards "consummation" or enlightenment. Many disciples reported experiencing mystical or paranormal states, and interpreted these as side effects of purification and their enhanced spiritual sensitivity. But they tended to downplay paranormal states, for it is considered bad taste or "showing off" to dwell on such phenomena.

It is important to note that the great majority of these Chinese practitioners espoused a scientific worldview when they first encountered Falun Gong, as products of a secular Chinese background and having been raised as members of the communist party.

Unlike nearly all the Westerners I spoke to, the Chinese claimed no prior interest in "fringe" spiritual matters. Their initial interest in *qigong* was, as they explained it, not as a spiritual path, but rather as an investigation of ancient Chinese "cultivation practices."

Li Hongzhi, unlike many of the successful *qigong* masters, brought a sophisticated, eclectic cosmology to the practice that pieced together disparate fragments of China's occult underground. Master Li taught *qigong*, but also added a moral vision, a creation myth, and outlined a spiritual path that leads to enlightenment.

I will describe these phases as they were communicated to me by my informants.

Healing (*Guanding*)

My first impression of Falun Gong was of a "Chinese Lourdes in the West," with a theory of disease that closely resembled Christian Science. During my research trip to Toronto in January 2000 I heard countless testimonials of miraculous healings. Later, I discovered that, although the healing power of Master Li's brand of *qigong* was certainly the strongest element in the initial appeal, it was by no means an ongoing concern for committed practitioners. Indeed, once healed, practitioners counted on Master Li to "take care of" their health, and tended to display an indifference to matters of the body. Master Li explains in *Zhuan Falun* (1999, 3) that "you cannot practice cultivation with an ill body ... I will purify your body." He claims disease is caused by karma.

An important factor influencing their choice was that Master Li's version of *qigong* is virtually free. One man compared it to another *qigong* master, Yan Xin: "The master charges a lot. Early in 1997 the group trip to New York cost $300 U.S. with no transportation, then it was $400 for a two-day seminar. Master Li is free." *Zhuan Falun* can be downloaded from the Internet, and one man recalls he was offered a tape by a practitioner for only $2.06. ("Gee, that's dumb business! You don't make any money that way!")

A Chinese bank worker explained, "I discovered I had diabetes when I arrived in Canada, and was expecting to face high medicine costs. I had no work insurance, so *qigong* was the last resort!"

The theory of illness advanced by Master Li is that disease is caused by karma, the result of bad actions. In Falun Gong, bad karma is believed to be a black substance in the body. *Qigong* is a process that purifies the body of (negative) karma and the Master "takes care of" the practitioners and helps free them of disease. A woman in her late fifties who had been diagnosed with breast cancer claimed to have found a cure simply by *reading Zhuan Falun*, even before she began practicing the *qigong* exercises. She described a dramatic healing experience through *guanding* (purification of karma):

> As I was sitting I could feel my karma that was attached to my body fall as if it were being pulled away! It was like being wrapped in duct tape, excruciating! Painful! I could sit in lotus for 1½ hours and feel my karma moving down my legs and out the soles of the feet. I would cry sometimes for a whole hour, not just physical pain. ... Sometimes I felt overwhelming remorse.

A sixty-seven-year-old Chinese woman had been diagnosed with cancer of the bowel in 1992. Half of her stomach was removed, and parts of her intestine and spleen. She was in the hospital expecting to die within six months, when a friend told her, "Master can save you!" and brought her *Zhuan Falun*. She decided to stop all medications and treatments to read "the Book." "I am thinking, if I only have six months, the *xinxing* will go up, my next life will be better! It will prepare me for next life." She rallied, took the long bus ride to New York to hear the Master, and is now walking in the Falun Gong parades and attending study sessions, although she says, "Sometimes I need a nap."

In Falun Gong, good health is seen as a natural by-product of the individual's spiritual progress, but so are renewed youth and increased beauty, as several practitioners pointed out:

> "Look at my mother-in-law's hair. It used to be all gray, but since she has been practicing Falun Gong, the black hair has grown back!"

> "Look at her, she is over fifty-five, but her period has come back!"

"Everyone looks younger than they really are!"

"My skin is lighter, more white than it used to be."

This "faith-healing" method is explained as "mind over matter." One man said, "If you worry about the disease, have doubts, you award it reality, existence. Disease is an illusion, a by-product of the human mentality." Relapses were explained as "karma working itself out."

Within the Falun Gong community there is considerable social pressure on practitioners to abandon conventional medicine, but they do not all necessarily do so. One Western woman rattled a bottle of her kidney stones in my face, while describing how they had been removed by a surgeon. Master Li does not actually go on record as telling practitioners not to consult doctors.

Moral Reform (*Xinxing*)

Once their health crises are resolved, practitioners tend to focus on the equally dramatic phenomenon of moral regeneration. Morality means the "giving up of attachments" (bad habits, selfish indulgences) and cultivating the virtues of *zhen-shan-ren*.[6] They report feeling less work-driven, less materialistic, more family-oriented.

A Taiwanese man of thirty-four said, "We are taught to take over responsibilities, make a better effort as family members, citizens. We take our gains and profits more lightly, let things go according to natural law, 'let the chips fall where they may'."

Other informants said that, "[by] doing things for others, we are increasing our *xinxing*," and that "now we are much more sincere. We don't exaggerate or tell stories. We refrain from criticizing other people."

---

6. Translated as "Truth, Compassion, Forbearance." These three qualities/virtues are depicted at the highest level of the pyramid of the *fa* (universal law) and as the only criteria for distinguishing good and bad people. See Li, *Zhuan Falun* (1999, 13–17).

Spiritual Salvation (*"Consummation"*)

Mystical experience in Falun Gong is often expressed as a vision of the *falun*, the wheel of law, spinning in space, with flashing colors. This *falun*, or "law wheel" is an energy center, equivalent to the Hindu *chakra*. As it rotates, it repels negative forces and attracts positive energy. Some informants described it entering their lower abdomen, and some felt a churning motion in their bellies. One Western woman claimed, "I saw the *falun* – it was yellow and purple, then I saw the nine colors." A middle-aged man, healed of diabetes, shared his vision of the *falun*, as follows:

> I had sitting meditation, and I saw with my flesh eyes the *falun* wheel in the air, coming from the skies. It came down and went right into my lower abdomen. Master Li said "for every practitioner, I will install a Law Body in your lower abdomen." Since then I no longer suffer from cold in the winter, nor any illness.

Another common phenomenon is to encounter the Original True Self (*yuanshen*). A twenty-year-old Western student reported:

> I felt a warm sensation as I was sitting, a warm current swept upwards from my toes to my head. I cry a lot, and I began to cry dramatically. Then when it subsided I looked up and saw my face in the mirror. I had found my Original True Self! She was there in the mirror, so beautiful. I smiled at her, "I found you at last!"

A recurring experience among practitioners is *guanding*, the purification of karma, accompanied by strong physiological sensations. A young Chinese man recollected:

> For the first few months I couldn't feel anything, while people around me were saying, "Hey, I feel energy! I can see!" Then, the fourth month, as I did the exercises, the second set in my room, I feel something – *guanding* – it clears the body, head to foot. I cried, the tears dropped on my legs. Oh! It's real!

I thought. I was shocked! I felt the energy rushing through me for the next 24 hours.

Prescient dreams, paranormal experiences, glimpses into alternative universes with beings in other dimensions, and miraculous avoidances of traffic accidents are common features in the practitioners' inner life. Many of my informants related visions of "the Book":

One night I fell asleep and dreamed I was reading the Book. I seemed to be in another dimension. The Book was golden, shimmering. I seemed to understand every word I read. Our teacher stood beside me, kindly turning the pages, showing me things I do not understand. It was a beautiful dream, and I was excited.

Apocalyptic Activism (*fa-rectification*)[7]

The fourth phase requires participation in public demonstrations against the PRC government's persecution of Falun Gong practitioners. At this point, the goal of individual enlightenment appears to be subsumed into a self-denying, sacrificial participation in the apocalyptic cosmic struggle between the forces of good and evil, known as "*fa*-rectification."

There is no formal invitation to join an activist team, no organized induction, nor does Master Li issue specific instructions on how to protest. Rather, these exercises are planned in local meetings at the grassroots level. The heroic roles of the protester and the martyr are modeled in testimonials and stories at the Experience Sharing Conferences.

One McGill Ph.D. student in his early thirties, whom I observed at the Montreal conference in February 2000, is a striking example of

---

7. Originally I was intending to call this section "Political Protest and Activism," but practitioners are adamant in insisting that Master Li is apolitical, and that they are interested not in making a political statement, but rather in protecting their fellow practitioners, defending the honor of China, and standing up for the *fa* and eliminating evil.

conversion to the protest movement. In his testimonial he described how he was inspired by the stories of protesters who had returned from the PRC. Until then, he had been practicing Falun Dafa at home and focusing on his studies in engineering, refusing to get involved in the demonstrations. But suddenly, he felt he had a "dirty heart" in valuing his diploma too much, and not wanting to let go of money and a good life. So he bought a $1,000 plane ticket and left for China the day before his final exams. His wife was opposed to this decision and became very angry. He departed early while she and the baby were still asleep, leaving a letter announcing, "I am going to Beijing for the appeal." On the airplane, he passed out Falun Gong pamphlets and had packed a 5-meter-wide banner for Tiananmen Square. On his arrival, the customs officer took away his passport and detained him, not allowing him into China, but on seeing he was a McGill student, did not arrest him. While waiting to return to Canada, the engineering student had a dream of a yellow hand standing on the ground. It was "the hand of opportunity" he decided, so he returned to Montreal just in time to take his exams, and passed with flying colors. But his wife had left home with their baby son by the time he returned.

Having proposed a four-phase model of conversion for the Chinese practitioners, I will now address some of the enigmatic features of their two-tier protest movement – that seems to combine an *exoteric* movement (that focuses on the rational and respectable pursuit of human rights, expressed in the international arena) with an *esoteric* movement (that focuses on an apocalyptic ideology and an ethic of martyrdom).

The Emergence of an Apocalyptic Theory

Li Hongzhi has forged an apocalyptic theodicy for making sense of the PRC government's suppression of Falun Gong, and for motivating his disciples in their civil disobedience. Li Hongzhi's apocalyptic ideology has been stimulated by and flourished in the hostile environment of the PRC, where oppression, persecution, and injustice have escalated steadily since July 1999. The United States-based Falun Dafa Information Center (2002) reported that 365 practitioners had died in custody, and over 50,000 were in prison, labor camps, or mental hospitals.

The emergence of Falun Gong's protest movement can be analyzed as the result of a give-and-take relationship between the charismatic Master and his disciples. While Master Li supplies the ideas, his disciples choose how to put them into action. Master Li then responds to their actions in his next article, either commending, encouraging, cautioning or castigating them for their actions. He provides occult interpretations of the ongoing struggle in China, and fresh spiritual motivation for their continuing dissent.

Apocalyptic undercurrents were already present in Li Hongzhi's speeches before the 1999 crackdown began. In *Zhuan Falun* terms like the "*dharma*-ending period"[8] or "Last Havoc"[9] are traditional, inherited from the Buddhist tradition. Master Li cited Nostradamus in his speeches (in Toronto, May 1999, and in Chicago, June 1999) as predicting the PRC's crackdown on Falun Gong. He identified Jiang Zemin as the "Third Antichrist," after Napoleon and Hitler, as prophesied by Nostradamus.

In 1999 Falun Gong was still fervently apolitical and optimistic that the PRC government would soon recognize practitioners as loyal citizens and grant them freedom to practice. Since Spring 2000, however, Li's articles on the www.minghui.net website began responding more directly to the suffering of his disciples.

As late as June 2000 the goal of individual consummation was still possible and relevant. Master Li was still advising practitioners to ignore the political climate, study the *fa*, and keep on practicing. But he also congratulated the martyrs of Tiananmen Square who had "consummated their own majestic positions" and presumably earned a posthumous enlightenment, or crown of martyrdom: "Whether

---

8. Master Li explains the *dharma*-ending period as beginning five hundred years after the death of Shakyamuni Buddha, when his *dharma* (teaching) would lose its salvific edge. See Li, *Zhuan Falun* (1999, 14).

9. In *Zhuan Falun* (1999, 14), this is explained as the third phase of evolution of the universe.

they are imprisoned or lose their human lives for persevering in Dafa cultivation, they achieve Consummation" (Li Hongzhi 2000a).

The Master's message was summarized in August 2000 as a call to battle at a time of "cosmic changes," with an insistence on activist involvement in "validating Dafa." The catchphrase "Power of Truth" as a means to defeat "malicious beings" was reminiscent of Gandhi's *satyagraha*. But prudence was advised. Disciples were urged to be "intelligent and flexible"; there were "various ways" to inform the public (*Minghui* Editors 2000).

Volunteering for death and imprisonment was not the only path to salvation, for "the police vans are not the [Law boat], the prisons are not the temples, labor camps are not the environment for cultivation. Going to Tiananmen Square to appeal is just one of the various means." The less-risky activist efforts in the West were commended, which "call[ed] for release of innocent arrested practitioners" (ibid.).

Master Li echoed this voice of caution in his letter of August 12, 2000, entitled "Rationality," in which he attempted to rein in his disciples' self-destructive impulses:

> Some students suggest that the best practice of cultivation is to get placed into detention centers or labor camps, or get sentenced to jail in order to validate the Fa. Students, it is not so. (Li Honzhi 2000b)

But he appeared to contradict this statement two days later when he urges his disciples to "let go of the thought of life and death under any circumstances." He appears to suggest martyrdom as he invites them to join the cosmic battle in the Three Realms (Li Honzhi 2000c).

By September 28, 2000, participation in *fa*-rectification had become the *only* path to salvation. Master Li condemned those who still sought individual enlightenment through the peaceful route of meditation: "In the midst of Fa-rectification ... no matter how he persists in studying the Fa and doing exercises at home, he is being controlled by demons and is enlightening along an evil path." (Li Hongzhi 2000d).

On October 21, 2000 Master Li emerged from hiding to deliver his first public speech since the crackdown began. In this speech he left his disciples no option but to participate in the cosmic battle as a great honor, since no other reality was left: "a tribulation like this has never taken place in history.... You ... are linked to the Fa." He warned, "no human attachment can be taken to heaven"; that "[fruit] status demands ... a massive test"; and that "evil demons are behind the tribulation" (Li Hongzhi 2000e).

At times Master Li seemed to advocate what his critics might interpret as a fanatical dehumanization process for the forging of fearless martyrs, as for example when he states: "a veteran disciple ... should ... regard himself as a particle of Dafa ... play the role of a Dafa particle" (Li Hongzhi 2000d). He consistently emphasized free choice, however, and the need for self-initiated actions. He kept insisting "it is not for him to spell things out" (personal communication from a confidential source, April 3, 1999).

A new development occurred in the important letter of January 2, 2001, "Beyond the Limits of Forbearance," in which Master Li urged practitioners to continue standing up against the "evil," but to develop some self-defence reflexes.

> Forbearance is not cowardice, much less is it resigning oneself to adversity. ... But Forbearance does not mean tolerating evil beings. ... If the evil has already reached the point where it is unsaveable and unkeepable, then various measures at different levels can be used to stop it and eradicate it. (Li Hongzhi 2001b)

He advised his disciples to stop cooperating meekly with their persecutors. He clearly identified Jiang Zemin's security officers as "evil beings" devoid of "human nature."

His next letters reaffirmed the apocalyptic significance of the struggle in China. He assured disciples that the evil regime in the PRC cannot last; that the cosmic war has already been won in the higher realms (Li Hongzhi 2001c). He prophesied the collapse of the "ruling party and its regime" due to the people's mistrust. He claimed the persecution was useful as a test: "to solidify *dafa* and remove cultivators' fundamental attachments so as to free cultivators from the shackles of humanness and karma."

In March 2001 he presented the vision of a large-scale judgment, where good will be separated from evil: "in the future several billion people are to obtain the Fa ... once this evil drama is over a large-scale elimination of humankind will commence" (Li Hongzhi 2001d). He awarded Jiang Zemin's regime cosmic significance as "old forces" that "utilized the evil." Falun Gong disciples were, in stark contrast, "sacred, magnificent."

In two of his letters Master Li came dangerously close to blaming the martyrs for getting themselves killed as the result of their own "human attachments" or "karma." He cryptically said, "I can tell you that if a person doesn't have that much karma, he won't have tribulations that severe" (Li Hongzhi 2000e). Another troubling letter threatened the crown of martyrs: "The most severely persecuted ones are precisely those students who harbor attachments. The more fearful they are inside, the more evil will go after such students" (Li Hongzhi 2001f). When I asked practitioners about these passages, they assured me he was referring only to the "reformed" apostates who broke under torture.

At the May 2001 Experience Sharing Conference in Ottawa, Master Li assured his students that they were "entrusted with a great historic mission ... amidst Fa-rectification." He made it clear, once again, that cultivation for the purpose of "improving themselves for Consummation" is not an option in these emergency times. He polarized the forces of good and evil and demanded a more forceful policy: "The contrast between this evil and our goodness is dramatic. So in the process of eliminating it, don't be lenient at all – just eliminate it! Here I'm not referring to humans but to those evil beings that manipulate humans" (Li Hongzhi 2001e). He advocated the cultivation of magical powers in order to overcome the enemy: "Actually my disciples all have abilities" and assured them they could levitate, given a correct understanding of molecular physics.

Towards a Philosophy of Protest

In order to understand Falun Gong's protest movement, I invited the practitioners to convey their own views of what the movement meant to them on spiritual and cosmological levels.

This was not easily accomplished, however, for there is no tradition of exegesis in Falun Gong. In a sense, the charisma of Master Li requires that the students confine themselves to an oral tradition.[10] The students read Master Li's writings over and over again in their reading groups, and resist any tendency to codify, summarize, or analyze their content. There is no priesthood or hierarchy of teachers. Since Master Li's statements are often enigmatic and his references ambiguous (not to mention his use of specialized Chinese terms), I was constantly asking disciples what he meant. They would always preface their comments with "according to *my* understanding" or "this is only *my* opinion," followed by a disclaimer to the effect that Master Li was coming from another, higher level of reality, so it was impossible for us to grasp his meaning completely.

Thus, Falun Gong is still essentially an oral tradition. Disciples read out loud from Li's published speeches, and do not question or summarize their content. While textual analysis is taboo, they are encouraged to relate personal anecdotes when a certain passage evokes memories. These communications were didactic and inspirational, and evidently facilitated a bonding between group members.

Three Directions in the Protest Movement

I found three different levels of interpretation of Master Li's philosophy of protest among the three Falun Gong communities I visited. The first emphasized the mythic, apocalyptic aspect of the Chinese

---

10. Usually "oral" means issuing directly from the mouth of the charismatic leader, whereas written revelations are indications of institutionalization. I would argue, however, that the freshness, flexibility, sacredness, and unaccountability of Master Li's Internet communications fit the characteristics of an oral tradition.

branch of the movement, the second focused on the global human rights and public relations aspect, and the third sought to expand a viable new religious movement among Chinese expatriate communities in the West while they engaged in demonstrations to release prisoners in the PRC.

When I visited the Ottawa Falun Gong community, mainly composed of Chinese couples in their mid-thirties, software designers and computer programmers who worked for Nortel, I asked them, "Why do practitioners stand up against the Chinese government?" Their responses showed a strong concern for the future of China. Some referred to China's divinely ordained central role in Master Li's apocalyptic vision. Most quoted the Master's apocalyptic statements; that it was necessary to "defend the Dafa" because we are in a "critical juncture in human history," the "dharma-ending period," and we must "face the tribulation" in order to assist in "rectifying the universe." One activist explained:

> We are in a special period, helping in the purification of the universe. We melt ourselves into the Law in order to protect the Law, like microscopic electrons. It is the Rectification. Millions are melting themselves into the Law in Beijing. In order to assist in the Rectification, they have left babies at home, quit their jobs.

Many of my Chinese informants regarded the victims of the crackdown as martyrs, who died for the Truth. They expressed their conviction that, because these people laid aside personal "attachments" and "melted into the *fa*," that they would be propelled instantly into "consummation." One woman said, "If we are quiet, then the Great Law won't be protected. We must be selfless and endure at this time. For some, who can put aside themselves, and stand up for Truth, for sure they will be enlightened!" But my impression was that consummation seemed to be a by-product of martyrdom, rather than its goal: "I don't think any of them thought about individual consummation before. They sacrificed their own body to awaken more people."

One couple held up the examples of Chen Zixiu and Chen Zhao Jinghua who had been tortured and chose to die rather than renounce their faith. "These individuals endured something that could not be endured by ordinary people," the husband said. "I feel part of their mind or body has the quality of enlightened beings or they could not endure."

Many testimonials I heard at the Experience Sharing Conferences conveyed the mystical or magical dimensions of the disciples' activism:

> I was incarcerated for 40 hours! Cultivation is superpersonal, Master Li will take care of everything.
>
> Endure the tribulation. Like a drop of water in the sea, we go to Beijing.
>
> Falun Dafa is experiencing such great disruptions and demonic interference, we must defend the Dafa.

I found a very different type of activism when I visited New York over the American Thanksgiving weekend in 2000. Western disciples, the spokespersons for the New York group, seemed reluctant to embrace the apocalyptic ideology behind Falun Gong's activist movement. For them, the goal of cultivation was still *personal* spiritual evolution, and the rationale behind the protest was a purely secular one – to stand up for human rights and social justice (Li Hongzhi 2001c).

I interviewed two friends, a man and woman, who had done extensive lobbying work with the media, embassies, and human rights groups. The man, a successful rock musician, described his moral regeneration through the practice of Falun Gong, which had enabled him to give up drugs and alcohol and to resist the advances of beautiful groupies. As an African American, he confessed to feeling like an outsider in the Chinese community of practitioners. I asked him what he felt was the point of the resistance movement in the PRC. "Why not ask, 'What's the point of Martin Luther King's civil rights movement?'" he rejoined. "Sure, a few people got hurt, but should we go ahead treating blacks as inferior to whites?" The woman added, "Why did Gandhi organize nonviolent dissent in India? It worked, didn't it?"

But when I asked them about whether martyrdom indicated a *post facto* state of consummation, or mitigated the bad karma of China, they dismissed these notions as idiosyncratic heresies emanating from individual practitioners' misinterpretations of the Master's wisdom. These Western disciples stuck to human rights, religious freedom, and social justice arguments. They were simply not interested in Falun Gong's emerging culture of martyrdom.

A third type of activism was found among the Chinese practitioners who were established in the United States. On February 26, 2001, I interviewed eight practitioners in Dallas, Texas, who were kind enough to meet me at the airport baggage carousel during a long stopover. They explained their understanding of the Master's recent message in "Beyond the Limits of Forbearance." "He's saying don't cooperate with bad people, these are devil peoples so we should stop trying to educate them," a young computer programmer explained, "but he makes it clear that there is to be no violence, no anti-government activity." A woman engineer added:

> Normally, we recognize that different people have different understandings; that when people hit you, you don't hit back. If they create trouble for you, you thank them, for this is how you make progress. But *this* article tells practitioners that, at this stage, when bad people hit you, they are *evil*. They are not helping you to upgrade your *xinxing*, so don't thank them. They are a danger to the Dafa.

I asked these Chinese Texans what Master Li meant by "*fa*-rectification." Their answers revealed a gnostic edge to Master Li's cosmology. A young software designer said:

> For example, I am a programmer. The program I created is running in the computer the way I designed it, even if I am not there in the office. So, the *fa*-rectification is kind of like a program still running in the computer, everything going the way it's meant to be. It works from the top down. In higher places the evil is already cleared up.

I found it significant that this group of activists felt no pressure to fly to China and participate in the protest in Beijing. "We can do much more useful work here in the United States," they said. They talked about demonstrations they had organized in front of the PRC consulate in Houston, Texas. They were also less quick to compose hagiographies for the Chinese martyrs or award them posthumous enlightenment, although they commended their selfless courage.

These different schools of thought within Falun Gong's resistance movement reflect the decentralized, grassroots quality of the organization that is united only through the Master's charisma, which is mediated through the Internet.

Conclusion

In previous studies of violent episodes occurring in new religious and spiritual movements, scholars have found that three important factors contributing to their volatility and violence are a sectarian stance towards society, a communal structure, and a relatively small size. Studies of the infamous "suicide cults" – the Solar Temple, Heaven's Gate, the People's Temple, the Branch Davidians of Waco (in which last case the cause of the fire that killed 86 members is still in dispute) – have shown that the intense commitment to a prophet's ideology that led to the voluntary suicide of his devotees was enhanced by (and indeed only possible within) the intimacy of a small, segregated communal society (Hall and Schuyler 2000; Wessinger 2000; Bromley and Melton 2002; Lewis 2011).

Falun Gong is, in contrast, a large, international, decentralized and diffuse movement. Its members are mainly professionals or graduate students in technology and the sciences and appear to be socially ambitious and materialistic in their goals.[11] As J. Gordon Melton noted, "We won't find mass suicides happening in Scientology – there are too many scientologists, scattered around the world, and

---

11. See the results of our 2000 membership survey in Palmer and Ownby (2000).

they are well-integrated into society."¹² Thus, if we are to interpret Falun Gong's history of martyrdom as an ongoing religiously motivated "mass-suicide," it clearly poses an exception to the theories expounded by NRM scholars.

Falun Gong appears to be undergoing a tug-of-war between the global aspirations of an international new religious movement, and the conservative, spiritual undercurrents that are concerned with saving China and preserving ancient "cultivation practices" amidst the expatriate communities of technocratic modernists in the Chinese diaspora.

The variety in interpretative responses is perhaps inevitable in a rapidly changing apocalyptic religion spearheaded by the enigmatic prophecies of Li Hongzhi, who is responding to the escalating tension surrounding his movement in China. Perhaps these different activist approaches contain the potential for schisms between the more secular human rights lobbying groups who focus on social justice and the spiritually oriented Chinese patriots who embrace martyrdom.

The content and tone of Master Li's articles on the Internet have shifted since the crackdown began. At the beginning, the Master's concern was peacekeeping, to placate the authorities. He insisted that Falun Gong was not "political," and urged practitioners to remain loyal citizens to the PRC. He instructed them to respond to even the most severe persecution with "forbearance" – meaning to turn the other cheek. But by November 2000, Master Li had identified Jiang Zemen as the "Third Antichrist" prophesied by Nostradamus and was referring to his minions as "demons" and urging his practitioners to stop cooperating with "evil" (Li Hongzhi 2000f). At the May 2001 Ottawa conference he showed them how to fight back against the "evil" by using magical techniques.

The Experience Sharing testimonials I listened to in January 2000 tended to focus on miraculous healings, and on resolving conflicts at home or at work, as disciples upgraded their *xinxing*. But in May

---

12. Presentation at the Society for the Scientific Study of Religion in Houston, Texas, in October 2000.

2001, the overriding concern was to "suffocate the evil" in China and participate in the apocalyptic struggle called *fa*-rectification.

This shift represents a familiar human response to suffering and injustice; to create theodicies, to seek transcendental meaning in the deaths that have already occurred, to demonize the oppressors, and to forge an esoteric ideology that strengthens and unites the protesters.

There is a heroic, inspiring aspect to Falun Gong's struggle for justice that resonates with Gandhi's *satyagraha* and the American civil rights movement. But this struggle might be seen as foolhardy, since Master Li Hongzhi has encouraged his practitioners to place themselves in situations where many have suffered incarceration and died painful deaths, while the PRC administration continues to adopt draconian measures of social control against Falun Gong, the "evil cult."

How will this struggle be resolved? Will potential martyrs continue to gravitate towards Tiananmen Square, testing their *qigong* magical defenses against evil? Or will Master Li encourage his students to continue lobbying for religious freedom and justice in the West, but to avoid public demonstrations in the land of "Mighty Virtue," where they can still wage their psychic battles from the safety and privacy of their own homes?

References

Bromley, David G. and J. Gordon Melton (eds.). 2002. *Cults, Religion, and Violence*. Cambridge: Cambridge University Press.

Falun Dafa Information Center. 2002. "List and Case Descriptions of the 365 Falun Gong Practitioners Linked in the Persecution," 8 February. http://www.clearwisdom.net/emh/special column/death list.html

Hall, John and Philip D. Schuyler. 2000. *Apocalypse Observed: Religious Movements and Violence in North America, Europe and Japan*. New York: Routledge.

Lewis, James R. (ed.). 2011. *Violence and New Religious Movements*. Oxford: Oxford University Press.

Li Hongzhi. 1999. *Zhuan Falun*. Taiwan: Universe Publishing Company.

Li Hongzhi. 2000a. "Towards Consummation," 17 June. http://www.clearwisdom.net/eng/2000/Jun/17/JingWen061700.html

Li Hongzhi. 2000b. "Rationality," 12 August.
http://www.clearwisdom.net/eng/2000/Aug/12/JingWen081200.html
Li Hongzhi. 2000c. "Eliminate Your Last Attachment," 14 August.
http://www.clearwisdom.net/emh/articles/2001/7/25/12527.html
Li Hongzhi. 2000d. "Serious Teachings," 28 September.
http://www.clearwisdom.net/emh/Sept/28/index.html
Li Hongzhi. 2000e. "Speech by Li Hongzhi at the Western U.S. Experience Sharing Conference of Falun Dafa," 21 October.
http://www.clearwisdom.net/eng/2000/Nov/05/JingWen/110500.html
Li Hongzhi. 2000f. "Prediction by Nostradamus on the Third Antichrist," 24 November.
http://www.clearwisdom.net/emh/articles/2000/11/24/6044.html
Li Hongzhi. 2001a. "Teaching the Fa at the 2001 Canada Falun Gong Cultivation Experience-sharing Conference," 31 May.
http://www.clearwisdom.net/emh/articles/2001/5/22/10271.html
Li Hongzhi. 2001b. "Beyond the Limits of Forbearance," 2 January.
http://www.clear-wisdom.net/net/eng/2001/Jan/02/JingWen010201.html
Li Hongzhi. 2001c. "Coercion Cannot Change Peoples' Hearts," 6 March.
http://www.clearwisdom.net/2001/Mar/JingWen030601.html
Li Hongzhi. 2001d. "Persons in Charge of the European Fa Conference and All Attendees," 20 March.
http://www.clearwisdom.net/eng/2001/Mar/20/JingWen032001.html
Li Hongzhi. 2001e. "Dafa Disciples' Thoughts Are Powerful," 25 April.
http://www.clearwisdom.net/eng/2001/Apr/25/JingWen042501.html
Li Hongzhi. 2001f. "Teaching the Fa."
http://www.clearwisdom.net/emh/articles/2001/5/22/10271.html
Lofland, John and Rodney Stark (1965). "On Becoming a World Saver: A Theory of Conversion to a Deviant Perspective," *American Sociological Review*, 30, 862–75.
Minghui Editors. 2000. "The Purpose of Stepping Forward to Validate the Dafa," 11 August.
http://www.clearwisdom.net/eng/2000/Aug/11/EDITOR081100.html
Minghui Editors. 2001. "Canada Falun Dafa Experience Sharing Conference Successfully Held in Ottawa" (www.falundafa.minghui.org), 22 May.
Palmer, Susan and David Ownby. 2000. "Falun Dafa Practitioners: A Preliminary Research Report," *Nova Religio: The Journal of Alternative and Emergent Religions*, 4:1 (October), 133–7.
Wessinger, Catherine (ed.). 2000. *Millennialism, Persecution, and Violence: Historical Cases*. Syracuse, NY: Syracuse University Press.

Williams, Philip F. and Yenna Wu. 2004. *The Great Wall of Confinement: The Chinese Prison Camp Through Contemporary Fiction and Reportage.* Berkeley: University of California Press.

Susan J. Palmer is an Affiliate Professor in the Religion Department of Concordia University, and a Research Associate at McGill University; also *co-chercheur* with the *Centre d'expertise et de formation sur les intégrismes religieux et la radicalisation* (CEFIR) at the Cégep Édouard-Montpetit Longueil, Quebec. Her research in the field of new religious movements has been funded by six federal grants from the Social Sciences and Humanities Research Council (SSHRC). She has published eleven book-length sociological studies of new religious movements, most notably *The New Heretics of France* (2011), *Aliens Adored: Rael's New Religion* (2004), and *Storming Zion: Government Raids on Religious Communities*, co-authored with Stuart Wright (2015).

4. Burning Faith
Interpreting the 1.23 Incident[1]

James R. Lewis

> It is in fact time to let go of your last attachments. As cultivators, you already know that you should ... let go of all worldly attachments, including the attachment to the human body. Dafa disciples [must rid themselves] of all ordinary human attachments, including the attachment to their human lives, in order to reach the realms of higher beings. (Li Hongzhi 2004a)

One of the most dramatic events in the ongoing conflict between the Falun Gong (FLG) movement and the People's Republic of China (PRC) was the self-immolation of five practitioners out of a group of seven – which included a talented young music student as well as a twelve-year-old girl – on January 23, 2001 (subsequently referred to as the "1.23 Incident"), which was the date of Chinese New Year's Eve in that particular year.[2] These followers chose Tiananmen Square as the site of their protest against the government's crackdown on FLG, a crackdown that had begun in earnest in 1999, following earlier protests in Tiananmen Square. Though security services dowsed the flames in short order, one practitioner died in the square and four were seriously burnt (one of the latter victims subsequently died).

---

1. An earlier version of this chapter appeared as "A Burning Faith in the Master: Interpreting the 1.23 Incident," *Journal of Religion and Violence* (2018), 6:2, 172–90.
2. The beginning of each new year is determined by the day of the new moon; thus the date varies from year to year.

According to the surviving self-immolators, this tragic event was set in motion by a dream reported by a fellow practitioner, Liu Yunfang. The following account is compiled from several different sources (e.g., Kaiwind 2007; Liu Yunfang 2012; Wang Jindong 2015):

> I dreamt that I traveled to Beijing. After arriving, and just before I walked onto Tiananmen Square, I drank a lot of gasoline, and poured gasoline on my body. Although I had brought along a lighter and matches, I also fixed an auto-ignition device on my arm (setting it for three minutes) for fear that the police might take away the lighter and matches. When I finally went into Tiananmen Square, the police immediately stopped me because of the strong smell of gasoline. Although the police stopped me from igniting the gasoline myself, the timing instrument set my body on fire, and the policemen had to let go of me. There was gasoline both in my stomach and on my body. When I spoke, gasoline spurted out of my mouth. And when I turned around with my mouth open, a big circle of fire enclosed me. The gasoline on my body also fell downward to the ground and the fire spread, forming a sea of fire around me. I talked about the merit of Falun Gong and how to practice it, and recited Li Hongzhi's scripture. When [I] finished, the fire got stronger and stronger. Then from amidst the fire, there emerged a shining Buddha. It was a Buddha just sitting there with Buddha light shining around him! At the time, I subconsciously thought that this was master Li Hongzhi, and that my self-immolation would prove that the "Dafa" was true!

Liu also felt that Li Hongzhi (LHZ; Falun Gong's founder leader) was spiritually communicating with him, requesting that he gather together other Falun Gong (FLG) practitioners for the purpose of carrying out a group self-immolation in Tiananmen Square. After the core group had been assembled, they decided to carry out their self-immolations on New Year's Eve. They chose this particular day because the legend behind Chinese New Year is that a terrifying mythical beast, Nian, who consumed livestock and human beings (including children), was driven away by villagers using the three things that Nian feared – the color red, loud noises, and fire.

By the time of the chosen day, there were seven protesters – Liu Yunfang, Wang Jindong, and Liu Baorong – and two mother–daughter pairs: Hao Huijun and Chen Guo; Liu Chunling and Liu Siying. These practitioners split into several groups and made their way into the square with Sprite bottles filled with gasoline hanging from their arms, underneath their armpits. They also carried two razor blades for slashing open the bottles and two lighters (in case one failed) to start a fire. They had pre-agreed that they would all begin setting themselves ablaze at the same time, 2:30 pm. Out of the original seven people, Liu Yunfang and Liu Baorong were stopped before they could set themselves alight. According to Liu Yunfang's account:

> I used the blade to cut open the bottle, and gasoline poured out onto my body. Dropping the blade, I immediately took the lighter ..., but there were several police on the spot to stop me. It made me disappointed, and I was desperately struggling, loudly shouting: "Falun Dafa is good!" "Truthfulness good and forbearance!" In less than 10 minutes, the police had put me into a car, and I was sent to the Beijing Detention Center. (Liu Yunfang 2012)

Over the years, Tiananmen Square has been a favorite place for protesters of various kinds, including Falun Gong practitioners, to demonstrate. As a consequence, there were numerous security personnel, both uniformed and non-uniformed, spread out around the square that day – a fact that undoubtedly saved the lives of most of the self-immolators. Several years after the event, Wang Jindong, one of the organizers, composed a substantial description of his own experience. Because it conveys a concrete sense of the incident, his account is worth quoting at length:

> No matter what other people would do, I [felt that I] must complete my task to defend Falun Dafa. When I got to the northeastern side of the monument, I found four policemen in plain clothes who then walked toward me with their eyes staring at me. I felt it would be too late if I did not take action. I used the blade I had prepared in my hand to cut through the clothes

and slice the bottle, and then I threw away the blade and took out the lighter with my left hand. At that moment, the policemen hurried towards me. They saw I was holding a lighter, but it seemed as if they had no idea of what I was about to do. They were stunned. When they were ten steps away from me, I struck the lighter. The fire instantly devoured me ... Being suffocated by the flames, I heard nothing but the whirr of the flame, but I thought my mission was about to be fulfilled.

At that moment, the policemen used something to put out the fire. (Later I learned from the video footage that it was a fire-extinguishing blanket.) I refused, twice. However, some other policemen managed to put out the fire with extinguishers. Greatly disappointed, I stood up and shouted, "Truthfulness, Compassion and Tolerance is the law of the universe; the law deserves to be respected by all people in the world. The Master [LHZ] is the supreme Buddha of the universe!" When the police were about to drive their car over to pick me up, we suddenly heard someone shout, "There is fire over there!" One of the police remained to take care of me, while the others rushed toward the places where my fellow practitioners had set themselves on fire. I kept on shouting slogans. Within ten minutes the police had driven their car to me. They then put me in the police car and sent me to a hospital. (Wang 2015)

Falun Gong quickly distanced itself from the event. Within 24 hours of its occurrence, FLG issued a press release which asserted that Chinese authorities had orchestrated the self-immolations as a way of framing the organization. New Tang Dynasty TV, an enterprise created by Falun Gong followers, also eventually produced a widely distributed video, *False Fire*, which seemingly supported the claim that the event was faked. The government, for its part, initially

> ... attempted to quash news of the event, even though Western journalists had been present and had recorded it; the tape was immediately confiscated by authorities. But soon the government realized they could use this as an opportunity to muster opposition to Falun Gong. A week after the incident had occurred state television broadcast some footage showing the twelve-year-old daughter of one of the practitioners, rolling

around in agony. The government framed the deaths as "cultic suicide," and discredited them as a form of protest. (Farley 2014a, 222–3)

Though there were accusations that the directive to immolate themselves came directly from Li Hongzhi, there are other possibilities, given the mostly decentralized structure of the movement at ground level.[3] There was also a spate of FLG suicides or attempted suicides in China at around the same time as the Tiananmen Square event – suicides to which few observers have called attention. Finally, there are certain aspects of suicide in Chinese culture that can be brought to bear on the interpretation of this tragedy.

The initial purpose of this essay is to assess the plausibility of conflicting interpretations of the 1.23 Incident. Naturally, the two major parties to the controversy which form the background for this incident – namely, the Falun Gong organization vs. the government of the People's Republic of China – dismiss each other's perspectives as self-evidently false. Specifically, PRC authorities consider that FLG's defenders have been duped by Falun Gong propaganda, while FLG supporters "summarily dismiss everyone" who gives serious consideration to the Chinese position "as either being on Beijing's payroll or mindless zombies, and every single piece of accusation against them as Beijing-backed propaganda" (Yue 2017).

Because I anticipate that many readers of this essay will be Westerners, and therefore inclined to automatically defend the human rights of "innocent" Falun Gong practitioners as "self-evidently" the correct position which any well-meaning person should take, let me preface my remarks by referring the reader to another essay in which I discuss why PRC authorities came to perceive FLG as a threat to the social order, as well as the esoteric theory of karma that motivates practitioners to "deliberately seek" (Palmer 2001, 17) being brutalized and even martyred (Lewis 2016). (In this regard, also refer to S. Palmer 2003.)

---

3. The question of FLG's organizational structure is thoroughly addressed in Tong (2002).

The intention of my earlier essay was not to completely absolve Chinese authorities of all responsibility for the conflict, but rather to argue (1) that there were at least two sides to the controversy, and (2) that the image of Falun Gong as an innocent, "passive and victimized group that needs to be 'saved'" (Liu 2005, 14) was a conscious creation of the FLG organization, designed to evoke support from non-PRC audiences. In another essay, co-authored with Nicole S. Ruskell (Lewis and Ruskell 2016), we analyzed the specific strategies by which FLG has been able to successfully promote this image to the world outside of China.[4]

Let me finally address my use of Chinese sources. I know that many Western observers – and especially Falun Gong adherents – automatically dismiss the accuracy of mainland sources, such as Facts on Falun Gong (facts.org.cn). I should thus note that, in a number of cases, I have been able to check media articles that have been re-posted on the Facts on Falun Gong (Facts) website against the originals, and found that they were reproduced faithfully, without modification, even when such articles included criticisms of PRC authorities. Additionally, Facts has always represented my work accurately, without exaggeration. Thus, while it is obvious that Facts has a strong critical point of view that focuses on the dark side of Falun Gong, from my experience they do not do so by inventing

---

4. FLG has been able to influence other media via its extensive presence on the web (Yu 2009, 132), through its direct press releases and through its own media. Falun Gong has also been able to propagate its point of view indirectly, through other, non-FLG sources, which creates the impression of multiple sources for the same narrative. Thus, for example, "The press often quote Amnesty International, but Amnesty's reports are not independently verified, and mainly come from Falun Gong sources" (Kavan 2005). Additionally, Falun Gong followers and/or sympathizers de facto control the relevant webpages in Wikipedia, a standard source for journalists operating under tight deadlines (Bell and Boas 2003, 287). On this last point, refer, e.g., to Sheng Jiang (2015) "Is Falun Gong's Wikipedia page objective?" https://www.quora.com/is-Falun-Gongs-Weikipedia-page-objective (accessed June 19, 2016) and User: Colipon/Falun Gong. https://en.wikipedia.org/wiki/User:Colipon/Falun_Gong (accessed June 20, 2016).

negative information. Lastly, though it probably does not need to be stated, the majority of references I utilize in my analysis of Falun Gong are not from PRC sources, with many from FLG sources or from sources supportive of Falun Gong.

To now shift to my analysis: The two basic opposing viewpoints were established almost immediately in the aftermath of the incident; these were: (1) the self-immolations were directly ordered by Li Hongzhi vs. (2) the immolations were staged by the PRC for propaganda purposes. The first of these interpretations of events was provided to the CNN reporters who were present in Tiananmen Square at the time: To quote from the initial CNN report:

> A CNN producer and cameraman saw a person sit down on a pavement, pour gasoline on his clothes and set himself on fire. Flames shot high into the air against a backdrop of a gray Chinese New Year's Eve afternoon with piles of snow packed onto the square. Police ran to the flames and extinguished them within minutes, as security personnel rushed to the area near People's Heroes Monument at the square's center. As military police apprehended the [CNN] crew and physically restrained them, the crew witnessed four more people immolating themselves. They raised their hands above their heads and staggered slowly about, flames tearing through their clothing ...
>
> Police issued the CNN crew a statement after their detention on Tiananmen Square confirming that one person had died and four were injured. Police said another person had been detained on the scene with two flasks of gasoline. According to the statement, the Falun Gong followers had burned themselves under the direction of Li Hongzhi, leader of the "evil cult." (MacKinnon 2001a)

Falun Gong's official response appeared so quickly that it was able to be included in a second CNN report the very next day:

> Falun Gong issued a statement saying: "This so-called suicide attempt on Tiananman Square has nothing to do with Falun Gong practitioners because the teachings of Falun Gong

prohibit any form of killing. Mr. Li Hongzhi, the founder of the practice, has explicitly stated that suicide is a sin." ...

The statement accused China's state-run news agency Xinhua, which also identified the burn victims as Falun Gong members, of lying. It said the Xinhua report was "yet another attempt by [China] to defame the practice of Falun Gong" and called on international media and human rights groups to investigate. The statement did not offer its own explanation of the incident (MacKinnon 2001b).

However, the Falun Gong organization eventually developed a sophisticated and detailed interpretation of the incident, asserting that it was a propaganda event staged by PRC authorities, as laid out in subsequent FLG publications (e.g., He 2014a, b, and c) and in the New Tang Dynasty TV documentary, *False Fire* (http://www.falsefire.com). For their part, Chinese authorities began a renewed media campaign, renewing the initial campaign that had been set in motion in 1999, following the official banning of Falun Gong:

> Television images of emotionally charged hospital scenes of self-immolation victims, particularly the repeated (contrasting) images of the young college student and the primary school girl before and after the incident, worked to dispel any initial doubt, indifference or even antagonism that many people had towards the state-led media campaign against Falun Gong. (Yu Haiqing 2009, 128)

Charges and countercharges regarding the interpretation of this event have repeatedly been hurled back and forth between Falun Gong and PRC authorities over the past sixteen years. A full analysis of these accusations would go beyond the task I have set myself in the present paper. Instead, I will restrict myself to discussing what I regard as strong points made by each side of this controversy regarding the details of the 1.23 Incident, and then put forward evidence to support an alternative interpretation of the event. First, let us examine Falun Gong's critical analysis of one particular point.

Liu Siying, the twelve-year-old girl who was set on fire by her practitioner mother during the incident, was subsequently treated in Jishuitan Hospital and lived for another two and a half months, until her death on March 17, 2001. None of her relatives were allowed to visit her during this time, and the only reporters allowed to interview her were from the Xinhua News Agency, China's official news agency, and from CCTV (China Central Television), another state-owned enterprise. Falun Gong spokespeople have called attention to the fact that Liu Siying was fully covered in gauze and that the CCTV reporter who interviewed her for a special televised program on the 1.23 Incident was not wearing a sterile mask or other protective clothing, further asserting that this would have been standard practice in burn wards. Though the latter point about standard practice can be disputed (a function of the severity of the burn and of how long it has been since the patient was burnt), the careful isolation of Liu Siying and the apparent effort to disguise her identity when she (or someone else posing as her) was interviewed by CCTV makes Falun Gong's counter-interpretation seem plausible. Video footage had been shot of Liu Siying in flames while screaming for her mother during the incident, and that footage was subsequently used as a core icon in the TV campaign against FLG. Thus it would have made sense for government authorities to have tried to manipulate every aspect of what the public knew about this young girl.

To get a sense of what I regard as the less compelling aspects of Falun Gong's analysis of the event, we can consider a sample detail in its discussion of Wang Jindong, one of the individuals who planned the self-immolations. Wang has been a central figure in the war of words over the proper interpretation of the 1.23 Incident (he passed away a number of years ago). Though he remained faithful to Li Hongzhi for some time following his self-immolation attempt, Wang eventually rejected Falun Gong, and subsequently authored a moderately lengthy statement in which he described the background leading up to the incident, his actions on the day of the self-immolations, and his subsequent reflections. The video recording of Wang setting himself on fire, as well as his later statements, have been subjected to minute analysis and criticism by FLG followers, who, echoing the organization's original response, have even denied that the individual in the video was ever a member. For example, Falun Gong analysts call attention to the shoes worn by the individual identified as Wang Jindong, asserting that they were the same as those worn by uniformed policemen – a coincidence easily explained by Wang as a gift from a former employer (on this point, refer to his 2015 statement).

For interpreting the 1.23 Incident, I tend not to be interested in these details. Rather, I find myself instead focusing on a statement attributed to Wang Jindong which makes an extremely compelling point, whether or not Wang was the actual author of this statement:

> Could the government arrange the 12-year-old student? Could the government buy over the two mothers and two daughters? I would like to ask the rumor makers, would you allow your family to self-immolate [even] if you were given 100 million Yuan? (Wang 2015)

The general point being made here is obvious: If the 1.23 self-immolators were not Falun Gong followers, then what could have motivated them to set themselves on fire? And however much one was being paid, could any mother have doused her daughter with gasoline and then set her alight?

Let me add that Wang's statement came vividly to mind when I met Chen Guo, the young music student who set herself on fire along with her mother on that fateful day. Formerly a talented musician who, as a young girl, had already won international acclaim for her mastery of the *pipa* (a traditional stringed instrument), Chen Guo struck me as quite sweet. Unfortunately, her face was a "blotchy mass of grafted skin with no nose and no ears" (Page 2002). I was forcibly struck by the depth of her tragedy when, upon leaving her house, I went to shake her hand, only to remember that she had lost both hands in the incident. Her explanation for why she and her fellow self-immolators had made their extreme sacrifice? "We wanted to strengthen the force of Falun Gong" (ibid.).

This spirit of devotion contrasts sharply with the tone of Falun Gong's initial press release, which bluntly denied that any of its members were involved in the incident:

> This so-called suicide attempt on Tiananmen Square has nothing to do with Falun Gong practitioners because the teachings of Falun Gong prohibit any form of killing. Mr. Li Hongzhi, the founder of the practice, has explicitly stated that suicide is a sin. (quoted in Schauble 2001)

It seems that by redefining the self-immolators as non-practitioners, they felt they could deny any connection with Falun Gong. However, over and above the question of what could have motivated non-practitioners (as FLG originally claimed) to set themselves and their children on fire, there is alternative evidence that the self-immolators were all followers. Thus, for example, with the exception of twelve-year-old Liu Siying, all of the self-immolators "had protested Beijing's actions against Falun Gong in Tiananmen Square previously, according to the Hong Kong-based Information Center for Human Rights and Democracy" (Pan 2001). (And note that this information center is not under the control of PRC authorities.)

It should also be noted that being abandoned by the Falun Gong organization did not seem to discourage other practitioners from following in the Tiananmen Square protesters' footsteps. These additional suicides are compelling evidence (1) that other followers independently interpreted Li Hongzhi's call to action as a call to make the ultimate sacrifice, and (2) that while one might be able to convincingly make the case that PRC authorities staged the 1.23 Incident, it is highly unlikely that the authorities staged multiple suicide events all over China – events that were neither videotaped nor later featured in Chinese news media:

> [On February 16, 2001,] Another member of the banned Falun Gong spiritual group committed suicide by setting himself on fire .... [S]tate television showed police officers covering the body with a sheet and quoted a witness as saying, "He poured gasoline over his head, lit it, and burst into flames." The news

> agency identified the dead man as Tan Yihui, a shoe shiner from Hunan province, in central China. It said Mr. Tan, 25, was dead by the time the police arrived and extinguished the fire … . Officials said they discovered a six-page suicide note nearby that identified him as a member of Falun Gong and that said he wished to "forget about life and death and achieve perfection in Paradise." (Rosenthal 2001)

> The self-immolations continued when on July 1, Luo Guili set himself alight in a city square in Nanning in southern China. Barely nineteen years old, he died the following day of severe burns and heart and lung failure. (Farley 2014b, 223)

> [O]n June 29 [of the same year], 16 Falun Gong followers in a labor camp in Harbin attempted mass suicide by hanging themselves with ropes fashioned from bedsheets. Ten of them, all women, died. [Additionally,] eleven sect members in a reeducation center had undertaken mass suicide and three died from the attempt (Chang 2004, 28).

There were also numerous cases of practitioners committing suicide by throwing themselves off buildings (Wang 2015; Li 2014). I should add that in October of 2016, I had a conversation with a former deputy provincial leader of Falun Gong who told me that at least eleven of her former associates had killed themselves by leaping from rooftops.

Regarding the labor camp and reeducation center suicides, Falun Gong's response was that these followers had been tortured to death and that "the camp had labeled their deaths suicide to cover up its crime" (Smith 2001). As was previously noted, in most disputes between Falun Gong and the Chinese government every major accusation is matched by a counter-accusation. However, in this case, I would argue that neither Chinese authorities nor the Falun Gong organization were the immediate causes of these various suicides and attempted suicides. Rather, the fact that they were carried out in no discernable pattern seems to indicate that they were not undertaken under the specific direction of either Li Hongzhi or the Chinese state.

At the individual practitioner level, there generally seems to be little or no direction from the Falun Gong leadership. (Though there are exceptions to this general pattern; e.g., I have spoken with former practitioners who report having been directed to participate in specific demonstrations – such as the Zhongnanhai demonstration in 1999 – by Falun Gong leaders.) In fact, the lack of such governance from the top has allowed schisms to develop under local leadership (e.g., see Thornton 2003, 264; Bell and Boas 2004, 282). Rather,

> In light of the Chinese government's persecution of Falun Gong, founder Li Hongzhi had fashioned an apocalyptic ideology to motivate his disciples to instigate and participate in civil disobedience. [However,] would-be activists were not formally invited to become a member of an activist team. There were no formal instructions on how to dissent. [Instead,] Civil disobedience actions were planned at local meetings. (Farley 2004, 224)

This does not, however, mean – as Li disingenuously has claimed (and as he explicitly instructs his followers to tell outsiders) – that "Falungong has no organization, but follows the formless nature of the Great Tao" (Palmer 2007, 264). Rather, the Falun Gong organization has people at all levels functioning as leaders (Lewis and Ruskell 2017; Zhao 2003, 216). And in contrast to the assertion that the founder was never in day-to-day control of the movement, LHZ could mobilize thousands of practitioners, seemingly overnight, for massive demonstrations in China prior to the crackdown (Palmer 2007, 252).

In the case of the 1.23 Incident, however, it is most probable that a group of ground-level practitioners organized and carried out the self-immolations. At least this was the scenario given in Wang Jindong's and Liu Yunfang's accounts, and in interviews with other survivors, as reported by Reuters:

> The victims said they had been inspired to burn themselves, though not specifically instructed, by Falun Gong leader, Li Hongzhi, who lives in exile in the United States and publishes

teachings mainly via the Internet. ... "We decided burning ourselves was the best way," said Chen, who also lost both her hands. "It was totally due to our own will. We were not forced by anyone."

Survivors made similar assertions to Chinese journalists, such as those that appeared in Chinese sources, including the *People's Daily*:

> Her face scarred with massive skin grafts and her hands missing, Chen Guo recalls the events which led her to set herself on fire in Beijing's Tiananmen Square more than a year ago.
> "I remember Li Hongzhi ... published a lecture entitled 'Beyond Tolerance' and after reading it, we decided not to wait any longer," Chen said. "We felt we must strengthen the force of Falun Gong in a special way and at that time we thought of self-immolation." ...
> [Wang Jindong added that,] "We went to Tiananmen Square on January 23, 2001. I was one of the main organizers and I burned myself first."
> "We went there just wanting to attain the 'all-round fulfillment' claimed by Li Hongzhi," he said. (*People's Daily* 2002)

As a background for understanding the motivations of these protesters, it should be understood that

> Mr. Li's cryptic exhortations to followers on the Falun Gong Web site [had] grown increasingly strident, chastising those people who cannot endure torture or even death in defense of his cosmology, which holds that Falun Gong is engaged in a struggle with evil beings for the redemption or destruction of the universe. "Even if a dafa cultivator truly casts off his human skin during the persecution, what awaits him is still consummation [and] Any fear is itself a barrier that prevents you from reaching consummation," Mr. Li wrote. (Smith 2001)

The apocalyptic teachings of Li Hongzhi could well have precipitated the self-immolations through a veiled call to civil disobedience and the promise of salvation for martyrs. Li teaches that the 'Ending Period of Catastrophe' is almost here, that contemporary society is degenerate and will be purged. The only ones who will be saved are those who are genuine Falun Gong practitioners. Li called Jiang Zemin, then president of the People's Republic of China, "the highest representative of the evil force in the human world" who is being manipulated by higher beings to persecute the Falun Gong. According to Li, only when the evil is eliminated can practitioners return home through Consummation to the Falun Dafa paradise. (Farley 2004, 224–5)

LHZ's essay mentioned by Chen Guo, the title of which is sometimes translated as "Beyond the Limits of Forbearance," paints a vivid portrait of the evil currently threatening to overrun humanity, instructing his followers that they should not merely continue to passively endure the advance of evil beings (especially those who persecute Falun Gong):

> Forbearance (*ren*) is not cowardice, much less is it resigning oneself to adversity. ... [Additionally,] Forbearance is absolutely not the limitless giving of free rein, which allows those evil beings who no longer have any human nature or righteous thoughts to do evil without limit. ... If the evil has already reached the point where it is unsaveable and unkeepable, then various measures at different levels can be used to stop it and eradicate it. ... the way the evil beings are currently performing shows that they are now completely without human nature and without righteous thoughts. Such evil's persecution of the Fa can thus no longer be tolerated. (Li Hongzhi 2001)

This is, of course, an overt call to action. However, as I have already indicated, there were no specific directions given for exactly how one should respond to this call. But why would the protesters (both the Tiananmen Square practitioners and other, later ones) choose martyrdom as their way of responding to the suppression of Falun Gong? It turns out that LHZ has both praised and encouraged martyrdom.

100 *Enlightened Martyrdom*

Thus, for example, at a gathering in Montreal in May 2001 that was attended by the sociologist of religion Susan Palmer,

> [Li Hongzhi] congratulated the martyrs of Tiananmen Square [seemingly referring, not to the 1.23 protesters, but to other protesters who had made the ultimate sacrifice] who have "consummated their own majestic positions" and presumably earned a posthumous enlightenment, or a crown of martyrdom: "Whether they are imprisoned or lose their human lives for persevering in Dafa cultivation, they achieve Consummation." (Palmer 2003, 356).

Palmer discusses the philosophy of karma and martyrdom behind these protests, and rightly notes that, "While Western politicians, journalists and human rights groups respond to social justice arguments, for the practitioners themselves, it is spiritual and apocalyptic expectations that fuel their civil disobedience" (ibid., 349).

Although Li Hongzhi made the remarks cited above by Palmer almost five months after the 1.23 Incident, he had articulated the same or similar ideas prior to January 23, 2001. Refer, for example, to his July 5, 1998 letter to Jian Xiaojun in which he asserted that a group of practitioners who died in an automobile accident in Hainan on a mission to spread Falun Gong had "obtained consummation" (Li 1998, reproduced in Kaiwind 2006). This would at least partly explain the many suicides of Falun Gong members that took place prior to July 22, 1999, the date on which FLG was formally banned in the PRC. Thus a news report published on March 22, 2001, under the headline "Falun Gong adherents who committed suicide before July 22, 1999 (partial list)," provides summaries of one hundred practitioners who killed themselves in a variety of different ways; e.g.:

> On July 4, 1999, Li Jinzhong (male, aged 51), a worker in Beigang Township, Tunliu County, Shanxi Province, joined with Li Jinzhong, a practitioner of Falun Gong, and a member of the Shanxi Coal Management Cadre College. They sat in meditation postures on a table. They poured petrol on

themselves and on the ground, and set themselves alight. They died of self-immolation. (*China News* 2001)

It is, of course, difficult to assess how many of these people were disturbed individuals who just coincidently happened to be practitioners. However, I think it fair to infer that at least some of these persons viewed their actions as being congruent with Li Hongzhi's teachings, perhaps believing that they too would "obtain consummation" like the practitioners who died in the automobile accident while on their mission to spread Falun Gong.

It should also be noted that Li Hongzhi himself never condemned followers who committed suicide in Falun Gong's name. And while the rate of practitioner suicides slowed down within a few years following the 1.23 Incident, followers continued to take their own lives. For example,

> On December 17, 2006, Zhang [Dongmei] telephoned her friend in another city: "My husband and I have been doing man-woman dual cultivation for a quite long period and our karma has been totally removed. Since our undertakings are completed, the day of Consummation is approaching." But her friend failed to fully understand her words and consequently, didn't pay much attention to [them]. However, three days later, the couple, following some eminent monks in the film, carried some gasoline to a remote place around the village, piled lumbers in the shape of lotus and set themselves ablaze for "Consummation," together with their beloved son Xiao Hu. When the villagers followed the flames to the scene, the couple had already died, and their son rolled down from the lumber stack because of the burning pain, with his head seriously burnt. After all-round rescue, the boy's life was saved. Neighbors were all deeply grieved to learn the sad news (Cheng Yun 2017).

If we want a broader understanding of the FLG suicides, it should first be noted that suicide as a form of political protest has taken place in a wide variety of different societies (Fierke 2013; Graitl 2014), including both traditional and contemporary China (Lee and

Kleinman 2003; Yu 2012). Self-immolation is especially popular because it is so dramatic that it tends to leave a greater impression on onlookers (Biggs 2005; Hedges 2015). Secondly, there is a long tradition of self-immolation in Chinese Buddhism (Jan 1965; Benn 2007) and, despite criticisms that they are not "really" Buddhist (Lao 2012), LHZ nevertheless claims that FLG belongs to the Buddhist tradition. (Though I should immediately add that pre-modern Buddhist self-immolations were not political protests, but were rather conceived as a "gift of the body.")

While there are plenty of precedents for Buddhist self-sacrifice in the Jataka Tales, it is Chapter Twenty-three of the Lotus Sutra – an important Mahayana Buddhist scripture – that provides the primary reference for later religious self-immolations. In this particular chapter, Sakyamuni tells the story of the bodhisattva Medicine King who, after anointing himself and his robes with fragrant oils and even drinking some of the oils, sets himself on fire. His body subsequently burns for 1200 years. He is then praised by numerous celestial beings and is reborn into a more fortunate realm, where he makes additional sacrifices (Benn 2009, 108–12). While there are discussions of self-immolations in other sutras, none have been as influential as the one described in the Lotus Sutra.

Although in the past there was a history of conflict between self-sacrificing Buddhists and the state (e.g., refer to Chapter 3 of Benn 2007), the contemporary deployment of self-immolation as political protest by Buddhists seems to have begun with Thich Quang Duc's self-immolation in Vietnam on June 11, 1963 (Biggs 2005, 173–5). Thich Quang Duc's dramatic self-sacrifice was intended to call world attention to the plight of Vietnamese Buddhists who were being persecuted by the dictatorship of Ngo Dinh Diem, who was a practicing Catholic. The event took place at a busy intersection in Saigon, where reporters had been invited to witness the self-immolation.

We should also note that there has been a fair amount written by scholars about religious suicide – and about suicide more generally – in the Chinese tradition, over and above suicides by Chinese Buddhists. I was, for instance, particularly impressed by Jimmy

Yu's *Sanctity and Self-inflicted Violence in Chinese Religions, 1500–1700* (2012). The final chapter in Elizabeth Perry and Mark Selden's edited volume, *Chinese Society* (2003), is entitled "Suicide as Resistance in Chinese Society." Its authors, Sing Lee and Arthur Kleinman, quote a dissertation in which the author asserts that "suicide is a hallmark of Chinese culture" (291). I have also recently been trying to learn elements of the Chinese language. In one text on learning to read Chinese, *Chineasy: The New Way to Read Chinese* (Hsueh 2014), the author observes that the traditional character for fire looks like "a person waving their arms, saying, 'Help! I'm on fire!'" (28).

The point I am making here is that there is a long tradition of suicide – particularly self-immolation – that is deeply embedded as a form of protest in China. The self-immolation of monks in Chinese Buddhism is part of this tradition, but is only one influence on that pattern. In other words, it is not that Falun Gong practitioners were directly influenced by Buddhist self-immolation but, rather, that Buddhism has contributed to a larger idea of suicide/self-immolation as a form of protest that in turn influenced practitioners. Of course, none of this absolves Li Hongzhi of his share of the blame. His writings and pronouncements were clearly the immediate cause of the tragedy.

To restate this point: I have recounted these various precedents – from suicides undertaken as forms of political protest to religious suicides in Buddhist texts – *not* to say that any particular set of events or any particular text directly influenced the Tiananmen Square protestors or the other practitioners who took their own lives. Rather, I am simply pointing out that protestors' decisions to self-immolate did not arise in a vacuum, and that there were numerous historical and contemporary examples of suicide as a form of resistance, both in China and elsewhere, that could have suggested self-immolation as an appropriate form of protest. When combined with Li Hongzhi's apocalyptic vision and his urgent but non-specific call to action, it is not difficult to see how these practitioners could draw the conclusion that they should go ahead and make the ultimate sacrifice to "defend the Fa."

To summarize, in this paper I revisited the controversy over the Tiananmen Square self-immolators, drawing from both primary and secondary material. However, rather than dwelling on the claims and counterclaims put forward by the Chinese government and the Falun Gong organization, I shifted my primary research focus to other factors that could shed light on this event. My conclusion was that rather than a PRC plot or an action directly ordered by the Falun Gong organization, it seems more likely that this was a demonstration planned and executed by local practitioners – though directly inspired by a combination of Li Hongzhi's violent apocalyptic vision, his call to non-specific action against the Chinese government, and examples of prior religious suicides and prior protest suicides.

References

Bell, Mark R., and Taylor C. Boas. 2003. "Falun Gong and the Internet: Evangelism, community, and struggle for survival," *Nova Religio: The Journal of Alternative and Emergent Religions*, 6:2.

Benn, James A. 2007. *Burning for the Buddha: Self-immolation in Chinese Buddhism*. Kuroda Institute Studies in East Asian Buddhism 19. Honolulu: University of Hawai'i Press.

Benn, James A. 2009. "The Lotus Sūtra and Self-immolation," in Jacqueline I. Stone and Stephen F. Teiser (eds.), *Readings of the Lotus Sūtra*. New York: Columbia University Press, pp. 107–31.

Biggs, Michael. 2005. "Dying Without Killing: Self-Immolations, 1963–2002," in Diego Gambetta (ed.), *Making Sense of Suicide Missions*. New York: Oxford University Press, pp. 173–208.

Chang, Maria Hsia. 2004. *Falun Gong: The End of Days*. New Haven: Yale University Press.

Cheng, Yun. 2017. "A couple burnt themselves to death for Consummation." http://www.facts.org.cn/Recommendations/201701/23/ t20170123_4790809.htm (accessed February 2, 2017).

China News. 2001. Falun Gong adherents who committed suicide before 22 July 1999 (partial list). http://www.chinanews.com/2001-03-22/26/80407.html (accessed January 22, 2017).

Farley, Helen. 2014a. "Death by Whose Hand? Falun Gong and Suicide," in James R. Lewis and Carole Cusack (eds.), *Sacred Suicide*. London: Routledge, pp. 215–32.

Farley, Helen. 2014b. "Falun Gong: A Narrative of Pending Apocalypse, Shape-shifting Aliens, and Relentless Persecution," in James R. Lewis and Jesper A. Petersen (eds.), *Controversial New Religions*, pp. 241–54. New York: Oxford University Press, pp. 249–50.

Fierke, K. M. 2013. *Political Self-sacrifice: Agency, Body and Emotion in International Relations*. Cambridge: Cambridge University Press.

Frank, Adam. 2004. "Falun Gong and the Threat of History," in Mary Ann Tretreault and Robert A. Denemark (eds.), *Gods, Guns, and Globalization: Religious Radicalism and International Political Economy*. Boulder, CO: Lynne Reiner Publishers.

Graitl, Lorenz. 2014. "Dying to Tell: Media Orchestration of Politically Motivated Suicides," in James R. Lewis and Carole Cusack (eds.), *Sacred Suicide*. Farnham, UK: Ashgate, pp. 193–212.

He, Daniel. 2014a. "54 Facts That Reveal How the 'Self-immolation' on Tiananmen Square Was Actually Staged for Propaganda Purposes – Part 1" (January 7). http://www.theepochtimes.com/n3/436255-54-facts-that-reveal-how-the-self-immolation-on-tiananmen-square-was-actually-staged-for-propaganda-purposes-part-1/ (accessed January 11, 2017).

He, Daniel. 2014b. "54 Facts That Reveal How the 'Self-immolation' on Tiananmen Square Was Actually Staged for Propaganda Purposes – Part 2" (January 7). http://www.theepochtimes.com/n3/436280-54-facts-that-reveal-how-the-self-immolation-on-tiananmen-square-was-actually-staged-for-propaganda-purposes-part-2/ (accessed January 11, 2017).

He, Daniel. 2014c. "54 Facts That Reveal How the 'Self-immolation' on Tiananmen Square Was Actually Staged for Propaganda Purposes – Part 3" (January 7). http://www.theepochtimes.com/n3/436312-54-facts-that-reveal-how-the-self-immolation-on-tiananmen-square-was-actually-staged-for-propaganda-purposes-part-3/ (accessed January 11, 2017).

Hedges, Paul. 2015. "Burning for a Cause: Four Factors in Successful Political (and Religious) Self-immolation Examined in Relation to Alleged Falun Gong 'Fanatics' in Tiananmen Square," *Politics and Religion*, 8, 797–817.

Jan Yin-hua. 1965. "Buddhist Self-immolation in Medieval China," *History of Religions*, 4(2), 243–68.

Kaiwind. 2006. "Zhang Yijun talks about the present and the past" (September 18). In addition to one of Li Hongzhi's letters, this webpage also contains a letter from Zhang Yijun, dated September 8, 2006. http://www.kaiwind.com/kfjc/ytflg/200711/t71263.htm (accessed October 27, 2016).

Kaiwind. 2007. "Chen Guo and her mother: Life of Tian'anmen 1.23 self-immolation survivors in the past and at present." http://www.kaiwind.com/kfjc/sszx/200711/t71287_5.htm (accessed January 23, 2017).

Kavan, Heather. 2005. "Print Media Coverage of Falun Gong in Australia and New Zealand," in Peter Horsfield (ed.), *Papers from the Trans-Tasman Research Symposium, "Emerging Research in Media, Religion and Culture."* Melbourne: RMIT Publishing, pp. 74–85.

Lao Cheng-Wu. 2012. *The Refutation and Analysis of Falun Gong.* Bloomington, IN: iUniverse, 2012.

Lee, Sing, and Arthur Kleinman. 2003. "Suicide as Resistance in Chinese Society," in Elisabeth J. Perry and Mark Selden (eds.), *Chinese Society: Change, Conflict and Resistance*, 2nd ed. London: RoutledgeCurzon, pp. 289–311.

Lewis, James R. 2016. "Sucking the '*De*' out of Me: How an Esoteric Theory of Persecution and Martyrdom Fuels Falun Gong's Assault on Intellectual Freedom," *Alternative Spirituality and Religion Review*, 7:1. https://www.academia.edu/12926903/Sucking_the_De_Out_of_Me (accessed January 13, 2017).

Lewis, James R., and Nicole Ruskell. 2016. "Innocent Victims of Chinese Oppression, Or Media Bullies? Falun Gong's In-Your-Face Media Strategies." Paper presented at the CESNUR Conference, "Religious Movements in a Globalized World: Korea, Asia and Beyond." Daejin University, Republic of Korea.
http://www.cesnur.org/2016/daejin_lewis_ruskell.pdf (accessed January 13, 2017).

Lewis, James R., and Nicole Ruskell. Forthcoming 2017. "Understanding Falun Gong's Martyrdom Strategy as Spiritual Terrorism," in James R. Lewis (ed.), *The Cambridge Companion to Religion and Terrorism.* Cambridge: Cambridge University Press.

Li, Cui. 2014. "Father Jumping off Building Because of Practicing Falun Gong."
http://www.facts.org.cn/Words/201407/22/t20140722_1787497.htm (accessed January 16, 2017).

Li Hongzhi. 1998. Letter to Jiang Xiaojun. July 5. Reproduced in Zhang 2006.
Li Hongzhi. 2001. "Beyond the Limits of Forbearance." https://falundafa.org/eng/eng/jjyz2_19.htm (accessed June 13, 2015).
Li Hongzhi. 2004a. "Eliminate Your Last Attachment(s)." http://en.minghui.org/html/articles/2000/8/14/9117.html (accessed November 4, 2016).
Li Hongzhi. 2004b. "Teaching the Fa at the International Fa Conference in New York." http://en.minghui.org/html/articles/2004/12/23/55877.html (accessed September 30, 2016).
Liu, Ying-Ying Tiffany. 2005. "Falun Gong, the Diaspora and Chinese Identity: Fieldwork among the Practitioners in Ottawa." Master of Arts thesis, Carlton University.
Liu Yunfang. 2012. "Planning '1.23' Self-immolation" Kaiwind (November 1, 2012). http://anticult.kaiwind.com/redian/tam/qlzzy/201501/20/t20150120_2268624.shtml (accessed November 11, 2016).
Lu, Yunfeng. 2005. "Entrepreneurial Logics and the Evolution of Falun Gong," *Journal for the Scientific Study of Religion*, 44(2), 173–85.
MacKinnon, Rebecca. 2001a. "Falun Gong members set selves on fire; 1 dies." (January 23). http://edition.cnn.com/2001/ASIANOW/east/01/23/china.falungong.02/ (accessed January 10, 2017).
MacKinnon, Rebecca. 2001b. "Falun Gong denies tie to self-immolation attempts." (January 24). http://edition.cnn.com/2001/ASIANOW/east/01/23/china.falungong.03/ (accessed January 10, 2017).
Østergaard, Clemens Stubbe. 2004. "Governance and the Political Challenge of the Falun Gong," in Jude Howell (ed.), *Governance in China*. Lanham, MD: Rowman & Littlefield, pp. 207–25.
Ownby, David. 2008. *Falun Gong and the Future of China*. New York: Oxford University Press.
Page, Jeremy. 2002. "Survivors say China Falun Gong immolations real." Reuters (April 4, 2002). https://culteducation.com/group/1254-falun-gong/6833-survivors-say-china-falun-gong-immolations-real.html (accessed January 12, 2017).
Palmer, David A. 2001. "Falun Gong: Between Sectarianism and Universal Salvation," *China Perspectives*, 35.
Palmer, David A. 2007. *Qigong Fever: Body, Science, and Utopia in China*. New York: Columbia University Press.

108 *Enlightened Martyrdom*

Palmer, Susan J. 2003. "Healing to Protest: Conversion Patterns Among the Practitioners of Falun Gong," *Nova Religio: The Journal of Alternative and Emergent Religions*, 6:2, 348–364.

Pan, Philip P. 2001. "Human Fire Ignites Chinese Mystery." *Washington Post*, February 4.
https://www.washingtonpost.com/archive/politics/2001/02/04/human-fire-ignites-chinese-mystery/e27303e3-6117-4ec3-b6cf-58f03cdb4773/ (accessed October 1, 2016).

Penny, Benjamin. 2003. "The Life and Times of Li Hongzhi: 'Falun Gong' and Religious Biography," *China Quarterly* 175, 643–61.

Penny, Benjamin. 2012. *The Religion of Falun Gong*. Chicago: University of Chicago Press.

People's Daily. April 8, 2002. "Falun Gong Survivors Speak of Self-Immolation."
http://en.people.cn/200204/08/print20020408_93635.html (accessed September 1, 2016).

Porter, Noah. 2003. *Falun Gong in the United States: An Ethnographic Study*. Dissertation.com

Rapsas, Tom. 2013. "Falun Gong and the dangerous, super-freaky side of Chinese spirituality."
http://www.patheos.com/blogs/wakeupcall/2013/10/falungong/ (accessed September 30, 2016).

Rosenthal, Elisabeth. 2001. "Another Falun Gong Member Reportedly Burns Himself in China." *New York Times*, February 17.
http://www.nytimes.com/2001/02/17/world/another-falun-gong-member-reportedly-burns-himself-in-china.html?src=pm (accessed January 22, 2017).

Schauble, John. 2001. "The Age: Falun Gong denies hand in deadly fire protest." http://en.minghui.org/html/articles/2001/1/25/5021.html (accessed October 5, 2016).

ShaoLan. 2014. *Chineasy: The New Way to Read Chinese*. New York: Harper Design.

Smith, Craig G. 2001. "Falun Gong Deaths Set Off Dispute on Suicide Report." *New York Times*.
http://www.nytimes.com/2001/07/04/world/falun-gong-deaths-set-off-dispute-on-suicide-report.html?_r=0 (accessed October 3, 2016).

Spaeth, Anthony. 1999. Interview with Li Hongzhi: "I am just a very ordinary man." TIME *Magazine*, vol. 154, number 4 (August 2).

Thornton, Patricia M. 2003. "The New Cybersects: Resistance and Repression in the Reform Era," in Elisabeth J. Perry and Mark Selden (eds.), *Chinese Society: Change, Conflict and Resistance*, 2nd ed. London: RoutledgeCurzon, pp. 247–70.

Tong, James W. 2002. "An Organizational Analysis of the Falun Gong: Structure, Communications, Financing," *China Quarterly*, 171, 636–60.

Tong, James W. 2009. *Revenge of the Forbidden City: The Suppression of the Falungong in China, 1999–2005*. New York: Oxford University Press.

Wang Ermu. 2015. "Exclusive: Li Hongzhi Changed His DOB." *Kaiwind*. http://www.facts.org.cn/Reports/China/201309/13/t20130913_1094287.htm (accessed October 1, 2016).

Wang Jindong. 2015. "Wang Jindong: My Personal Statement on the Tiananmen Square Self-immolation Incident." http://www.facts.org.cn/krs/wfem/201501/06/t20150106_2232364.htm (accessed November 5, 2016).

Yu Haiqing. 2009. *Media and Cultural Transformation in China*. New York: Routledge.

Yu, Jimmy. 2012. *Sanctity and Self-inflicted Violence in Chinese Religions, 1500–1700*. New York: Oxford University Press.

Yue, Tom. 2017. Response to: "Why Is Falun Gong Bad?" https://www.quora.com/Why-is-Falun-Gong-bad (accessed January 13, 2017).

Zhao, Yuezhi Zhao. 2003. "Falun Gong, Identity, and the Struggle over Meaning Inside and Outside China," in Nick Couldry and James Curran (eds.), *Contesting Media Power: Alternative Media in a Networked World*. Lanham, MD: Rowman & Littlefield Publishers, pp. 209–26.

James R. Lewis is a much-published researcher in the field of new religious movements, and is Professor of Philosophy at the School of Philosophy, Wuhan University, China. At present, he edits or co-edits four academic book series, and is the general editor for the *Alternative Spirituality and Religion Review*, and Associate Editor of the *Journal of Religion and Violence*. Recent publications include *New Age in Norway* (Equinox, 2017), *Cambridge Companion to Religion and Terrorism* (Cambridge University Press, 2017), and *Oxford Handbook of New Religious Movements* (Oxford University Press, 2016).

5. Devil Killing and the Essence of Falun Gong

Fang Yong

Introduction

This paper examines incidents of "devil" killings by cult organizations in China. In one well-known murder case from May 2014, several members of the "Almighty God" group killed an innocent diner at McDonald's restaurant in Zhaoyuan, Shandong Province. The murder took place because the victim was considered to be a devil, i.e., a being that should be eliminated from the Earth. It was not until this moment that the public saw clearly that "Almighty God" was a destructive religion. There have also been a number of other "devil-killing" cases, many of which have involved followers of the Falun Gong organization. Although many of these tragedies occurred years ago, they remain of importance in the context of Chinese socio-culture and the activity of such groups today.

Devil Killing by Falun Gong Practitioners

In many cases, Falun Gong practitioners have killed people for the sake of eliminating so-called "devils." These cases can be divided into several categories, as follows:

1. Those who attempt to hinder the practice of Falun Gong
Such people are considered to be devils. A typical example is the case of Wu Deqiao, a male aged thirty-six, who was employed at Jiangsu Wujiang Supply and Marketing Cooperative. On the

evening of February 25, 1998, during Falun Gong practice at home, Wu was struck suddenly with the feeling that someone wanted to kill him. He ran to the local police station, yelling "Earthquake! Earthquake!" before returning home. He felt that he had "externalized his power" and become Buddha. His wife, Shen Yuzhen, then tried to prevent Wu's erratic behavior by interrupting his practice. As a consequence, Wu stabbed Shen to death with a kitchen knife.

2. Those who belittle the practice of Falun Gong and seek to prevent it

Again, such people are considered by Falun Gong practitioners to be devils. For instance, on the morning of April 8, 1998, Falun Gong practitioner Wang Anshou (a male aged thirty-six, who worked at Shandong Xintai Taishan Machinery Factory) beat his father to death with a pole and a spade. Wang, who had first encountered Falun Gong in February of the same year, had come to regard his father and stepmother as the "tiger demon" and "fox demon" respectively due to their opposition to his practice of Falun Gong. On the day in question, Wang's father had said that it was a waste of time to practice Falun Gong in the morning when there were so many other things to be done, a statement which led to Wang's frenzied attack.

3. Those who are perceived as having the potential to harm Falun Gong followers

In some instances, Falun Gong practitioners have come to believe that a particular individual poses a threat to their safety. For example, Yuan Runtian, a female graduate of Guangzhou Light Industry Vocational School, murdered Huang Daisheng in the Lanhe Township of Panyu, Guangdong Province, on the evening of February 6, 2000. Yuan had begun to practice Falun Gong while still at school, and had become very unsociable and introverted around that time. Although Yuan found a job after graduation, she was dismissed after a short time, which led her to devote all her time to Falun Gong. Around November 1999, she became delirious, believing that she was in another world. She often dreamed of "Master" Li Hongzhi (the leader of Falun Gong), and she came to fear a number of local men, whom she felt wanted to take sexual advantage of her or even kill her. One of these men was Huang Daisheng, to whom Yuan had never spoken before, but who she believed had hurt her in another world. Yuan concluded that Huang was a devil, and must be killed. She broke into his house and stabbed him in the face until he died.

4. Those who announce their decision not to believe in or practice Falun Gong

Such people are also labeled devils by Falun Gong followers. In one particular case, Wei Zhihua, a Falun Gong practitioner from the Longgang District of Shenzhen City, turned her back on the organization, stating openly that she would "never … be a Falun Gong disciple," after coming to realize that many of Falun Gong's actions were harmful to society. This led to her being tied up and suffocated to death on February 20, 2001 by a group of twelve Falun Gong members, including her husband.

5. Those who appear to be possessed by the devil

In some of the Falun Gong-related murder cases, victims have been selected based solely on their appearance. Between April 19 and 22, 2002, Guan Shuyun (a Falun Gong practitioner from the Meixi District, Yichun City, Heilongjiang Province) took part in Falun Gong practice with dozens of other practitioners. All of a sudden, she was struck by the impression that her young daughter, Dai Nan, was possessed by devils. Guan then took hold of her daughter, who was not yet nine years old, and strangled her to death in front of the entire group. In a similar incident on the evening of March 25, 2010, four people were beaten to death in the Fanshan District of Beijing City. The principal perpetrator was Tang Shuling, the mother of Li Yuandong, who was one of the victims. Tang also thought that her daughter looked as if she was possessed by devils and thus believed that her actions were in her daughter's best interests.

In every case but number 5, the victims themselves were considered to be devils, who needed to be eradicated to prevent them from threatening the practice of Falun Gong. In the last example, it was not the victims themselves who were considered to be devils; rather, the individuals were thought to be possessed by devils. In such cases, it appears that the murderers believed that they were "rescuing" their victims from devils. Here, the murderers may attribute the victims' deaths to their own lack of competence in exorcising the devils or to the exceedingly strong power of the devils, which cannot be overcome without death occurring. Either way, it appears that the perpetrators thought they were acting for the good of the victim.

Where such "devil-killing" cases are concerned, then, we must ask four fundamental questions. First, what are the characteristics of devils in the eyes of Falun Gong practitioners? Second, what is a "devil" considered to be in Falun Gong? Third, why do Falun Gong members feel that they have to kill devils? Finally, what do devil-killing activities reveal about the nature of Falun Gong?

The Characteristics of Devils, as Defined in Falun Gong

In the writings of Falun Gong, all the troubles encountered by practitioners are labeled "devil disasters," indicating that devils are the root cause of anti-Falun Gong beliefs and actions. Falun Gong leader Li Hongzhi's basic thinking on the topic of devils can be distilled into three points, as follows:

1. Devils are tools through which practitioners are tested. This can be gleaned from such statements as:

> If you want to do something good, you must also overcome troubles and distractions. The theory of mutual reinforcement and neutralization brings about this requirement. It is because of this theory and the distractions caused by devils that nothing can be achieved easily. Through struggle and effort, you can overcome many hardships, until you achieve what you wish. It is only then that you will be able to taste real pleasure and treasure its value. Only through success can we appreciate delight.

114 *Enlightened Martyrdom*

> Without the theory of mutual reinforcement or the distractions caused by devils, everything could be achieved easily. But if there were no devils whatsoever, you would not value what was in your hands or be able to taste the delights of success. (Li Hongzhi 1996)

On this point, Li continues:

> Some may ask me why I don't get rid of devils. If I killed all the devils, you would have no chance to improve. Nothing could be used to test your loyalty to Dafa. Without the distractions caused by devils, some of you could not abandon your preoccupations or eliminate karmic obscurations. (ibid.)

2. Devils exist only in the "low-level" world, i.e., the present world inhabited by human beings. Their existence is banned in the "high-level" world that Falun Gong practitioners seek to inhabit. In other words, once a practitioner attains a high level of cultivation, devils will no longer exist in his or her world. Additionally, in order to reach a level of existence higher than the common people inhabit, devils must be eradicated.

3. Devils often cause trouble for Falun Gong practitioners in the pursuit of a higher level of cultivation. As Li Hongzhi puts it,

> We can indeed find that some devils might interrupt your cultivation. It's never groundless. There is one widely-accepted method of practicing Falun Gong that invites devils. To be more specific, before you learn to practice Dafa, you may find yourself in a quiet environment. But once you learn to practice Dafa, you will suddenly find yourself in a very noisy environment. Car horns are sounding, and there is noise from people walking, talking, and slamming cupboard doors. Outside, there are also radios playing. If you don't practice Dafa, your environment will seem quite good. But once you practice Dafa, your environment will worsen immediately. Few of us have explored the reasons for this further; most practitioners just feel surprised or frustrated. In fact, it is the devils that are causing trouble. They assign someone to make

trouble for you. It's the simplest form of distraction and it prevents you from ever practicing Dafa. You are improved through cultivation, but you are thwarted by them. They feel unhappy, so they try to stop you. (Li Hongzhi, *Zhuan Falun*)

Here, we see that desire for retribution (and, more specifically, karmic retribution) is given as the key reason for devils distracting Falun Gong practitioners.

Definition of Devils in Falun Gong: the Common People and the Devil Figure

At this point, we shall explore the question of what a devil actually is, according to Falun Gong practitioners. To begin with, Li Hongzhi categorizes human beings into two groups: common people and Falun Gong practitioners: "As real practitioners, we should approach this problem at every level, but not from the perspective of common people" (*Zhuan Falun*, Lecture Six). Li adds that the common people have fallen to the bottom rung of existence due to their decadence:

> ... human lives do not originate from the society of the common people. In fact, real human life comes from the universe. This universe contains many different types of matter. Owing to the interaction between them, these types of matter can generate human lives. In other words, the earliest human life originates from the universe. The universe itself is kind hearted, so we can find truthfulness, compassion, and forbearance there. Human beings and the universe have the same characteristics. But, as more and more human lives are generated, social relationships appear between groups of people. Some people gradually become selfish, and so they fall to a lower level. They cannot maintain their level and they degenerate. But they cannot even remain at this lower level; they continue to degenerate further. At last, they drop to the current level of human beings. (Li Hongzhi, *Zhuan Falun*, Lecture One)

Li also states that, from the standpoint of the great enlightened beings, all common people should be eradicated: "Human society as a whole remains at one level. It has fallen to this low level. From the perspectives of the practitioners and the great enlightened beings, these human lives should be destroyed" (ibid.). This quotation reveals the anti-human element in Falun Gong's doctrine. He argues that the common people survive only because of the great enlightened beings' great mercy. Without this, he claims, society would degrade to the point at which it would be destroyed completely: "But the great enlightened beings give them another chance, out of mercy. So, we are left with this particular environment and space" (ibid.).

For Li Hongzhi, Falun Gong practitioners differ from the common people in three ways. First, a Falun Gong follower should have a desire to rise above the level of the common people and go back to "nature" (i.e., to that from which human beings came). He explains,

> The lives in this space are different from those in all the other spaces in the universe. People in this space can't see the lives in other spaces or the truth of the universe. So, these people become lost. In order to cure diseases and overcome troubles and eliminate bad karma, they must practice Dafa so they can go back to nature. This can be seen widely in different practices. For human beings, the ultimate purpose is to go back to nature. If a person wants to practice Dafa, we can conclude that his Buddha nature has been born. This is something precious because it means that the person hopes to go back to nature and leave the level of the common people. (ibid.)

Additionally, Li teaches that "there's nobody but me who can do this ... who can move the common people to a higher level." He further asserts that "opportunities of this kind can rarely be found. After all, I can't teach Falun Gong forever." In this way, Li Hongzhi portrays Falun Gong as a great opportunity. His words imply that he is a greatly enlightened being himself, whose ideas about leaving the level of common people and going back to nature are unquestionable.

Devil Killing and the Essence of Falun Gong

The second way in which Falun Gong followers differ from the common person is that they have to be purified in order to work toward a higher level of existence – a process which is instigated by Li Hongzhi himself. He states, "You can't cultivate yourself if you're sick with disease. I've got to purify your body. But physical purification is only available to those who appreciate the real intentions behind practicing Dafa" (ibid.). Finally, the practice of true Falun Gong is not open to all; it is for a select group only: "After your body has been purified, I will give you access to the whole cultivation system so that you can commence high-level cultivation immediately. But this is made available only to those who come here for real cultivation" (ibid.).

According to Li, once you have been selected by him, purified by him, and installed with a "Falun," you become a real practitioner of Falun Gong. Rather than Falun Gong practitioners cultivating Falun, it is the Falun that cultivates them:

> This is the case with your Falun. It rotates. It can solve the problems that common people meet in their everyday practice of Dafa. As a result, people have to practice Dafa for a longer period. How come? It rotates all the time. It keeps absorbing energy from the universe, and then transforms this energy. When you're at work, it's cultivating you. Sure, we install not just a Falun in your body, but also lots of other functions and mechanisms. The Falun in you operates and evolves automatically. Dafa automatically transforms people. In this way, "Falun Gong cultivates people" or "Dafa cultivates people." Whether you practice Falun Gong or not, Falun Gong keeps on cultivating you all the time. (ibid.)

In other words, practitioners of Falun Gong are cultivated and protected by the Falun at all times. As Li states, "If you're a real practitioner of Falun Gong, you will be protected by our Falun" (ibid.). This protection comes from our own dharma bodies and authority, according to him:

> ... as I've said, my dharma can protect you. In fact, I haven't said any more about it. Everyone has bodies in other spaces.

> With power, a person's body can become bigger. When I cultivate myself, my body becomes very large. To what degree? Some ask me, "Master, you're in the United States. How can I continue to practice Falun Gong? Can you still protect me?" As I have said, my dharma bodies can protect you. What I want to say is that a considerable space – including some parts of the universe – is still within my belly! Wherever you go, you're within my easy reach. (Li Hongzhi 1994)

Li adds, "My roots are in the universe. Anyone who does something negative to you also does the same to me. Frankly, they're doing something negative to the universe" (Li Hongzhi, *Zhuan Falun*, Lecture One). We can see, therefore, that anyone who harms a Falun Gong practitioner is also thought to be harming Li Hongzhi – and even the universe. This is a bold claim, but it should also be pointed out that the so-called protection offered by Li is actually a form of control. Those protected by Falun are said to be under the control of Li's "dharma bodies"; this is the factor that differentiates them from the common people.

It should be stated here that, although they are said to be protected by Falun, practitioners of Falun Gong are not granted immunity to devils' actions: "People have different ideas and long-term arguments, but can't reach a consensus. They're exploited by the devils that damage Dafa. If you cling to your wrong ideas, it becomes a personal preoccupation" (Li Hongzhi 1999). These words are Li's response to the presence of internal conflicts within Falun Gong. They can be interpreted as meaning that any ideas which deviate from Li's beliefs are not welcome within the context of Falun Gong. Li claims that such ideas emerge when Falun Gong practitioners are used by devils or when their bodies and minds are not purified completely.

Further still, Li insinuates that devils are his own creation, being a method through which to test his disciples:

> There are some devils, for sure. Why? I have recently dealt with some problems, including matters of this kind. Just think about it. These things often happen across the country or at

Devil Killing and the Essence of Falun Gong 119

> some of our cultivation stations. Some damage our Dafa or curse me. Some claim that Dafa is really bad. Their actions do significant damage to our cultivation. But why not consider these things as positive? In the whole process of cultivation, you have to face problems – your ideas about the nature of Dafa and your attitude toward Dafa. Your determination is tested until your cultivation is achieved at last. (Li Hongzhi 1994)

Elsewhere, he expands on this point:

> The lives of practitioners of Falun Gong are well planned. But there may not always be eighty-one troubles. It depends on your basis. This has much to do with your attainable level. Practitioners must go through some of the same things as common people. It's an extremely painful process. Where the things that you can't do without are concerned, we'll try our best to help you get rid of them. Your nature can be improved only through devil-based cultivation. (Li Hongzhi, *Falun Gong*, Chapter Five)

Despite the argument that Li Hongzhi has sent the devils to test Falun Gong practitioners, the devils themselves are not innocent of blame. On the contrary, it is the guilt of the devils that makes them prepared to distract Falun Gong practitioners. In other words, the devils' guilt is pre-existing; Li merely capitalizes upon it to test the resolve of his followers. The sins of these devils are considered so negative that all necessary measures should be taken to eliminate them. According to Falun Gong, those common people who remain beyond the protection of Falun Gong and have never been purified by Li Hongzhi are mostly utilized by devils, whether knowingly or unconsciously. This intrinsic devilish nature will only worsen over time, hence the concept that such devils must be destroyed.

For Li Hongzhi, devils use three methods to take advantage of common people. First, they trigger their devilish nature. This is closely followed by the second method, in which devils possess common people:

120 *Enlightened Martyrdom*

> Some less sincere people are possessed by devils. Their primary consciousness cannot control them. They think it's something called Gong. Once physically possessed by devils, they act crazily and cry loudly. Some outsiders may be frightened to see this kind of Falun Gong practitioner. How can we think of this as cultivation? It's the lowest level of disease treatment and healthy body maintenance, but it's really dangerous. Once you get used to it, your primary consciousness cannot keep you under control. In such a case, your body will be controlled by a secondary consciousness or by external information – through possession. They [the devils] may do something dangerous or destroy our cultivated world. (Li Hongzhi, *Zhuan Falun*, Lecture Six)

In the third method, common people are transformed into devils. In other words, devils assume the form of common people. This point is more complicated, however, because in some cases Li claims to have prepared and sent the devils to test practitioners. If this is true, then can Master Li Hongzhi actually be considered the master of devils? According to the doctrine of Buddhism, all beings – even Buddha and devils – are the same. In Li Hongzhi's doctrine, however, the notion of theodicy is complicated by his positioning as the controller of devil-related activity. Notably, it is a topic that Li seems to avoid in his speeches, meaning that the matter cannot be discussed any further here due to insufficient evidence – but it is a point worthy of further investigation in future.

If we leave to one side the claim that devils are assigned the task of testing practitioners of Falun Gong by Li Hongzhi himself, then the rest of the evidence indicates that, according to Falun Gong, devils are ordinary people. We could even conclude that all people are devils. If this is the case, though, we must return to the same point: as Li Hongzhi is a human being, surely he must also be a devil? At the very least, he lives in the world of devils, making the idea of separating Falun Gong practitioners from devilishness more complex.

Falun Gong's Basic Attitude Toward the Common People: Deliverance Through Destruction

As we have seen, Falun Gong practitioners are in a bind, in the sense that they seek cultivation and elevation, but must live among the devils of everyday society, who threaten the achievement of these aims. If one chooses to practice Falun Gong, one must therefore confront the fundamental contrast between common people and Falun Gong practitioners. In particular, opposing ideas about what is "good" pose a problem here. On this point, Li Hongzhi states the following:

> As a practitioner, you must learn to cultivate yourself in the environment populated by common people. You must temper yourself and gradually get rid of your preoccupations and desires. As ordinary human beings, we may think that something is good, but once we attain a high level, we may think otherwise. In the eyes of the common people, one should gain more material things to live a better life. For a great enlightened being, however, such a person is only getting worse. What's wrong with this? The more he gains, the more damage he does to others. He gets something he doesn't deserve, and he turns more attention to things like fame and money. There is a heavy price to pay: morality. Your level can never improve if you don't focus on the cultivation of your true nature. (Li Hongzhi, *Zhuan Falun*, Lecture One)

It is imperative, then, that Falun Gong practitioners cultivate themselves while they reside in society alongside common people. It could be suggested, therefore, that common people are not without value where Falun Gong is concerned; they permit the chosen few to make the comparisons necessary to elevate themselves above the general social level. We can identify three main ways in which Falun Gong understands the value of the common people:

1. *The common people are worthless.*
   In terms of this belief, the common people should have been destroyed. After all, such human beings continue to

degenerate until they die: "Human society as a whole remains at one level. It has fallen to this low level. From the perspectives of the practitioners and the great enlightened beings, these human lives should have been destroyed" (Li Hongzhi, *Zhuan Falun*, Lecture One).

2. *The common people are tools used to test Falun Gong practitioners.*

Here, ordinary people are envisaged as the enemy. This idea can be seen in Li Hongzhi's lectures: "Some may ask me why I don't get rid of devils. If I killed all the devils, you would have no chance to improve. Nothing could be used to test your loyalty to Dafa" (Li Hongzhi 1996).

3. *The common people provide energy for Falun Gong practitioners.*

In some Falun Gong literature and practices, the common people can be seen as fodder for practitioners. This can be seen in the case of Fu Yibin, who killed members of his family for the sake of cultivating his "primordial baby." When being interviewed in jail, Fu stated, "After they're killed, their 'primordial spirits' and 'true beings' can gain direct access to my lower abdomen. So, the universe – including the sun, the moon, and the Earth – will be structured. Inside my lower abdomen, the public region can rotate ceaselessly. It's where the basis of 'Zhuan Falun' can be found." Such ideas originate from Li Hongzhi's belief that the Falun continuously rotates inside Falun Gong practitioners, absorbing and transforming the universe's energy. One reason, then, for killing common people is to absorb their primordial spirits.

In this way, the killing of the "devils" that reside in common people can be interpreted as a method of achieving deliverance for common people. What is more, common people should be grateful for this deliverance. It is believed that when people are physically destroyed by Falun Gong practitioners, their primordial spirits are released from their bodies. The energy released thus enables otherwise "useless" non-practitioners to become valuable in some way.

Devil Killing and the Essence of Falun Gong 123

To summarize, then, the value of common people lies not in their physical body, but in their internal spirit. They also have an associated value, which is that of being a tool to test Falun Gong practitioners. Once they lose their value as a tool, they are delivered via the physical death of the body. This may seem extreme, but one must remember that, from the perspective of the Falun Gong practitioner, all human emotions must be left aside, if s/he wishes to attain a higher level of existence. The final use that is then made of common people involves the absorption of primordial spirits into the bodies of Falun Gong followers. This coincides with the destruction of the devils inside the physical body of the common person. Unfortunately, this belief has led to a number of murders in the name of deliverance.

Li Hongzhi typically justifies devil killing in one of three ways, as indicated by the following quotations:

1. "Those who damage Dafa are devils. These devils should be killed" (Li Hongzhi 1994).
2. "If devils are unavoidable, then measures should be taken to suppress and eliminate them" (Forbearance Is Limited).
3. "Nothing can change today's people. Do you understand what I mean? Let me tell you. It's because people, with their mutated thoughts, can't discern things. It's because you can change their consciousness, but you can't change the mutation of their natures, no matter what form of cultivation is used" (Li Hongzhi 2000a and b).

Ultimately, all three of these types of justification indicate two things: (1) nobody outside Falun Gong is really pure and (2) the impure people must be eradicated. In this way, deliverance through death is justified in Falun Gong.

Conclusion

The words of Li Hongzhi suggest that lives in the known universe can be divided into two groups: the cultivated and the non-cultivated. Similarly, the people in today's world fall into two categories: Falun Gong practitioners and non-Falun Gong practitioners. The former belong to the world of cultivation, whereas the latter includes common people and devils. Given Li's comments on the relationship between common people and devils, it can be concluded that non-practitioners are considered devilish. Li proposes that common people should be destroyed, using the notion of devil killing to justify this stance. It is evident that, in essence, Falun Gong is intolerant of non-Falun Gong practitioners. This intolerance is further evidenced by the use of common people as tools to test practitioners.

Additionally, in Falun Gong doctrine, non-practitioners who are killed are expected to feel gratitude to Falun Gong for delivering them from evil. Hence, the devil-killing process is construed as enabling primordial spirits to be released. These spirits can then be used by Falun Gong practitioners as energy, enabling them to cultivate primordial babies. In this way, common people are stripped of value, becoming mere tools and sources of energy. Arguably, then, the practice of Falun Gong can lead only to the perpetration of more acts of violence against non-followers.

References

Li Hongzhi. *Zhuan Falun.*
Li Hongzhi. 1994. "Interpretation of Falun Dafa, Proposals at the Counselors Meeting of Beijing Falun Dafa," December 17.
Li Hongzhi. 1996. Lecture at Beijing International Exchange Meeting, November 11.
Li Hongzhi. 1999. Lecture at the Australian Conference of Falun Dafa, May 2–3, Sydney.
Li Hongzhi. 2000a. Lecture in Ann Arbor, December 9.
Li Hongzhi. 2000b. Lecture at Falun Gong Conference in Great Lakes Region, December 18.

Fang Yong is an Associate Professor in the School of Philosophy at Wuhan University. His research interests include ethics, religious studies, and political philosophy, with a special focus on Christian and Buddhist ethics. He has published one book in Chinese and five translations of books from English into Chinese.

6. The Self-contradictions in Li Hongzhi's Statements about Illness

Cao Yan

Li Hongzhi, Falun Gong's founder-leader, uses several methods to attract followers. First, he utilizes many Buddhist terms in the construction of the "Falun Dafa" doctrine, such as "Buddha," "Falun," "Dharmakaya," and "sickness karma," thus giving his ideas an aura of authority. Second, he capitalizes on people's notions of faith, emphasizing concepts typically found in religious teachings – such as truthfulness, compassion, and forbearance – in order to appeal to his target audience. Despite Li's appropriation of Buddhist terminology and sentiment, the Buddhist community rejects Falun Dafa's claim to be a legitimate religion. Additionally, certain previous studies have argued that Falun Gong is not only anti-science, but also anti-society and even anti-humanity. One of the factors supporting such arguments is Li Hongzhi's theory of illness, in which the use of medical treatment is discouraged.

The Rejection of Medicine and Medical Treatment for Illnesses

According to Li Hongzhi, diseases are caused by karma and thus cannot be escaped; the only option is to suffer the pain of illness. Part of this belief includes Falun Gong's opposition to medicine and medical treatment for diseases. Li claims that bad karma can only be dissipated through consciously enduring illness:

> Once ill, the person takes medicine or seeks various kinds of treatments, which, in effect, press the sickness back into the body again. This way, instead of paying sickness karma for wrongdoings from a previous life, he will do additional bad things in this life and hurt others; this brings about new sickness karma and leads to different kinds of sicknesses. Nevertheless, he continues to take medicine or to use various treatments that press the sickness back into his body. Surgery can only remove flesh in the superficial, physical dimension; the sickness karma in another dimension has not been touched at all – it is simply beyond the reach of modern medical technology. When the sickness recurs, the person will seek treatment again. When a person is reincarnated after death, any sickness karma that has been accrued will be pressed back into the body again. This cycle goes on one lifetime after another; it is unknown just how much sickness karma accumulates in a person's body. (Li Hongzhi 1996, 36–7)

Here, Li suggests that modern medicine and surgical treatments cannot access sickness karma – medicine can work on the physical body only, while the root cause of the disease exists in another dimension. Thus, the treatment of illnesses via medical methods merely returns the sickness to the body, prolonging the existence of bad karma. Interestingly, he holds a similar belief regarding alternative treatments like *qigong* – he argues that they cannot tackle the root cause of illness. Li does state, however, that there is a solution to illness; he claims to be invested with a magical power, through which his disciples' diseases can be cured:

> For us cultivators, beyond the karma that Master has eliminated, we must still pay a portion ourselves. You will thus feel physically uncomfortable, as if you were suffering from sickness. Cultivation practice cleanses you of your life's origins. The human body contains layers, like the rings of a tree; each ring contains sickness karma. So, your body must be cleansed at the very center. Were all the karma to be pushed out at once, however, you wouldn't be able to take it; it would endanger your life. Only one or two pieces can be pushed out every once in a while, thus allowing you to overcome the karma and pay

Self-contradictions in Li Hongzhi's Statements about Illness   127

for it through suffering. But this is only that little bit that is left for you to endure after I have eliminated most of the karma from you.

Even basic *qigong* treatments push karma into a person's body. When a person has too much karma and is still doing bad things, he faces destruction – the complete destruction of both body and soul. Death here is total extinction. When treating a sickness in a human being, a Great Enlightened Being can completely eliminate the karmic cause of that sickness, but this is done mainly for the purpose of saving people. (ibid.)

Li indicates that it takes too long for practitioners to overcome bad karma through suffering. Moreover, the karma hinders their practice of cultivation. He states, therefore, that he can eliminate most of the negative karma and sickness karma in a follower's body through his magic power – although, as stated above, he leaves a small portion for them to endure. In Li's understanding, this residual karma facilitates the practice of cultivation, allowing his disciples to advance to a higher level of existence quickly. Where certain "insubordinate" latecomers are concerned, however, Li shows less mercy, as reflected in the following quotation:

Here, we do not teach you to treat illness. We lead you to the Great Way, the righteous way, and we elevate you. Thus, in my lectures, I always say that practitioners of Falun Dafa are not allowed to have treatment for illnesses. If you treat an illness, you are not a practitioner of Falun Dafa. Because we lead you toward the righteous path through In-Triple-World-Fa cultivation practice, your body will be purified continually until it is completely transformed by high-energy matter. How can you practice cultivation if you are still collecting those dark things in your body? Those things are karma! You will be unable to practice cultivation at all. With too much karma, you will be unable to bear it. If you suffer too much, you will be unable to practice cultivation. This is the reason why I have made this Dafa public, although, even so, you may not know what I have taught. Given that this Dafa can be made public, it is necessary to find ways to protect it. If you treat illnesses in others, I will take back everything given to your body for cultivation. We cannot allow you to casually ruin something so precious for fame and self-interest. If you do not follow the requirements of the Fa, you are not a practitioner of Falun Dafa. If you want to be an everyday person, your body will be reset to the level of everyday people and the bad things will be returned to you. (Li Hongzhi 1999, 77–8)

Contradictions in Li Hongzhi's Statements about Illness

The quotations given above indicate a major contradiction in Li Hongzhi's statements about illness. Li purports to be powerful enough to eliminate illness and bad karma, but he also states that he can return this karma to any practitioner who does not follow the Falun Gong doctrine sufficiently. We must ask, then, how is it possible for Li to return bad karma that has already been eliminated? Can he really claim that his ability to eliminate illness and karma is plausible, while maintaining that he can restore bad karma?

It is a matter of basic semantics that what has been eliminated no longer exists. Logic dictates that is impossible to return something that does not exist. Indeed, if Li does claim to have such a power, then this can be construed as an admission of creating a sort of evil – something which is not natural and which will also have an adverse effect upon the recipient. Such actions preclude his ability to maintain an image of himself as a divine or merciful person. Indeed, his statements contradict his positioning of Falun Gong as a faith for "the true, the good, and the tolerant." If the so-called elimination of bad karma can be interpreted as a severing of the connection between bad karma and a Falun Gong practitioner, and, relatedly, the returning of bad karma can be understood as the re-establishment of that connection, then it can be suggested that Li advocates – and, indeed, perpetrates – the pollution of cleansed people with disease, an act which can be considered evil.

As Li posits that he can restore this bad karma, we must also question where the bad karma resides after it has been removed from a practitioner, if it is not eliminated altogether. We can only

Self-contradictions in Li Hongzhi's Statements about Illness 129

assume that he transfers the bad karma of others to himself during this process. If this is so, then Li should not be considered a divine being or Buddha. The quality of divinity would enable him to eliminate bad karma once and for all, thus rendering it impossible for it to be returned. Only one other option remains: that surplus bad karma is converted into something good through Li's religious practice. If this were the logic at work here, however, then how could he justify turning the good back into evil and then transferring it to other people? If Li Hongzhi does have the power to turn good into evil, then it only means he can create more evil than others, for other people can only create evil. They certainly are incapable of turning the good into evil. We can conclude that Li Hongzhi is the only person in the world, then, with the power to transform bad to good and back again.

We are left with a situation that raises more questions than it answers. The elimination of bad karma might mean taking evil out of a person's body and storing it elsewhere so that it can be returned if necessary, but then can bad karma be converted or eliminated at all? Or perhaps Li Hongzhi actually does wish to suggest that he has the power to convert bad karma to good, or to eliminate bad karma altogether – but can the initiation of such an act necessarily be viewed as good? To tentatively suggest some answers, we can turn to Li's *Falun Gong – Essentials of Diligence* (Li Hongzhi 1996), which contains a chapter dedicated to the topic of illness. Here he states that to practice transcendental law is to practice the purest *arhat*, which is a space in which no karma or illness exists. We can surmise, therefore, that in Falun Gong's doctrine, bad karma can be truly eliminated through practice. If Li were claiming simply to transfer his disciples' karma without eradicating it, then this would be no different from a medical treatment or an alternative therapy like *qigong*, both of which he criticizes for failing to transform bad karma. In such circumstances, illness can only be pushed back inside the patient's body – in other words, if karma was transferred, it would have to be returned to the body sooner or later. We might suggest here that Li Hongzhi's power to "remove" bad karma could actually be described better as the power to reduce its impact upon the patient, but if this was the case, then there would be no need to remove the karma from the patient's body because it would not be a true removal – the dimension in which the karma resides would not have been accessed. Once more, this aspect of his teaching is rendered problematic because it is, of course, not possible to return something that has never been removed in the first place.

Given Li Hongzhi's insistence that editing even a single word in his books or sutra is not allowed (this would be considered "disobeying the law"), an explanation is required for the contradictions evident in his ideas if they are to be considered credible.

Li Hongzhi's Statements as an Abuse of Human Rights

As discussed extensively in the previous section, the notion that Li Hongzhi can eliminate bad karma from others is highly dubious, given the contradictions inherent in his statements. Indeed, Li's speeches and texts can be understood, at least in part, as propaganda, designed to attract followers to Falun Gong. A close inspection of the data reveals contradictory statements that call the credibility of his doctrine into question. He wants his disciples to believe that his faith is good, but he threatens them with disease, which cannot reasonably be considered an aspect of a good and honest religion. Moreover, Li Hongzhi specifically targets the disobedient, threatening to damage his disciples' spirits and bodies, thus demonstrating a lack of tolerance or forbearance – qualities which are supposed to be important in Falun Gong. However, what we see here is a propensity for threatening disciples as a way of controlling them – Li's statements become a means through which to maintain power over his followers.

This goal of such control is implicit in Li's writings. When he asserts that, "If you do not follow the requirements of the Fa, you are not a practitioner of Falun Dafa. If you want to be an everyday person, your body will be reset to the level of the everyday people and the bad things will be returned to you" (Li Hongzhi 1999), he is warning his disciples to avoid abjuration of their belief in Falun Gong. It can be surmised that Li wants to avoid Falun Gong gaining a negative image that might be associated with abjuration. Indeed, he repeatedly asserts that abjuration is unwise, disloyal, and even evil. In this way, he exerts control over his disciples, preventing them from making free choices.

What is problematic here is that, in Buddhist scripture, Buddha indicates that abjuration as an action is neither good nor evil. In the ancient Buddhist Abhidharma texts, it is stated that "Whatever the nature of the doctrine, not gaining itself is neutral" (T 29.1562. 399a 20–1). "Not gaining" here can be understood as referring to abjuration and deprivation – that is to say, no matter what doctrine is abjured, abjuration itself is not good or evil. This concept of "not gaining" belongs to Non-covered Dharma (无覆法), a set of principles in which disengagement is not hindered (as opposed to Covered Dharma [有覆法], in which disengagement is discouraged). In the quotation here, the idea that abjuration is "neutral" can be understood to mean that it is neither a negative nor a positive act. Thus, an interpretation of Buddhist teachings suggests that abjuration can be understood as a basic human right. If it is neutral and does not cause any harm, then no individual or group should be deprived of the right to abjuration under any circumstances.

In Buddhism, the opposite of abjuration is "gaining" or attainment. As stated in the Abhidharma, "Believing in good doctrine helps to gain good. Believing good, evil or non-*ji* doctrine (无记法), people gain good, evil or non-*ji* accordingly" (T29.1562. 398c9–10). In other words, gaining is judged as either good or evil according to the doctrine being followed. In this light, an action or achievement can be evaluated as either good or evil, depending on the context. When one is uncertain about whether or not an action is good or evil, or when the nature of an act is uncertain, then choosing to undertake it bears ethical risks. On the contrary, abjuration of either a good or an evil act involves no such risks. To expand on this, obtaining can be good, evil, or "non-*ji*" and, as such, the legitimacy of the act needs to be supported by the certainty that it is not evil. Abjuration, on the other hand, is not good or evil, and so the legitimacy of abjuration needs no further support; it speaks for itself. At play here is the zero-sum principle; the loss and gain associated with abjuration balance each other out, so that the consequence amounts to nothing – it is neutral. As such, the right to abjure should be given to every person, and the decision to do so should be respected.

If one abjures a contract in business, that abjuration should not be judged as good or evil; there is unlikely to be a claim for compensation for mental damage. Usually, all one is expected to do is to pay a penalty, in accordance with the terms of the contract. Any mental damage caused can be considered the result of a misunderstanding of the ethics associated with abjuration – terminating a contract is much better than acting passively and causing intentional delays to the fulfillment of contractual obligations because, in such a case, abjuration allows the other party to select a new contract partner rapidly.

Where Falun Gong is concerned, however, it seems that Li Hongzhi regards the abjuration of belief as evil. He punishes disciples who disobey him and abjure Falun Gong, actions which run contrary to Buddhist doctrine. This is problematic, given that Li positions himself as the "Great Buddha." Indeed, his threats of action and punishment for abjuration can be considered a violation of the basic right to abjure belief. Here, he takes advantage of people's misunderstanding of the ethics of abjuration. The popular saying "Put away the cleaver and the butcher becomes a Buddha" is of relevance in this context – in everyday life, we appreciate those who abjure evil and criticize those who abjure good. If someone can become good by refraining from those things that made him seem evil, then the opposite must also be true: if we see someone abjuring former good deeds, then we believe that this is an evil act.

Buddhism, however, promotes choice. When a person considers converting to Buddhism, it is suggested that he or she should learn about the faith first in order to decide whether it suits him/her. Furthermore, if a disciple who has converted to Buddhism comes to believe that s/he has chosen the wrong path, then s/he is considered to have the right to abjure at any time. In Buddhist doctrine, the faith is never forced upon others; Buddha respects people's free will and their basic human right to abjure. But in many of the groups that have been accused of being "cults," one finds a denial of the right to abjure the faith. For instance, some such religions threaten their disciples with doomsday in order to frighten them into not leaving. Often, if a disciple has any thoughts that run contrary to those of his/her leaders, then that person is singled out as not being a true believer. Such leaders might use the threat of a dissenter no longer being protected by the gods, asserting that unfaithful actions will attract bad karma. The desire to leave such religions is often positioned as disloyal and, indeed, evil. Sometimes the individual and his/her family become subject to threats that are designed to prevent dissent.

In groups like Falun Gong, there is little room for objections or criticism. The techniques used to maintain a following, such as the fear tactics discussed above, render it difficult for many disciples to abjure their belief. They become frightened of the consequences of bad karma and of being branded evil because of abjuration. Such a rigid and closed form of organizational management, however, is not at all in line with the democratic, free spirit of the contemporary world. In this paper, we have sought to emphasize that abjuration is a basic human right that should not be denied. Rather than believing that the faith must be maintained at all costs, society should be educated to understand that one's right to abjure is sacred.

References

Li Hongzhi. 1996. "Sickness Karma," in *Falun Dafa: Essentials of Diligence* (法轮大法·精进要旨).

Li Hongzhi. 1999. "The Issue of Pursuit," in *Falun Dafa.* Nei Menggu: Nei Menggu Culture Press.

T: *The Taisho Edition of the Chinese Tripitaka* (大正新修大藏經). Taipei: Xinwenfeng, 1983.

Cao Yan is Associate Professor in the Department of Religion, School of Philosophy, at Wuhan University, in Wuhan, China. His research interests include Buddhism, Hinduism, and Sanskrit.

7. Scientific or Anti-scientific
A Critical Analysis of "Science" Discourses in Falun Gong[1]

Wang Chengjun

As many researchers have argued, the use of science to justify beliefs has long been a popular "legitimation strategy" in new religions (see Rapport 2016, 278). The recently emerged religion[2] Falun Gong has also made use of this strategy for the purpose of propagating its teachings (e.g., the term "science" is mentioned 38 times in Li Hongzhi's *Zhuan Falun*, one of Falun Gong's principal scriptures; see Farley 2011, 155). Indeed, if one were to compile terminological statistics from all the publications and speeches of Li Hongzhi, Falun Gong's founder, then one would find that "science" is one of the most frequently used terms.

In contrast with other new religions that have adopted science as a source of legitimation, however, Falun Gong's use of "science" discourse is confusing and inconsistent. While it is sometimes claimed by Falun Gong that its doctrines, creeds, and beliefs can be well explained by modern science, at other times its teachings

---

1. This paper was written in Chinese first and then translated into English for the CESNUR 2017 conference "Holy Lands and Sacred History in New Religious Movements." I must thank Professor James R. Lewis of the University of Tromsø for his kind help with adapting the content into English.

2. Scholarly opinion is divided over whether or not Falun Gong is a religion. Some do not believe that it qualifies as a religion, understanding it rather as a meditation group or a cult. Others suggest, however, that it can be considered a religion in the full sense. (See Penny 2012, 4–8.)

are positioned as transcending the realm of natural science. This second position precludes the possibility of using science to understand or verify Falun Gong's teachings. In general, Falun Gong has been positioned as a science in itself – or, more specifically, as the "ultimate science" or "super-science." At the same time, however, Li Hongzhi has also taught that science, in the general sense of the term, is defective and hazardous, both theoretically and practically speaking. This can be seen in Li Hongzhi's suggestion that natural science masks the truth and is harmful to human beings' moral cultivation. Li has even gone as far as to suggest that science is responsible for many different types of modern social "disease" (including social and environmental problems). It has also been suggested that Falun Gong practitioners should refuse to use modern science and technology in their daily lives, with Li going as far as to say that his students should not visit doctors when they fall ill. In the face of such contradictions and controversial ideas, we are led to wonder, then, what place do "scientific" discourses have in Falun Gong? Has this new religion used science successfully as a legitimation strategy? And, if not, to what extent should we seriously entertain its doctrines?

In this paper, I will offer critical reflections on the science-related discourses present in Falun Gong. First, I will analyze such discourses, arguing that they fall into three different categories. Second, I will trace these discourses back to their origins in order to suggest that, even if science-based legitimation of the faith is effective in persuading its practitioners, it is by no means successful in a wider sense. Finally, I will conclude with some more specific remarks on the ways in which "science" discourses have been used by Falun Gong.

Three Types of "Science" Discourse in Falun Gong

A careful examination of texts related to Falun Gong reveals at least three types of science-related discourse. I term these "scientific," "sci-fi," and "para-scientific" discourses.

1. Scientific Discourse

Scientific discourse in Falun Gong can be divided into two subtypes: (1) references to standard terms or authoritative theories established in the traditional natural sciences, and (2) discussions of theories and/or claims in a scientific-sounding way.

The first subtype appears in Falun Gong's texts very frequently. For example, in the earliest Chinese version of *Zhuan Falun*, Li Hongzhi states at the beginning that

> *Buddha dharma (fo-fa)* is the most profound, abstruse and super-science ... *Buddha dharma* comprises all truths and offers insight into the mysteries of all things – from particles and molecules to the whole universe; from the smallest to the largest things. (Li Hongzhi 1994, 1)[3]

In the same text, Li argues that *qigong* (a popular dance-type exercise, from which the Falun Gong movement originated) was part of "pre-historic culture," and makes no hesitation in appealing to Darwinism for authentication: "According to Darwin's theory of evolution, humankind evolved from aquatic plants to aquatic animals" (Li Hongzhi 2014, 19). Such examples of Li Hongzhi's use of science to legitimize his claims are not unusual; indeed, it is easy for a reader to find multiple examples in his scriptures and speeches.

The second subtype of scientific discourse involves Falun Gong's own science-like definitions of its theories. For example, in the

---

3. Researchers might have noticed that the scripture texts of Falun Gong have been slightly revised by Li Hongzhi in recent years. The passage cited here was translated by me from the original Chinese version of *Zhuan Falun*, published in December 1994. In the newest English online edition (2014) of this scripture, a new introduction (entitled "On *Dafa*"), written by Li Hongzhi in May 2015, is added, and the verses I cite here have been revised as "*Dafa* is the wisdom of the creator. It is the bedrock of creation, what the heavens, earth, and universe are built upon. It encompasses all things, from the utmost minuscule to the vastest of the vast, while manifesting differently at each of the cosmic body's planes of existence" (Li Hongzhi 2014, I).

paragraph from *Zhuan Falun* quoted above, Li gives "empirical" proof to demonstrate that the aforementioned "pre-historic culture" did in fact exist. Some of his examples include the following: (1) that human beings have found ancient buildings beneath the ocean; (2) that a certain American scientist found a human footprint in a trilobite fossil; (3) that a 30,000-year-old stone carved with a pattern of a man with a telescope has been found in Peru; and (4) that a scientist has discovered a uranium mine in Gabon which was probably a nuclear reactor. Li uses such "proofs" to conclude that, according to his observations, "the humankind has undergone complete annihilation 81 times. With a little remaining from the previous civilization, only a small number of people would survive and enter the next period, again living a primitive life (ibid., 24). This manner of validation involves following a "hypothesis, empirical proof, theory" procedure. Clearly, Li uses unreliable data here as proof, thus rendering his theory dubious at best. But the method can be understood as following that utilized in the pursuit of scientific knowledge. In this way, Li Hongzhi and Falun Gong take an alternative, competing "scientific" position regarding the evolution of human beings and human culture – areas which geoscientists, biologists, and anthropologists also continue to address in their work.

We can see, then, that many of the alternative scientific claims made by Falun Gong about nature and the universe are not supported by reliable empirical proofs. Li also alleges that matter and spirit are unified, asserting his belief that thought is material and that all material beings in the universe are spiritual (ibid., 32). He adds that the Earth has a history of 100 billion years, stating that there were "big men, middle-sized men, and small men" in the first half of this history. Li also claims that the moon was made by man at an earlier stage of Earth's history and then sent into outer space (Li Hongzhi 2002). He argues that there are both new and old universes, and that all living beings in this (the old) universe will be destroyed when *Authentic Dharma* (*zheng fa*) comes (ibid.). Again, these claims lack solid evidence and are thus hard to believe – they are quite different from the realms of common sense and standard science. In order to discuss these ideas further, it is useful to first examine the other two types of "science" discourse identified in this paper – the sci-fi discourse and the para-scientific discourse.

2. Sci-fi Discourse

The sci-fi discourse category relates to topics often found in sci-fi movies and literature – for example, aliens, UFOs, and other things considered as being supernatural. A reading of Li Hongzhi's writings and speeches reveals that such themes are prevalent. In *Zhuan Falun* (2014, 226), Li suggests that the so-called "dual cultivation of a man and a woman (*nan-nü-shuang-xiu*) actually did not originate from this planet of ours. It came from another planet." The text also mentions flying saucers twice, arguing that they surpass any human-made technologies (ibid., 71, 349). Further study of Li's theories reveals that he became particularly fascinated with this sort of discourse after traveling to the Western world to promote Falun Gong. In his later speeches and interviews, aliens are regularly featured, and what is perhaps most interesting is that his portrayal of these figures differs here from portrayals in earlier texts. After visiting the West, Li's earlier suggestions that aliens are real and use highly advanced technology developed into claims that human beings are subjects for alien experimentation. Li begins to assert that human society is controlled by alien forces – in his version of events, the Earth has been invaded by aliens, who have assumed a humanlike appearance. According to Li, these aliens will take over the Earth completely.[4] Li also strives for consistency here by indicating that the aliens were the inhabitants of the "past earth" that he talked about in earlier writings (Li Hongzhi 2002). Li further justifies his alien narrative by suggesting that, although human beings were created to be greater than the aliens, the supremacy of the aliens will be reinstated if human beings fail to embrace the teachings of Falun Gong (ibid.).Thus, a closer look at the Falun Gong alien narrative indicates that it is a tool through which to encourage disciples' adherence to the principles of the faith.

4. On the development of Li's alien narrative, see Penny (2012, 130–2).

3. Para-scientific Discourse

The third type of "science" discourse in Falun Gong, the "para-scientific" discourse, concerns subjects outside the scope of traditional science that cannot be explained via accepted scientific theories or tested using conventional scientific methods. Again, two subtypes can be identified within this category: (1) references to scientific concepts or claims that cannot be verified using any conventional scientific theory/method; and (2) references to Li Hongzhi's assertion that Falun Gong is the ultimate science (or a "super-science").

The first subtype occurs in Falun Gong rhetoric so frequently that it can be found easily in any Falun Gong text one might open. Li Hongzhi seems to have great interest, for instance, in creating a new cosmology – he posits that there may be as many as 3000 universes of various ages and argues that "there are two kinds of matter in the high and micro cosmos." Such examples are only the tip of the iceberg; it appears that Li aims to transform a wide range of scientific fields. As Helen Farley (2011, 155) comments, he "creates an alternative paradigm where science as we know it is untenable; in contrast, he promises his own approach would represent breakthroughs in physics, geophysics, astrophysics, astronomy, chemistry, history, geography, philosophy, social science and so on."

One of the most notable examples of this type of discourse is what Li calls "heavenly eye" or "celestial eye" (*tian-mu*). This is a reference to the "material organs" connected to the pineal gland that lie between the eyebrows of the human being, which, for Li, are at present "degenerate," but which have the potential to develop special powers via the practice of Falun Gong (Li Hongzhi 2014, 55–84). Such development would enable human beings to see tiny particles, thus giving them visual access to the essence of things. Indeed, Li even claims that the training of the eyes could bestow X-ray-type vision upon people, as well as granting them the ability to see into other spaces and times, thus enabling the foretelling of the future (ibid.).

The second subtype of para-scientific discourse – the idea that Falun Gong is the ultimate science and transcends any other type of science – can be traced back to *Zhuan Falun* and the origins of the Falun Gong faith. At the very beginning of the book, it is announced that the *Buddha dharma (fo-fa)* that Falun Gong teaches is the "most profound, abstruse and super-science" (Li Hongzhi 1994, 1). This super-science is described as being inexplicable via the traditional, "limited" methods associated with natural science. Li is also careful to draw a clear line between the Falun Gong "super-science" and superstition/the supernatural (i.e., anything that has been identified as non-scientific).[5] In what ways, though, is this so-called "super-science" different from superstition, religion, and the supernatural? This is a particularly important question, given that Li refers to gods, devils, ghosts, and other supernatural or religiously spiritual beings in positive ways in various places. Li never provides explanations for the contradictions in his doctrine, thus rendering his position on para-scientific discourses ambiguous.

The division of Falun Gong's "science" discourse into three categories should be understood as being fairly flexible. Indeed, the three categories should be considered interrelated. They do not

5. When Falun Gong originated, Li Hongzhi stated that he wanted to separate the so-called "*fo-fa*" (*Buddha dharma*) from religion. Regarding the propensity for academia to define new movements in religious terms, he said, "[W]hat on Earth is this *fo-fa?* Is it a religion? Is it a philosophy? These are all that modern Buddhist scholars know …" (Li Hongzhi 1994, 1). In 1995, in a letter to his disciples (entitled "Broad and Immense"), he added, "The principles of *Falun Dafa* can provide guidance for anyone's cultivation practice, including for one's religious beliefs. This is the principle of the universe, the true *Fa* that has never been taught. People in the past were not allowed to know this universe's principle (the *Buddha Fa*). It transcends all academic theories and moral principles of human society from ancient times to this day. What was taught by religions and what people experienced in the past were only superficialities and shallow phenomena" (Li Hongzhi 1997a, 5). During his first *Fa* conference in North America in 1998, Li also explicitly stated, "*Falun Dafa* is not a religion, and I will never engage in religion. Our *Falun Dafa* is absolutely not a religion." This is because, for him, religion is "created and acknowledged by human beings" and is therefore "corrupt and evil"; it "can never be the salvation of people" (Li Hongzhi 1998a).

appear independently in Li Hongzhi's texts and speeches; rather, the three areas meet and mingle, so that some statements might be considered to contain elements of all three – the scientific, the sci-fi, and the para-scientific. Take, for example, the idea of "heavenly eyes" mentioned above, which is discussed in relation to "special powers," while, at the same time, terms from modern medical science like "pineal gland" are used. It is clear here that the "heavenly eyes" theory could fall into both the scientific and the para-scientific discourse categories.

The Origins of the Falun Gong "Science" Discourse

As noted by earlier researchers, Li Hongzhi has no specific educational background in science, his formal education having ended after high school.[6] Despite this, since Falun Gong was founded in 1992, Li has regularly appealed to science as a legitimating resource. Given Li's lack of scientific training, this could be considered a risky strategy – after all, upon what could his theories be based? This approach to legitimation becomes less surprising, however, when one examines the origins of Falun Gong.

The development of Falun Gong can be related to the "*qigong* fever" that swept mainland China in the 1980s – I myself remember this phenomenon from childhood.[7] I can still recall thousands of people – young and old – flooding out of their homes every morning and evening to gather in squares, gardens, and other public spaces to practice *qigong* during the 1980s and 1990s. If you entered a bookstore in China at that time, you would find that the best-selling book would always be a book about *qigong*. There were countless *qigong*

---

6. On Li's life and background, see Penny (2012, 77–111).

7. Much research has been conducted regarding the relationship between *qigong* and Falun Gong. For a clear, concise explanation of *qigong* fever and the development of Falun Gong, see Penny (2012, 8–18) and Farley (2011, 150–3). On the general development of *qigong* fever in China, see Chen (2003).

groups and masters, and these masters often asserted that they had special powers that had been bestowed upon them via the practice. Even the official Chinese media discussed *qigong* to the point where some *qigong* masters became well-known, godlike, public figures. Up until the Chinese government decided to ban Falun Gong and demythologize these masters in the late 1990s, *qigong* remained a prominent social and cultural phenomenon.

One reason for the development of *qigong* fever may have been the fact that the practice functioned as a social event for Chinese people. It allowed them to feel freer from their labor and to have a sense of enjoying leisure time. In the 1980s and 1990s, the Chinese economy was developing quickly and, accordingly, the nation was becoming less introverted. There were not many forms of public life or social events available to ordinary Chinese people, however. As such, *qigong* facilitated greater social interaction. Additionally, the country's underdeveloped medical system encouraged the Chinese to embrace *qigong*. One of the main problems the government had to tackle in the 1980s was the lack of generally available healthcare. In such circumstances, the (unsubstantiated) notion that *qigong* had healing powers was exaggerated, thus increasing the popularity of the practice. It was thought that *qigong*, like *tai chi*, could improve general bodily health, and some even believed that it could help to heal diseases as serious as cancer and HIV.

The *qigong* craze also involved a more supernatural element. Some practitioners believed that they could attain special powers through *qigong*, like mind control, the ability to fly, the ability to become invisible, and the power to penetrate through solid matter. In other words, they thought that *qigong* would enable them to become Superman-like beings. It was culturally normal not to question such beliefs – indeed, some political and scientific authorities put forth similar points of view. The military even founded an institute based on *qigong* to promote an area of study termed "body science," which concerned such "superhuman" powers. So, why did people believe such claims, even when it was easy to find evidence that contradicted them? The simple answer is that, in many people's eyes, *qigong* was "scientific." It was believed that the so-called "body science" would lead to huge breakthroughs in the study of human beings, thus placing China at the forefront of a new scientific revolution. The Chinese did not question the reliability and authority of science. Thus, the scientization of *qigong* led to its widespread adoption and acceptance. This scientization process included the framing of practically all *qigong*-related activities as "scientific" via the introduction of scientific terms and theories into the practice. As society began to accept *qigong* as a sort of science, the idea developed that, sooner or later, its mysteries would be revealed through scientific study. A number of authoritative Chinese scientists also backed this notion. Thus, "science" became an unavoidable term where *qigong* was concerned. When Falun Gong developed as a subsection of *qigong* in the 1990s, therefore, the movement was automatically associated with the term "science." Metaphorically speaking, science thus provided Falun Gong with access to a market; the science label allowed the movement to attract customers and to thrive. We can see, then, that Falun Gong's science discourse is integral to its existence, particularly where the first category that we have identified – "scientific discourse" – is concerned.

The second category of science discourse – "sci-fi discourse" – can also be traced to a 1980s Chinese craze. A mania for UFOs and alien stories arose in China alongside *qigong* fever, influenced in part by the global popularity of US sci-fi movies at this time. As a result, many unofficial associations and institutes for UFO research were founded, and large numbers of books and magazines about UFOs became popular. It was widely believed that UFOs existed, particularly because the official media reported on UFO-related news. It can be argued that the UFO narrative was accepted so readily because it satisfied people's curiosity about mysteries and also provided escapism from the mundaneness of everyday life. This can be understood as a backlash against restrictive Confucian philosophy, which had warned the Chinese to shun devils and gods for thousands of years. The UFO narrative thus fostered people's imaginations and gave them hope that there was a universe beyond what was known. We can interpret this sort of appeal of UFO and alien culture as a Messiah-type narrative, in which aliens are viewed as having the potential to save ordinary people from the drudgery of earthly life. Despite the lack of empirical evidence for UFOs, such stories were accepted because of the failure of existing scientific theories to explain particular events and occurrences. In this way, UFO mania led to the perpetuation of at least three types of belief among the Chinese, all of which are important in Falun Gong: (1) the idea that we are not alone in this vast universe – there are many other intelligent beings beyond the Earth; (2) the notion that those intelligent beings are far more advanced than we are, being able to do what human beings cannot; (3) the theory that intelligent alien beings have already come to our planet many times, having established connections with us – even if we are not always aware of it. A cursory analysis of the science discourse in Falun Gong indicates clearly that the sci-fi element is borrowed directly from these beliefs. The UFO craze can therefore be considered an important source, leading to the emergence of a sci-fi discourse in Falun Gong.

At this point, we can turn to the origins of the third strand of the Falun Gong science discourse. Here, it can be argued that the concept of Falun Gong as a "super-science" emerged from the sublime status of science in mainstream Chinese culture.[8] For the Chinese, the word "science" is not a neutral noun that refers to a particular system of knowledge; it also has a specific axiological meaning related to the terms "true," "right," and "good." To clarify, in some

---

8. As James R. Lewis and Olav Hammer (2011, 8) point out, the synonymity of science with truth is one of the main reasons for the appeal to science as a legitimation strategy in new religious movements. Jeremy Rapport (2016) also emphasizes this point. It should be noted, however, that the status of science has developed in different ways in the Western world, when compared with the Chinese case. More specifically, Chinese society's understanding of science as truth is not influenced by what Rapport terms "Baconianism" (the idea that science is a way to explore the secrets of God). Baconian and Christian ideas have had little influence in China due to its mainly atheist history. Rather, the status of science in China has been influenced by the Marxist and materialist ideologies of the nineteenth century. On science and scientificism in China, see Xiao (2011, 45–50).

cases, the term "science" could be replaced by "truth" or "righteousness" in the Chinese context. In the mainstream view, science represents the summit of human reason and knowledge, and is therefore a symbol of that which is true and good (Xiao 2011, 45–50). For example, the Chinese government would call its version of socialism "scientific socialism" and would refer to China's development as "scientific development." When judging whether a belief, statement, or act was right or wrong, a Chinese person would state that it was or was not "scientific." In China, then, if a set of beliefs claim to be "scientific," the authority of those beliefs is likely to be accepted. This explains why the *qigong* movement appealed to science with no hesitation in order to legitimate itself. The same can be said for Falun Gong: the use of a science discourse facilitates popularity and acceptance. It is my belief, therefore, that Falun Gong would have gained a following even without the *qigong* "fad"; the status of science is so high in Chinese culture that Falun Gong was bound to be successful, as long as Li Hongzhi used science-type ideas for its basis. In fact, the credibility associated with anything termed scientific in Chinese culture can help us to understand why there are contradictions in Falun Gong's science discourse; even when Li began to turn away from a belief in natural science after visiting the West, it suited his purposes to retain the idea of Falun Gong being a "super-science" because it enabled the movement to retain its air of authenticity.

The Failure of Science-based Legitimation in Falun Gong

Thus far, we have analyzed the science discourse found in Falun Gong, identifying three categories within this discourse, and tracing their origins. We have also seen that Falun Gong utilizes this science discourse to legitimate or justify itself. The purpose of such legitimation, according to Jeremy Rapport, is to "establish a person's, or a group's, right to exercise authority over others." More specifically, this approach can be said to "make their claims seem authoritative, and so are used to explain and to justify the exercise of power" (Rapport 2011, 551). The evidence given above makes it clear that Falun Gong appeals to science in this way. The question remains, however, whether or not this use of the science discourse is successful.

The three types of science discourse analyzed earlier are used by Falun Gong in two main ways: (1) the utilization of terms and theories borrowed from traditional science as evidence of the veracity of its core beliefs and as a way of dismissing skepticism about them, and (2) the application of the science label in order to make these core beliefs seem acceptable to the general public.

It should once again be noted that these two applications of science discourse are not independent from one another; their relationship is rather complicated and intertwined. For example, in Li Hongzhi's *Falun Dafa: Essentials for Further Advancement* (*Jingjin-yao-zhi*) – a text that is considered a guidebook for Falun Gong practitioners – it is stated that "truth, goodness, and forbearance" (*Zhen, Shan, Ren*) are "the highest attributes of the universe." In more detail:

> This is because matter is composed of microscopic matter, which is in turn made up of even more microscopic matter – this goes on and on until the end. Therefore, Zhen consists of Zhen-Shan-Ren, Shan consists of Zhen-Shan-Ren, and Ren also consists of Zhen-Shan-Ren … In a very high and very microscopic dimension of the universe there exist two different kinds of substances. They are two forms of material existence manifest by the supreme nature of the universe, Zhen-Shan-Ren, at certain dimensional levels in the universe. They pervade certain dimensions from top to bottom, or from the microscopic level to the macroscopic level … Any kind of matter or life in the universe is composed of microscopic particles that make up larger particles, and these then form surface matter. Within the scope covered by these two kinds of matter of differing properties, all matter and lives possess dual nature just the same. For instance, iron and steel are hard, but they oxidize and rust when buried in the earth. Pottery and porcelain, on the other hand, do not oxidize when buried in the

earth, but are fragile and easily broken. The same applies to human beings, who possess Buddha-nature and demon-nature at the same time. (Li Hongzhi 1997a, 28–30)

In this passage, science discourse is utilized in both of the aforementioned ways. When explaining the relationship between truth, goodness, and forbearance, Li borrows terms from physics to argue his case. When explicating how matter has a dual nature, however, Li seeks to integrate physics into his self-made theory about the construction of truth, goodness, and forbearance.

By marrying these two types of discourse, Li seeks to demonstrate that his theories are grounded in scientific fact and are therefore worth believing. But, is this legitimation strategy successful? This question is difficult to answer. In general, there are two standards by which one can assess the success or otherwise of a legitimation strategy, which will here be termed the "extrinsic" and "intrinsic" standards. The extrinsic standard refers to the idea that the successful legitimation of a set of beliefs can be measured via the acceptance of the authority of this set of beliefs by a target audience. The intrinsic standard, on the other hand, can be defined as a measure of the extent to which a legitimation strategy makes a set of beliefs seem so rational and systematic that all people (especially those who are indifferent to that set of beliefs) find it credible and reasonable. Obviously, a legitimation strategy could be successful extrinsically while not necessarily being successful intrinsically, and vice versa. Moreover, even if some of the beliefs within the set went against reason or common sense, or contradicted each other, they could still be seen as legitimate and accepted by society, if various methods were used to prevent disbelief – for example, brainwashing, deceit, or even force. Likewise, sets of beliefs that seemed rational, reasonable, and consistent to society could fail to gain any authority and could thus be rejected by the target audience due to obstacles such as prejudices and stereotyped thinking. In the history of science, the battle between the heliocentric and geocentric models of the solar system exemplifies this perfectly. Given such complexities, it is hard to decide whether a legitimation strategy can be considered successful or not.

If we take the intrinsic standard as a means by which to examine Falun Gong's science-based legitimation strategy, then it hardly needs to be said that the strategy used has been successful. Problems here include the misuse and abuse of scientific terms, concepts, and theories – a situation which also pertains to the science discourses of many other new religions. Furthermore, in Falun Gong doctrine, the deployment of science has been carried out in an inconsistent way, thus further reducing the legitimacy of the movement's authentication efforts. Indeed, inconsistencies can be found not only in the scientific, sci-fi, and para-scientific strands of Falun Gong's science discourse, but also in the movement's theoretical and practical methods.

One of the most obvious issues here is as follows: Falun Gong uses science to explain and defend itself, thus disguising the illegitimacy of its claims. On the other hand, it also criticizes and denounces modern science by proclaiming itself a "super-science." We suggest, therefore, that Li Hongzhi has two different conceptions of science: one is an empirical understanding of science, which relates to systematic knowledge about nature and the universe, based on data and reasoning; the other is a scientific rendering of Falun Gong's belief system – a system that Li posits as being the ultimate truth. There is a notable tension between these two conceptions of science. Of course, modern science has never claimed to be the embodiment of ultimate truth; on the contrary, it is based on the need to question and to conduct research. However, where Falun Gong is concerned, the concept of "super-science" excludes any possibility of questioning the veracity of the movement's doctrine. What we see here, then, is not just an extreme claim about the importance of Falun Gong; it is also a sharp criticism of natural science – the word "super" in itself suggesting something greater than the norm. We might liken Falun Gong to Janus here due to its self-contradictory stance.

It is interesting that Li maintains a distinction between natural science and this "super-science" throughout his appeals to the former for legitimating his doctrine. He states often that natural science

Scientific or Anti-scientific 149

is nothing but "humankind's science" or "modern people's science," thus emphasizing the limitations of the field. In his own words, natural science is "very shallow" and "far lower" than the science of Falun Gong – he even goes as far as to use the term "pernicious."

Li Hongzhi's repeated attacks on the authority of natural science include claims that: (1) modern science has developed on "a wrong basis" and has therefore rendered itself false as a whole;[9] (2) many of the scientific theories and laws that society accepts are totally false, including the theory of evolution ("the current civilization's

---

9. In a speech at a *Fa* conference in San Francisco in April 1997, Li stated: "I often say that today's science has developed on a flawed understanding and a wrong basis since its establishment. So it is confined to that framework alone. As for true science, from what we've really learned of the universe, life, and matter, today's science can't be considered a science because the wondrousness of the universe could never be discovered by following the path of this science" (Li Hongzhi 1997b). Additionally, at a *Fa* conference in Switzerland in September 1998, Li argued, "The basis of almost all understanding in science is flawed, and that includes the basis for understanding matter, the universe, and life" (Li Hongzhi 1998c).

10. In 1998, while teaching about *Fa* at a *Fa* conference in Europe, Li stated: "Yet people say that humans evolved from apes. This is something brought about by modern science. Isn't it ridiculous? Darwin's theory of evolution is full of holes. If you don't believe it, then carefully re-examine it: During the evolution from apes to humans and from primitive organisms to modern organisms, the intermediary links are totally absent. Yet people have nonetheless accepted the theory. Now *that* is blind faith! And this is the current civilization's worst disgrace and scandal. That's what is truly bizarre!" (Li Hongzhi 1998b). In Los Angeles in February 2006, Li claimed, "This evolution has never existed," going on to posit that "Today's education leads people to solely base their thinking on the false theory of evolution and to believe that human beings evolved to this state, that society has achieved a high level of scientific advancement, and that mankind created its own civilization – created modern civilization. That's not the case at all" (Li Hongzhi 2006).

11. At a *Fa* conference held in Canada in May 2001, Li stated: "You know, the theory of gravity science believed in nowadays is totally wrong" (Li Hongzhi 2001).

worst disgrace and scandal"[10]) and Newtonian mechanics ("totally wrong"[11]); (3) modern science is "imperfect" and "blind" to itself, and, as such, can never reveal the true nature of the universe (i.e., the truths Falun Gong has preached), thus making it less important even than the work of "past civilizations"[12]; (4) all scientists are common people and are therefore "really insignificant."[13]

Li Hongzhi's criticisms do not stop there; he goes even further to say that natural science is not just lacking authority and truth; it

12. At a Fa conference in Sydney in August 1996, Li claimed, "In addition, this empirical science of modern man is imperfect. For instance, this modern science cannot prove the existence of gods, nor can it verify the existence of other dimensions. It cannot see the lives and the existing forms of matter in other dimensions. It does not know that there is the manifestation from the matter of virtue on the human body. Nor does it know that there is the manifestation from the matter of karma around the human body either. People all believe in modern science and, yet, modern science is unable to verify such things." He added, "The way modern empirical science develops now is very clumsy and slow. It is really like a blind person groping an elephant. It cannot recognize the existing form of matter in the entire universe and cannot recognize the existence of the characteristics of the universe" (Li Hongzhi 1996). Two years later, speaking at a *Fa* conference in Europe, he stated: "Although I've incorporated modern science in telling you these principles, I can tell you that I don't approve of this science. First off, in light of the entire, immense cosmos, this science is like kids' stuff. But as humans see it, it has brought about modern machines, making things seem so much better than in ancient times. In fact, I can tell you that this science falls far behind when it's compared with that of the last human civilization" (Li Hongzhi 1998b).

13. In a paragraph of *Falun Dafa: Essentials for Further Advancement (Jing-jin-yao-zhi)* entitled "What Is Wisdom?", Li writes, "People think that the renowned persons, scholars, and different sorts of experts in human society are great. In fact, they are all really insignificant, for they are everyday people. Their knowledge is only that tiny bit understood by the modern science of human society. In the vast universe, from the most macroscopic to the most microscopic, human society is exactly in the very middle, in the outermost layer, and on the outermost surface. Also, its living beings are the lowest form of existence, so their understanding of matter and mind is very limited, superficial, and pitiful" (Li Hongzhi 1997a, 11).

Scientific or Anti-scientific 151

also hazardous. This is because, Li argues, it has been "imposed on human beings by the aliens," who have evil plans for human society.[14] Furthermore, Li claims that natural science is responsible for a series of problems faced by humankind, including moral corruption and environmental pollution.[15] As such, he judges modern science as "the hugest disaster for human beings," which ultimately will lead to a situation in which "the entire earth disintegrates and is gone."[16]

The peak of this attack is Li's declaration that natural science is nothing but an "evil religion" (*xie-jiao*). For him, the positioning

---

14. This claim has been made at *Fa* conferences in Singapore (August 1998), Switzerland (September 1998), Atlanta (November 2003), and New York (November 2004). For Li, this imposition enables the aliens to "assimilate human ways of thinking and living, and replace human beings in the end" (Li Hongzhi 1998c).

15. For example, at a *Fa* conference in Europe in May 1998, Li stated: "The new generation raised on modern science dauntlessly kills, commits arson, and does bad things. Gangsters and organized crime have appeared in society, and people use drugs, traffic drugs, do prostitution ... they stop at no evil. There's a lot of filthy and obscene stuff. People do anything they please, they do whatever they want. Think about it, everyone: Isn't this sort of society appalling?! This is the biggest disaster that science has brought to us." He added here: "[But] the consequent disasters it also brings about are quite substantial. What I was referring to are disasters that humans can't see. The disasters that people can see, such as environmental pollution and ecological damage, are also quite appalling. This science has brought a whole series of social problems" (Li Hongzhi 1998b).

16. At the *Fa* conference in Atlanta in 2003, Li said the following: "Did you know this? Science's development in the microcosmic realm is even more terrifying. In its study of the more microcosmic particles, it makes the more microcosmic particles undergo fission, which causes the microcosmic particles to have continuous, chain-reaction fissions, which explode and split nonstop. The scientists have become aware of this and now they're afraid of it. If the explosions continue on like that, it won't take long before the entire earth disintegrates and is gone. At present none of the scientists who did those things are able to stop this type of explosion, and the fission and disintegration keeps on going ... And what science has brought upon mankind doesn't stop at that – isn't it terrifying?" (Li Hongzhi 2003).

of the science field as the arena of absolute truth renders science a religion. As such, its practitioners – i.e., scientists – are a type of "clergy." He sees this "religion" as evil for the following reasons:

> And yet, this science is not advanced. Its development is limited to only the boundaries of the present dimension. It's not able to prove the existence of gods. Neither does it know about retribution for wrongdoing. It will brand you superstitious if you speak about the existence of gods. If you say that a person who does bad things meets with retribution, that a person is rewarded for doing good, and that a person has to cherish virtue to be a good person, science will declare your words heretical and wicked. In fact, this science is attacking human beings' best side: their innate quality of being truly kindhearted. It doesn't tell people to cherish virtue, nor does it tell people to be kind. It encourages people to unleash all their desires, destroying the environment that man needs in order to exist, along with the innate nature and standards for mankind.
> (Li Hongzhi 1998b)

The paragraph above concludes with the sentence, "This science is nothing but an evil religion." The phrase "evil religion" should not be considered here to have been chosen arbitrarily or casually; it is a deliberate attempt to devalue natural science. The term "religion" has long been associated with blind faith and superstition in China. Coupling such a word with "evil" only accentuates the negative connotations which Li wishes to impose upon the science field.

We must ask, then, why does Li criticize natural science so severely? It is perhaps obvious that such a tactic enables him to position Falun Gong as true science. The problem remains, however, that such a stance is inconsistent with Li's use of science for legitimation purposes. One cannot support a set of ideas in one breath and denounce them in the next, if one is to be seen as credible. In Chinese, such contradictions could be called "slapping on your own face" or "stoning your own feet." Interestingly, Li Hongzhi does not seem to trouble himself about this inconsistency, despite the fact that it arose as soon as he began to term Falun Gong a "superscience." As his anti-science attitude has become more and more extreme, this problem has become increasingly obvious. Ironically, the super-science continues to appeal to natural science for legitimation, while decrying that sphere of knowledge at the same time.

Perhaps the area of greatest concern regarding Falun Gong's criticism of natural science is not the theory that is proposed, but the actions and attitudes that are promoted in practice. This can be seen in two particular rules that Li Hongzhi expects his disciples to follow:

1. Falun Gong practitioners are forbidden to talk about science. Li declared this for the first time in a speech in 1996. His reasoning is that scientific discussions might shake their faith; perhaps the real reason, however, is that it enables Li to create and maintain some credibility around the para-scientific discourse of Falun Gong. When questioned about why he himself discusses science so often, Li answered that it was to "give proof of Falun Gong to the intelligentsia" – in other words, to lend the faith some sort of academic credibility (see Li Hongzhi 1997a, 27). Li has been forced to justify his approach further, however, in the face of additional questioning from his disciples. He has said that any uncertainties about the science discourse in Falun Gong arise not from his teachings, but from the disciples themselves, who must elevate themselves above the common level in order to let go of such judgments (Li Hongzhi 1998a). In other words, Li uses rhetoric to dismiss questions. He supports his points by positioning Falun Gong as the ultimate science, which cannot be questioned, since its authority is greater than anything known by humanity. If Falun Gong's teachings seem to contradict common sense or natural science, then, this is because common sense and natural science are at fault. Those who do not accept this are branded commoners who lack the ability to see the truth. The difficulty here, of course, is that Li has never offered proof for his claim that Falun Gong is a super-science that contains the ultimate truth.
2. Practitioners are also discouraged from using modern science and technology, being warned, for example, not to trust

doctors when they are ill. The justification is that a reliance on modern science indicates a lack of faith in Falun Gong (ibid.). It is perhaps unsurprising that many practitioners have died as a result of following this rule.

This negative and even harmful attitude toward science and technology in practice is deeply ironic, considering that Falun Gong has perhaps relied more than any other religious movement on technology to spread its message. Li Hongzhi depends significantly on the internet for information sharing, despite claiming to be able to share his knowledge via a self-alleged "super-power."[17] It becomes evident, then, that Falun Gong is inconsistent, not just where its theoretical statements about science are concerned; there are also discrepancies between its theory and its practice.

Importantly, although Falun Gong's theoretical inconsistencies prevent its legitimation strategy from being successful on the intrinsic level, the movement does seem to have had achievements in terms of the extrinsic standard. If it had failed totally in this respect, the movement would probably have vanished years ago. The fact is that Falun Gong still has a large population of followers, both in China and overseas, most of whom accept all facets of Falun Gong science discourse.

So, how is it possible that Falun Gong has recruited and retained so many disciples if these disciples are rational beings who should be able to see the contradictions inherent in the movement's science discourse? A quick look at the educational background of the majority of Li's followers provides an answer to this query. Just as with the practitioners in most other offshoots of *qigong*, the disciples of Falun Gong tend to be the less educated – they lack scientific knowledge, and cannot discriminate between true and false science discourses. In any society, this is also the group of people most likely

---

17. As Helen Farley has observed, "It is intriguing that even though modern science is seen as the enemy of virtue and is the means by which hostile aliens gain control of humanity via computers, the spread of *Falun Gong* is almost entirely achieved by the use of modern technology ..." (2011, 160).

to submit to the authority of a science-based idea, if the society in question holds science in high esteem. Couching a set of beliefs in scientific terms enables a movement like Falun Gong to strengthen its own image and, at the same time, discourages people from questioning these beliefs. In this way, Falun Gong has established its authority over its followers effectively and can thus be considered to have utilized science successfully as a legitimation strategy, from an extrinsic perspective – even if the discourse in question does not appear to make rational sense.

Further Remarks on the Science Discourse in Falun Gong

We have identified and traced the origins of the various types of science discourse present in Falun Gong's teachings – the scientific, the sci-fi, and the para-scientific – and have established how the movement uses these discourses to legitimate itself. We have seen that, although Falun Gong's use of a science-based legitimation strategy seems to have been successful extrinsically speaking, efforts to utilize science to appear legitimate on the intrinsic level have failed. Furthermore, we have found that this failure lies in the inconsistency within the movement's deployment of science discourses – especially the fact that it both appeals to natural science and denounces natural science at the same time. Natural science is depicted as false and even evil in order to enable Falun Gong to be positioned as the absolute truth. We have also noted that Falun Gong practitioners are subject to control where science is concerned – being forbidden to talk about the field or to rely on modern technological developments.

Can any rational person accept Falun Gong's science-based claims and beliefs? For me, the glaring inconsistencies in Falun Gong's science discourse mean that the movement's doctrine must be rejected wholesale. This is not to say that we should call Falun Gong's disciples stupid for being deceived; after all, there is no moral obligation for a person to accept or reject a belief on the basis of rationality. What I am trying to say here is that practitioners of Falun Gong should be given sympathy, rather than being blamed for their choice, since they are in a certain sense deceived and brainwashed by Falun Gong's science discourse.

As a scholar, I feel that it is my duty here to point to the areas in which Falun Gong's science discourse becomes a social concern. In some respects, Li Hongzhi may be right in suggesting that science has many limitations (for instance, our scientific knowledge remains incomplete, and science has no understanding of spirituality). We can even agree with Li that science can be related to a number of social problems in modern society (for example, increasing environmental damage, which is connected with global industrialization and the modern-day scientific and technological revolution). It cannot be said, however, that these limitations render it wise to incite opposition to the theory and practice of natural science. Such hostility to science could undermine the positive functions of that sphere, which are, undoubtedly, of great benefit to human well-being. This is perhaps part of the reason why religions in general, whether old or new, seldom seek to deny the merits of science. Although many religions have, of course, come into severe conflict with science (take, for example, Christianity), they have also sought to maintain a peaceful relationship with the field – some faiths have even made efforts to incorporate modern science into their belief systems. In such a culture, Falun Gong's negativity regarding natural science is surprising. As Hegel famously states, there is no need to throw out the baby with the bath water. Prohibiting followers from utilizing modern science and technology altogether is foolhardy at best and, at worst, threatening to humankind's existence.

One aspect that may seem contradictory is the notion of a religion criticizing science – after all, shouldn't religion deal with that which is valuable and meaningful? It is the general consensus in society that, while science and religion are important aspects of human life, they are separate. Science tends to deal with natural facts, answering questions about how the universe operates. Religion, on the other hand, concerns supernatural subjects, seeking to determine how humankind can live a righteous existence. The two spheres handle very different subjects and have very different purposes. Likewise, the language used in the two areas is dissimilar. Here, I will quote the eminent evolutionist scientist Steven Jay Gould (2002), who argues that science and religion should be seen as two "NOMAs" (Non-overlapping Magisteria). That is to say, science should not invade the field of religion or brand religious belief absurd, and religion should not intervene in scientific affairs or pass judgments upon scientific practices. An analysis of Falun Gong reveals that this movement has intervened in science to such an extent that it has opened itself to ridicule. Not only does it denounce natural science; it also puts forward many competing scientific claims, none of which are backed by any real proof. Arguably, it is not the role of a religion to obtrude upon science in this way.

I wish to conclude by putting forth my contention that Falun Gong is based on an extreme form of exclusivism, which has been subtly hidden in its carefully compiled science discourse. In proclaiming itself the "ultimate" truth and branding all else false and evil, in condemning disbelievers as "common people" controlled by devils, and in denying its followers the right to question, Falun Gong manifests this troubling exclusivist inclination. In a world in which pluralism has become a fact and is accepted by most rational people, extreme exclusivism is not only provocative; it is also deeply concerning.

References

All web pages were accessed for a final check on October 15, 2018.

Chen, Nancy N. 2003. *Breathing Spaces: Qigong, Psychiatry, and Healing in China*. New York: Columbia University Press.
Farley, Helen. 2011. "Falun Gong and Science: Origins, Pseudoscience, and China's Scientific Establishment," in James R. Lewis and Olav Hammer (eds.), *Hand Book of Religion and the Authority of Science*, pp. 141–64.
Gould, Stephen Jay. 2002. *Rocks of Ages: Science and Religion in the Fullness of Life.* New York: Ballantine Books.
Lewis, James R., and Olav Hammer. 2011. "Introduction," in James R. Lewis and Olav Hammer (eds.), *Hand Book of Religion and the Authority of Science*, pp. 1–20.

Lewis, James R., and Olav Hammer (eds.). 2011. *Hand Book of Religion and the Authority of Science*, Brill Handbooks on Contemporary Religion. Vol. 3. Leiden and Boston: Koninklijke Brill NV.

Li Hongzhi. 1994. "Lunyu," in *Zhuan Falun*, pp. 1–3.

Li Hongzhi. 1996. "Lecture in Sydney," August. http://en.falundafa.org/eng/lectures/1996L.html

Li Hongzhi. 1997a. *Falun Dafa: Essentials for Further Advancement (Jing-jin-yao-zhi)*. http://en.falundafa.org/eng/jjyz.htm

Li Hongzhi. 1997b. "Teaching the *Fa* in San Francisco," April 6. http://en.falundafa.org/eng/lectures/1997L.html#_Toc511984050

Li Hongzhi. 1998a. "Lecture at the First Conference in North America," March 29–30, New York. http://en.falundafa.org/eng/lectures/19980329L.html

Li Hongzhi. 1998b. "Teaching the *Fa* at the Conference in Europe," May 30–31, Frankfurt. http://en.falundafa.org/eng/lectures/19980530L.html

Li Hongzhi. 1998c. "Teaching the *Fa* at the Conference in Switzerland," September 4–5, Geneva. http://en.falundafa.org/eng/lectures/19980904L.html

Li Hongzhi. 2001. "Teaching the *Fa* at the 2001 Canada *Fa* Conference," May 19, Ottawa. http://en.falundafa.org/eng/daohang_3.htm

Li Hongzhi. 2002. "Touring North America to Teach the *Fa*," March. http://en.falundafa.org/eng/lectures/200203L.html

Li Hongzhi. 2003. "Teaching the *Fa* at the 2003 Atlanta *Fa* Conference," November 29, Atlanta. http://en.falundafa.org/eng/lectures/20031129L.html

Li Hongzhi. 2006. "Teaching the *Fa* in the City of Los Angeles," February 25, Los Angeles. http://en.falundafa.org/eng/lectures/20060225L.html

Li Hongzhi. 2014. *Zhuan Falun* (4th English edition). http://en.falundafa.org/eng/zfl2014/ZFL2014-002.html

Li Hongzhi. 2015. "On Dafa (*Lunyu*)," in *Zhuan Falun* (2014). http://en.falundafa.org/eng/zfl2014/ZFL2014-002.html

Penny, Benjamin. 2012. *The Religion of Falun Gong*. Chicago and London: The University of Chicago Press.

Rapport, Jeremy. 2011. "Christian Science, New Thought and Scientific Discourse," in James R. Lewis and Olav Hammer (eds.), *Hand Book of Religion and the Authority of Science*, pp. 549–70.

Rapport, Jeremy. 2016. "New Religions and Science," in James R. Lewis and Inga B. Tøllefsen (eds.), *The Oxford Handbook of New Religious Movements*, Vol. II. New York: Oxford University Press, pp. 278–86.

Xiao Ming. 2011. *The Cultural Economy of Falun Gong in China: A Rhetorical Perspective*. Columbia: University of South Carolina Press.

Wang Chengjun has a PhD in philosophy and is a lecturer at Zhongnan University of Economics and Law and member of the International NRM Research Center of Wuhan University. His main areas of study include medieval philosophy, philosophy of religion, and religious studies.

8. "You Don't Want to Have That Kind of Thought in Your Mind"
Li Hongzhi, Aliens, and Science

Stefano Bigliardi

In one of the most puzzling and astounding (and, indeed, most ridiculed) claims made by the Falun Gong leader Li Hongzhi (b. 1951), technology and science[1] are said to have been introduced to Earth by sinister aliens. Such aliens manipulate human beings (whose bodies they regard as desirable prey), keeping them in a state of discord and corruption, and planning eventually to take over the whole planet. Some of these aliens, it is said, already live on Earth, disguised as human beings. Their presence can be discerned, however – despite their varied appearances – by certain extraordinary individuals, who are able to neutralize the aliens' manipulative techniques. Master Li counts himself among this number of extraordinary people. Such teachings emerged initially in Falun Gong's literature but were made known to the public in a 1999 interview for *Time* magazine (Dowell 1999). These ideas have also been reiterated by Master Li at various conferences and in later texts.

---

1. For the sake of brevity, the term "science" is used in an inclusive sense in the title of the present chapter, and throughout. It should be understood to include technology as well.

Li Hongzhi, Aliens, and Science 161

Master Li's "alien theory"[2] or "alien theology" can be studied from a number of different perspectives. One might be interested in disproving it by examining the logic of the theory and contrasting it with scientific data. One could investigate how widespread such a doctrine is among Falun Gong practitioners, considering how and why they can entertain such beliefs, given modern technological and scientific knowledge. This chapter adopts a third method: I am interested here neither in *debunking* Li Hongzhi's theory nor in investigating its *diffusion among*, and the *reasons for its acceptance by*, specific individuals who identify as Falun Gong practitioners. Rather, I focus on alien-related claims made by Li Hongzhi in order to try to reconstruct their role within his teachings as a whole, looking in particular at his conceptualization of science.[3] More specifically, I offer an extensive list of references to aliens in Li Hongzhi's writings, analyzing them meticulously in order to demonstrate both the persistence of the alien theme in his thought and the gradual changes in his rhetoric over time.

The first section of the paper reconstructs Master Li's 1999 interview. The second section expands upon the "alien narratives" that are introduced or emphasized by him in other texts, both preceding and following the famous interview. The final section offers a detailed analysis and interpretation of Master Li's "alien teachings," which also makes reference to proponents of analogous popular narratives within other new religious movements.

    2. In the present analysis, I use the terms "theory" and "narrative" interchangeably. "Theology" is also an acceptable term, but it automatically projects the aura of religion onto Li's theory, which is problematic, given that the accuracy of terming Falun Gong "religious" has long been a matter of debate.

    3. I refer in particular to Li Hongzhi's conceptualization of science as analyzed by David Ownby (2008). Other scholarly works that examine Falun Gong's "alien theory" in relation to Master Li's conceptualization of science and his ideas more generally include Penny (2012) and Farley (2014). It should be noted that such works do not offer a comprehensive collection and comparative analysis of all of the references to aliens found in Li Hongzhi's writings. In contrast, the present chapter offers more detailed textual analysis.

The 1999 *Time* Interview

During an interview on May 10, 1999, with the journalist William Thatcher Dowell in New York, Li Hongzhi refers to aliens when discussing the two causes of the "chaos" that he identifies on present-day Earth and in human society. In 2017, Dowell recalled and evaluated the circumstances and the content of the interview as follows:

> [The interview] was done in a modern apartment near Battery Park in lower Manhattan. Teddy Thai, a photographer for *Time*, was also present during the interview. ... Li was pudgy and unassuming, but clearly felt that he had an inner knowledge that ordinary people would have difficulty understanding. He had been made an honorary citizen of Houston, Texas. He showed me the certificate that the city had given him. I called the city hall to ask about it, and they said that it had been under an earlier administration and they knew nothing about it.
>
> We had a seemingly ordinary conversation until he casually mentioned that the world is in chaos. I acknowledged the fact, and asked him why he thought that was the case. He said there were two reasons. The first was that people had abandoned religion. Then he hesitated. I asked him what the second reason was. He said that about a hundred years ago, the world had started to be invaded by extra-terrestrials, in other words, visitors from outer space. I looked at Teddy, who started to roll his eyes, and suppressed a smile. Obviously, from the perspective of *Time* that promised to make a great story. I asked him what these alien beings looked like. "I could tell you," he said, "but it is so horrible that if I did, you would never be able to sleep again." I said that I could take that risk. He then described them as having exposed bones in their faces, and other terrible physical abnormalities. I asked him what he thought their purpose was. He said that it was to convince us to forget about being human beings and to convince us to replace humanity with technology.
>
> ... I was interested in how he came to that conclusion. He eventually explained that as a young child he had been sent to spend months in various monasteries in northern China. It

struck me that if you were a monk, cut off from the rest of the world, and tried to reconcile the modern world with your acquired knowledge of reality, given the limitations of being confined to a mountain, then Li's explanation would make sense ....

Li practiced Qigong, an established theory of channelling the internal energy of a human being. He explained that he had extraordinary power and asked me to hold out my hand. He then tried to concentrate the energy from his hand to enter my hand. I felt nothing, but wanted to be polite and said that I could see what he was talking about. Li felt that if followed to its limit, Qigong could enable people to levitate, pass through walls and return from the dead, or at least have everlasting life. He was nervous about revealing these secrets to an unbeliever. In other words, he thought that an uninitiated individual needed to be brought into the circle slowly. I had the impression that he was completely sincere and believed everything he was saying. ... Philosophically some of his thinking was probably justified, although it was based on a shaky framework of mythology rather than cold scientific deduction.

What further struck me about Li was that he had surrounded himself with a number of acolytes, usually attractive Chinese women, who were well educated and should have known better. One of his aides was currently enrolled in Harvard. How they could believe something so surreal struck me as unusual. ... For a while I stayed close to the movement, and they held regular exercise practices in Central Park almost exclusively for non-Asian Americans. I attributed that to the fact that there are many aspects of Qigong which do make sense and are attractive.[4]

In the published interview, Master Li states that the first cause of modern-day world chaos is that people have abandoned "orthodox religion." To this, he adds that, since the beginning of the twentieth

---

4. William Thatcher Dowell, private communication, March 5, 2017. The original e-mail is in the author's archives. The text has been edited slightly, and redundant/non-relevant passages have been eliminated. It is published with William Thatcher Dowell's permission.

century, "aliens" have "begun to invade the human mind and its ideology and culture." Master Li claims that these aliens have come from "other planets," adding that the names that he "use[s] for these planets are different" (presumably from current astronomical vocabulary) and that some aliens come from thus far undiscovered "dimensions." Furthermore, he states that such aliens have "introduced modern machinery like computers and airplanes." For Master Li, therefore, a clear sign of the presence of aliens since the beginning of the twentieth century is the unprecedented development of "culture." He adds that "inspiration" has been induced in scientists by the aliens. Although it is believed that scientists invent independently, they are actually manipulated, according to Master Li. Humankind, he stresses, has become spiritually and culturally dependent on science; in this sense, it can already be said to be controlled by aliens.

According to Master Li, however, the main instrument of alien control and domination is cloning. After pointing out that the "spirit" is what constitutes the difference between a living body and a dead one, he states that a cloned body is not provided by the "gods" and thus has no soul. For Master Li, this means that the aliens would be able to enter such a body. One by one, he believes, all humans will be replaced in this way. Eventually, the aliens/clones will assume power and will "introduce legislation to stop human reproduction." Master Li also argues that wars and weapons are used by the aliens to control human beings. He sees these areas as being linked strongly to science, since "the military industry leads other industries such as computers and electronics." He explains further that the human body "is the most perfect in the universe," hence the aliens' desire for it. Additionally, he states that "U.S. technology has already detected" some of the aliens, as well as adding that they can be enormously different from one another.

After an initial refusal to describe aliens in detail ("You do not want to have that kind of thought in your mind"), Master Li elaborates, upon the interviewer's insistence: "one type [of alien] looks like a human, but has a nose that is made of bone. Others look like ghosts." He also adds a remark concerning his own relationship with the aliens: "At first they thought that I was trying to help them. Now they know that I am sweeping them away." Master Li also states that human society is on its way to destruction, independent of the alien invasion, citing reasons such as air pollution for this belief. He also argues that science cannot determine the magnitude of the damage. He concludes the interview by stating twice that he is not against science ("I drive a car," he specifies), but he continues to emphasize that, nonetheless, "science is destroying mankind."

Aliens in Falun Dafa Literature and Master Li's Conference Talks

According to data taken from the official Falun Dafa webpage entitled *Books & Recent Writings of Mr Li Hongzhi*,[5] the earliest

---

5. Available at http://en.falundafa.org/falun-dafa-books.html and http://en.falundafa.org/falun-dafa-recent-writings.html. In the interests of clarity and scholarly integrity, it should be made clear that I have written the present essay in my capacity as an expert in "alien narratives" in new religious movements; I am neither a Falun Gong specialist, nor a speaker of Chinese. The analysis is based, therefore, on the Falun Dafa literature available in English online. I have searched primarily for the terms "alien(s)" and "extraterrestrial(s)," conducting supplementary searches for "UFO(s)" and "planet(s)." In the following descriptions, page numbers are not given for the sources; instead, URLs are given. The texts under scrutiny are examined one by one and the references made to aliens are highlighted. The URLs for each of the sources are given in the footnotes. Where different translations/versions of the texts were available, I selected the earliest example for analysis. Due, in all likelihood, to the varying standards used by different translators (the names of whom are not given in the documents in question), some words appear with different spellings or in different formats, depending on the text at hand; the term "Earth," for example, is rendered "earth" in some texts, and "gods" sometimes appears as "Gods." The texts are quoted here without modification. The Chinese term for "extraterrestrial" or "alien" is 外星人 [*wài xīng ré*], consisting of the terms "outside," "star" (or "sphere"), and "being." I give hearty thanks to David Ownby and Hind Lebdaoui for their advice concerning Falun Gong and the

reference to aliens in Falun Dafa texts appears in "Teaching the Fa in Beijing at the Zhuan Falun Publication Ceremony" (Li Hongzhi 1995). Here, Master Li discusses the ability of (Western) science to investigate the nature of matter, about which he has doubts: "the path along which Western science has been developing is the slowest, and humankind chose the most imperfect way of developing it." This does not mean, in his opinion, that other kinds of science cannot uncover deeper understandings of reality or create more advanced scientific techniques. Rather, the aliens are taken as a point of comparison with humans' scientific and technological capabilities. Master Li states:

> You know about aliens, right – those flying saucers that fly back and forth, that come without a trace and leave without a shadow, and that travel at a high speed and are hard to fathom. A flying saucer can even change its size to be bigger or smaller. How is that so? It is just that its methods for researching and developing science and technology are different. It can travel in other dimensions. Because of the difference in time-space, it can come, get to where it's going, and leave at will.

This point, however, is not expanded upon further. The idea of aliens then surfaces again in "Fa Teaching Given in San Francisco." Here Master Li states: "Humankind believes that only humans are the sole beings in the universe – they're just extremely pitiful, pitiful to this extent. Aliens have in fact visited our earth and their visits have even been captured in photos, yet people still don't believe in their existence. It's because people have been restrained by this science" (Li Hongzhi 1997).

Aliens are also mentioned in passing in conference proceedings in 1998, in New York (Li Hongzhi 1998b). Here, they are described as manipulating humanity: "I can tell you that the development of the current society and its entire developmental process has, in its formation and evolution, been controlled and pushed forward by

---

Chinese language, as well as to Jim Lewis for reading preliminary versions of this chapter and discussing them with me.

alien beings." Later on, Master Li states: "If you have the ability, take a look at this world and you'll see that there are many alien beings. Yet they look like human beings and you can't tell the difference. All these need to be dealt with" (ibid.). In response to a question concerning the reasons why beings inhabiting a higher dimension would need flying devices, he explains:

> ... there are particularly more places like those of alien beings. They need to fly and need to use flying devices. I can't tell you about all those, leading your thinking toward those places and encouraging curiosity. Beings are extremely complex. There are worlds of all kinds and there's great diversity in the cosmos. Now we only have white, yellow, and black races of humans on earth; over there, there are also green and blue ones, and even multi-colored ones. (ibid.)

Extensive mention of aliens is made in three sets of conference proceedings from May 1998 (Frankfurt), September 1998 (Geneva), and February 1999 (Los Angeles). In his Frankfurt speech (Li Hongzhi 1998c), he mentions aliens when discussing the similarities between science and religion. After pointing out that both fields are highly institutionalized, he differentiates between them by emphasizing two points. First, whereas religion teaches one to "believe spiritually," science teaches one to "perceive materially so as to elicit people's spiritual trust and support." Second, and perhaps most importantly, "science ... is not something gods imparted to humans. Instead, it was passed down to humans by alien beings inside the Three Realms [Heaven, Earth and the Underworld], and for the purpose of controlling humankind." Master Li states that people believe in science more than in anything else, and that this has brought about "the degeneration of morality." Science, he argues, can neither detect fundamental spiritual dynamics (like changes in karma), nor can it prove the existence of "heavenly paradises," both of which are essential, in his view, for understanding the meaning of human life and reaching salvation. For Master Li, this lack of vision explains why scientists deem such ideas merely superstitious.

168 *Enlightened Martyrdom*

Later on, when asked whether it is possible "to communicate with intelligent beings beyond Earth," Master Li answers in the affirmative, but adds that people should not assume, as "movies" and "imaginative stories" tend to suggest, that such a possibility is open to everyone. Indeed, he states that an ordinary person would be put in danger by trying to communicate with higher beings such as aliens:

> Lives beyond Earth are just lives on other planets within this physical dimension that our human eyes can perceive. Yet those lives don't regard people as human beings. They think people are beasts, a kind of animal. They slaughter people at will and experiment on you at will. They kidnap people to their planets, lock them in cages, and put them on display as animals. Many of Earth's people who have gone missing were taken by them. (ibid.)

According to Master Li, it is the aliens themselves who have created science and passed it on to humans. He reiterates the idea that the aliens "covet" human beings' "flawless" bodies, continuing to say the following: "They [the aliens] have added their things [*sic*] into one layer of human beings' molecular cells. That's already been done now and it has formed on a large scale." He asserts that one of the clues that an alien intervention in human history has taken place is the unexpectedly rapid development of computers – devices which can be understood as powerful instruments of control. He is careful, however, to reassure Falun Gong students, while warning them about the aliens' strategies: "Aliens have registered everyone who knows how to operate a computer. For real. As to our students, I've cleaned all of that up for them, so that they won't be interfered with by aliens when they use computers."

As Master Li proceeds, his alien narrative becomes even more complex:

> Why are there aliens? Some aliens originate from their planets. Why do some aliens always come to Earth? It's because they were once humans on Earth. But it wasn't the Earth of our

Li Hongzhi, Aliens, and Science 169

time. It was the previous Earth that existed at the same location as this Earth. Earth has been replaced many times. Each time it was replaced, there was a portion of lives – living beings created by gods with different appearances, some of whom were similar to today's humans, some of whom had different forms – who were relatively good at the time and were thus preserved. (ibid.)

The problem with the beings that were preserved, explains Master Li, is that, "due to a slackening in overseeing them, they have developed, and they have created all kinds of scientific methods according to their schemes"; in fact, he argues, they have "deteriorated." For this reason, "all aliens are in the process of being completely eliminated. They are being eliminated throughout the entire universe. At present, those up there have been eliminated. What's left are only those who have escaped to Earth, who are mingling among people or who have attached to human bodies." Master Li concludes this discussion on an optimistic note: "I'm watching all of them. Let them do their outrageous things for the time being. It won't be long before they're eradicated." According to the transcript of the speech, this statement was followed by enthusiastic applause.

During the Swiss conference, Master Li is recorded to have spoken about aliens in response to a specific question: "Teacher said that when the universe was cleaned up, there were alien beings who escaped onto the earth. Do they exist in the form of possessing spirits or in some other form?" As a reply, Master Li states, "at Earth's position there were Earths that existed before. Those previous Earths were discarded. Some exploded. It happened many times – the number has been quite large" (Li Hongzhi 1998d). Each time an Earth was discarded, he expands, a certain number of human beings (the "good" beings) was preserved and placed on the new planet by the gods. This number has increased over time, according to Master Li. He continues, "The gods in each time period created humans with a different appearance, so the differences are quite substantial, and there are some who were created on other planets. These are alien beings." Such beings thus constitute a sort of "record" of the universe's history. He adds that the technology that was preserved and traveled with these beings to other planets was more advanced than modern technology:

> Their bodies can enter other dimensions and adjust to the mode of those dimensions they are in. ... Those things they ride in that fly back and forth – those aircraft that human beings call flying saucers – can enter other dimensions and fly into other space-times. ... The types of fuel they use aren't in the least the kinds of substances conceivable by the technology, theories, or concepts of modern science. (ibid.)

Master Li is at pains to stress that, although alien beings have been "developing and metamorphosing," the changes are actually characterized by deterioration: "Greed and lust have caused something like Star Wars to actually happen over where they live. They haven't yet threatened humankind because humankind doesn't have the ability to pose a threat to them. So they haven't attacked humankind. They would attack humankind if you were to threaten them." However, he explains once more that the aliens view the human body as perfect "and want to steal it." This is why "they saturate all domains of humankind with science. ... When human beings' thoughts and way of existence are completely assimilated to theirs, they just have to replace people's souls and humans will become them, and they will eventually replace the human race." According to Master Li, then, aliens have been present on our Earth throughout its history, but "their full-scale arrival began when Caucasian society entered the industrial age." Prior to that, he states, aliens did not control people.

Additionally, Master Li asserts that the mixing of races on Earth is a major asset for the aliens in the pursuit of power:

> [aliens have] chosen a few nationalities as the vanguards of their future, total control of humankind. Japan is the vanguard that drives technology. The United States is the vanguard in breaking away from all ancient cultures on earth. ... England was the vanguard in the manufacture of machinery during the early stages, and Spain was the vanguard for mixing the human races. The way alien beings get human beings to shake free of

the gods is to mix the races, causing human beings to become rootless people, just like the plant hybrids people make nowadays. South Americans, Central Americans, Mexicans and some people in South East Asia – all of these races have been mixed. (ibid.)

Master Li then goes on to explain his belief in the "layer" of the alien body within the human body, which, he reassures his students, can be eliminated by him, once a disciple "obtains the Fa." To this, he adds another explanation as to why aliens feel that they have the right to replace humans: "they have this idea that human beings are no longer any good, their morality has degenerated, and everything is perverted. So they think it's all right to just replace them, given that they are going to be eliminated all the same."

Master Li continues on a positive and combative note, which, curiously, is not devoid of some compassion for the aliens themselves:

> They don't know that this thing I'm doing has been systematically arranged, so no matter where they run to they can't escape. They have to pay for all of the bad things they've done, for sure. ... As for how their lives will eventually be dealt with, alien beings definitely won't exist in the future. If there are truly good ones among the alien beings, then their lives can reincarnate as other lives. Bad lives will be eliminated. (ibid.)

He adds that some of the aliens, being aware that they could not escape, "have married Earth dwellers." He continues, "But it's not that they marry legitimately, because no one would marry them. They catch a village woman to leave behind their offspring. And there are those who are hiding among ordinary people. They can't stay under cover no matter how they hide." He explains this idea further:

> Some of them have assumed man's appearance and walk the streets. You have no idea who they are. Some have hidden and don't come out. But the number is now small, very small. In the past they could hide, and their flying saucers could fly up and go to another dimension. But the other dimensions have

172 *Enlightened Martyrdom*

> all been cleaned up. Immense Gong is rushing here and they can no longer hide. (ibid.)

In the Los Angeles conference transcript, Master Li mentions aliens while discussing science – a field which, in his opinion, is "actually not scientific. It is merely something imposed on man by aliens, something that has penetrated the entire society and pervaded it in every respect." However, science, according to him,

> can't detect or know the real heavens because it crawls within only the current material dimension ... And the science imposed upon man by aliens is thus confined to this. Aliens are living beings in this dimension as well, and they are similarly incapable of knowing the truth of the universe. (Li Hongzhi 1999a)

Master Li insists, though, that he does not wish his students to abandon science: "I'm not telling you to oppose this science, nor am I teaching you to break free from it. That's not what I mean. I am telling you what science is." Nonetheless, he does reiterate that science is both shallow and harmful: "For instance, scientists nowadays ... say that damage to the ozone layer has occurred at the South Pole, where a hole has appeared. ... Science is incapable of realizing the role played by gods, so people say that the hole was caused by damage to the ozone layer."

During this lecture, Master Li explains that the aliens started to come to Earth in droves during the Industrial Revolution: "They started with mathematics and chemistry – started from the shallow, simple knowledge of the earliest days – and penetrated on through to modern machinery, and eventually they developed up to today's computers. As development continues further their ultimate goal will be to replace human beings." Once again, he clarifies that this replacement has started to happen via the creation of a layer of cells in almost every individual's body:

> Almost everyone has a layer of the body that was created by aliens. Why do I say that? It's because all of the science that

they instilled in you has created a warped human mind set in your mind. There have never been humans like this in any of mankind's previous civilizations. When the mind is like that, so is the body. As you know, every cell in your body is you, and your brain is connected to the brain in every cell. In that case, the thought processes inside the countless cells in your body are all the thoughts of warped human beings, and the entire body has become like that. (ibid.)

Master Li adds here that cloning is the main technology that will allow aliens to replace humans. His explanation focuses on the fact that a cloned body is one that no spirit has entered, so it can easily become possessed by another:

> Why doesn't a person keep living after he [sic] dies and the body is laid down there, since it's the same body after all? It's because all of his [sic] main spirits have left. That is, if a person isn't given a spirit and isn't allowed to reincarnate at the time of birth, he [sic] will still be dead after he is born. So what will happen? Aliens will enter. This is the ultimate means that aliens will use to replace man – that is, cloning humans. Man is being used by aliens to destroy himself [sic], yet he [sic] is not aware of it and is still protecting this science, destroying the human race. If humans are cloned en masse in the future, those beings will all be aliens that have reincarnated in human bodies, and there will be no more human race. (ibid.)

The topic of aliens is also taken up during the question-and-answer session at the Los Angeles conference, with Master Li ending once more on an optimistic note:

> I said last time that everybody who operates a computer has been catalogued by aliens with a number. That's absolutely true. But our disciples don't have this problem. I have cleaned it out for them, and moreover, aliens are in the final stage of being cleaned out. Yet there are still some that are hiding, but they are rarely seen now. They used to hide in those super-material dimensions in order to control human beings. (ibid.)

174 *Enlightened Martyrdom*

Another brief mention of aliens is made by Master Li in a speech at a conference in Singapore, with the discussion being in line with the aforementioned narratives:

> Today's science has been imposed on humankind by alien beings. No people in any historical period or in any civilization ever had science like this. ... Gods arrange how human society develops. For example, in ancient China a god was sent down to invent paper-making, and another god was sent down to invent the compass. (Li Hongzhi 1998e)

Concerning the problem of how to deal with science, he adds:

> I'll give you an example. While cleaning up the alien beings, I said to them: "You've deformed the human race. Your system of things has seriously damaged human society and distorted people's thinking." Since they couldn't offer any justification, they came back with this argument, "But you're making use of us, too." I do travel by car and use other modern tools. "Yet," I said to them, "even if I wanted to travel on horseback these days, there are no settings that would allow me to do so, for you've destroyed them all. Isn't that true?!" So we can only live with it, right? (ibid.)

Aliens are also mentioned in a lecture given at a New York conference on March 27–28, 1999. Master Li states: "The day they [i.e. human beings] have really cloned a person is the day aliens formally start to replace human beings." He then argues: "Gods won't arrange for a cloned human being to have a soul, so the person that's produced will be just like a corpse. Without a soul it's dead at birth. What happens, then? Aliens will take advantage of this by entering into those bodies, and they will become their souls" (Li Hongzhi 1999b).

At a conference in Sydney (May 2–3, 1999), the same concepts are reiterated. He declares: "If human beings replicate human beings, then people will have truly begun to destroy man himself. Aliens wearing the skins of humans would be replicated en masse, occupying the bodies of humans." To this, he adds:

> Today's society isn't good because what today's society worships is science and not gods, and that's why people can see less and less. In addition, this science was created for human beings by aliens, who are also beings in this dimension. It's only that they are beings from other planets. (Li Hongzhi 1999c)

In a conference speech given in Toronto (May 23, 1999), Master Li shows some awareness of the criticism directed at the "alien narrative" by the press. Answering a question concerning humanity's reincarnations, he states:

> You may have read in the newspaper someone's article about my addressing the issue of aliens, and he found it to be laughable. Think about it, everyone: There has never been a human race like this in history, yet there have been periods of time in history when the technology of the human race was more advanced – far, far, more advanced than it is today. Human beings nowadays can't build a moon and place it in the sky, yet in the history of the human race, human beings were able to do so. (Li Hongzhi 1999d)

Once again, he expands on the idea of the "alien cellular layer" in the human body:

> The things invented and created by scientists are in fact not the creations of human beings. Whose creation are they, then? They were created by the structure that is controlled by extraterrestrials and that has formed in man's brain. And that structure is precisely something tightly controlled by the extraterrestrials. They will give you an inspiration and have you invent something. They have begun to replace the human race in a systematic manner. (ibid.)

Once more, Master Li also warns his students of the risks of cloning:

> A human body is like a piece of clothing: when it is worn by a human being, it is alive; if it's not worn, it is dead. Think about it, then: What will happen if gods don't place a soul

176 *Enlightened Martyrdom*

inside a cloned being on account of its having been created by human beings and gods surely not acknowledging it? An extraterrestrial will fill the vacuum by placing itself as the soul of that human. So then it will have a human body and will occupy a human being. There will be more and more of these types of beings. And owing to their desires, human beings will be ordered to continuously make them. More and more of them will be made. These beings will become the majority, and they will become members of the human race, and they will be smarter than man. The minds of human beings already have a layer of their particles in them and are being controlled by them. So they will formulate laws that won't allow human beings to give birth from a certain point on. All [lives] will have to be cloned. And that is when they will invade the earth on a large scale. On the surface they would look like human beings, but would not be; they would be alien lives. Think about it, then: In no way am I spinning tall tales for people. (ibid.)

After the turn of the millennium, the topic of aliens is touched upon more sporadically by Master Li. On December 9, 2000 in Ann Arbor, he mentions the aliens to his students, but rather briefly. Here, he adds no new elements to the narrative and, once again, he seems to be aware of the ridicule of his theories in the press: "Some reporters who didn't understand or who even harbored ill intentions made stories out of it. I don't care about what the reporters might say – I just do whatever I should. People in the future will understand" (Li Hongzhi 2000).

A brief mention of aliens is also made in a conference lecture transcript from July 21, 2001 in Washington, DC. Here, Master Li states: "As you know, I often talk about alien beings. Why do I talk about alien beings? Because in the past *they* were the real human beings in this environment of the Earth. During different periods of history and in an even more remote history, they were the proper inhabitants here" (Li Hongzhi 2001; original emphasis).

In a text entitled "Touring North America to Teach the Fa," dated March 2002, Master Li repeats similar ideas: "Why do I always talk about alien beings? It's because no matter how many Earths were renewed in the past, the main beings here at this Earth's location were like alien life-forms. There were differences in each time period, but none of them had the image of man" (Li Hongzhi 2002). He also reiterates the idea of the perfection of the human body, as well as the aliens' envy of it: "The body structure of humans was created by Gods, so it is the most perfect human body system in this dimension. All the alien beings sigh in admiration when they see it!" (ibid).

In the "Fa-Lecture During the 2003 Lantern Festival at the U.S. West Fa Conference," aliens are mentioned just once, while Master Li is talking about the Earth's past: "It was for the existence of human beings that so many things, like water, plants, animals, and so on, were created on this Earth. The beings and the environments that were on the planets here before were worse. The highest-level beings there were like aliens. In other words, there weren't any human beings at this place" (Li Hongzhi 2003a).

In New York in April 2003, Master Li claims:

> The beings on the previous Earths all had the appearances of aliens, and their natural environments were extremely harsh. That's because having beings at the worst place who are in the image of Gods wasn't allowed. Human beings have the images of Gods, so those on the previous Earths all had the ugly appearance of aliens. To have Fa-rectification things take place here and make it possible for all sentient beings in the entire cosmos to be saved – even sentient beings at the most surface level – the Three Realms and human beings were created here. Why were human beings created, rather than have beings like aliens listen to the Fa? The reason is, if those kinds of beings were to listen to the Fa of the cosmos and become my disciples, that'd be the same as insulting the cosmos and all Gods. (Li Hongzhi 2003b)

At a speech given in Atlanta in November 2003, Master Li comes back to the idea of the "cell layer" created inside human beings: "I've told you before that because of alien science and technology, one layer of the human body, one of the human body's layers of

178 *Enlightened Martyrdom*

particles, has been placed fully under the control of aliens. It consists entirely of alien planets' elements, including numbers, mechanical structures, electronic components, and so on. It consists of that stuff [*sic*]." Likewise, he reiterates his theories about aliens, science, and pollution: "The pollution of water has gotten way too severe, and what pollutes it are not normal factors of human substances, but rather, what pollutes it are modern science's industries which were brought over by aliens. So it can't be purified to that degree anymore, and that's why we say that after it has warped nothing can purify it" (Li Hongzhi 2003c).

In the transcript of Master Li's lecture at the International Conference in New York in 2004, aliens/extraterrestrials are referred to briefly once more:

> During ages even longer ago, in this dimension where mankind is, ... mankind simply did not exist. Through exploration modern people have discovered that extraterrestrial life exists. Yes, in the past it was such beings that were spread out over this plane composed of molecules, ... Why did gods create man later on? Because the cosmos was to be reconstructed. (Li Hongzhi 2004)

Master Li continues, "If you say that the skyscrapers in Manhattan are the same as those in the heavens, that's not true, because they were brought about by modern science, and modern science was brought about by aliens" (ibid.)

Aliens are mentioned again in a speech in 2006 in Toronto, in which the same ideas are repeated once more:

> Why have extraterrestrial lives come to the earth so frequently? They have had many reasons. And those aside, they are in awe of the human body, in which they have seen so many things they had never seen before. The reason is, in the cosmos of the past, this environment – that is, these dimensions where the Three Realms now exist – was inhabited by a variety of lowly creatures, including what we refer to today as aliens. They are in fact lowly creatures that have gained a certain technological expertise. [But then] suddenly this cosmic body went through

enormous changes, and human beings came into being as the world was created; a being such as man came into existence. Those [alien] creatures think, looking from that technological standpoint of theirs, that the composition of the human body, the entire design and functioning of the human body, is just so perfect. (Li Hongzhi 2006)

In the speech "What Is a Dafa Disciple?" at a New York conference, Master Li states that:

The old forces created what in this world is the wicked party's regime, with the intent to make things difficult for sentient beings. Along with this, they cooked up a slew of crazy theories as well as modern ideas and things of that sort, making this world terribly complicated, with both good and bad things in it. At the same time, they added to the mix certain warped factors as well as alien biotechnology, so as to disorder man's traditional, proper thinking. In Western society, it was basically enough for them to just get some evil and sinister things up and running. (Li Hongzhi 2011)

To this, he adds: "Even alien life forms, whose technology is remarkably advanced, must seek salvation through Fa-rectification amidst the cosmic cycle of formation, stasis, degeneration, destruction" (ibid.).

Similarly, in a lecture in Los Angeles, aliens are touched upon during a description of an apocalyptic, "evil vs. good" scenario:

Although in Fa-rectification this Earth may be small, all lives in the cosmic body saw that it was a safe haven. Everywhere else planets are dissolving and exploding. You're aware of the information astronomers have disclosed, right? Explosions are happening all throughout the cosmos. Why are there so many alien beings [here]? They saw that Earth was the safest place, and so they hurried over here. Of course, a large number of them were blocked and forbidden from coming to Earth. Those who had come in earlier times have been forbidden from fouling things up, or else the societies on this Earth would have fallen into chaos long ago. The latecomers were told to hide near the

180 *Enlightened Martyrdom*

> sun. Even those on the moon were early arrivers. They all saw that it was safe here. And why is that? The Fa-rectification is taking place here; this is the heart of Fa-rectification. Gods from throughout the cosmos – even very great ones – have reincarnated here. But as for whether it will ultimately be safe here, whether it will be a success or failure, depends on how the Fa-rectification goes. If the Fa-rectification doesn't succeed this time, this Earth will not be kept, and even the cosmos will be no more. (Li Hongzhi 2013)

A single mention of aliens is made during conference proceedings in 2014 in New York. Here, Master Li expands on the concept of "planes" – i.e., the different levels of the universe and of reality – explaining the possibility of knowing about them and acting in accordance with this knowledge:

> Human society is the lowest plane. "Saving sentient beings" refers to all beings, not just human beings – all lives. As you know, this dimension in which human society exists is not only occupied by human beings. People now realize that there are aliens. Do you know how many types of beings there are? People cannot imagine how many beings of various forms there are, and yet there are still other beings existing at different planes. This space here is but the lowest of dimensions. Only when the Fa is taught here, can each of the planes, from higher to lower, throughout the cosmic body, as with each and every life form, possibly obtain the Fa. If it were done at one plane higher, the lives below would not be able to obtain it; and if they weren't able to obtain it, that plane would cease to exist after the Fa rectifies the cosmos – it would be no more. That is why it is at the lowest plane that the Fa is taught, at the lowest plane that things are done, and this lowest-plane language is used. (Li Hongzhi 2014)

Master Li also takes up the issue of aliens following a question from a disciple in October 2015, in Los Angeles. The disciple states that he is concerned that people at his workplace do not communicate much; they share information rarely – and when they do so, they rely on technology as the means. Li Hongzhi answers:

Without knowing the specifics of the situation I can't say much. But you touched on an issue, which is, that people don't directly communicate with each other even when they see each other, and instead they send text messages. I can tell you that that's what aliens do. Human beings are supposed to interact with one another. For thousands of years of human societies, with traditional, god-given culture in place, human beings never went without interacting.

Then what kinds of beings don't interact with each other? As you may know, there are no emotions over on the planets of alien beings. But how scary to think of Earth becoming like that! Yet for cultivators, emotions are an attachment. Breaking free of emotion is a challenge put in place for cultivators, and it helps you to eliminate karma and human thoughts and attachments as you cultivate. The existence of emotions also serves to sustain the human way of living. Aliens, meanwhile, cannot cultivate, and they don't have this special environment that human beings do. But "aliens" are dubbed as such by the people on Earth. They are just odd creatures, strange entities. Strictly speaking, man was created from clay by gods. Gods regard the basic particles of the Three Realms to be soil, or dust in the cosmos. As I see it, aliens climbed out of a garbage dump, as they are lower than humans.

They don't have emotions, so what holds their societies together? Technology. Whoever's technology is superior has a higher status there. And whoever's technology is even higher gets to be the leader. They live for technology. Initially they were just a lowly life form, existing for no real purpose. As they gradually came to use technology to maintain their existence, technology came to be their top priority. That's how they are. They don't understand humankind's thinking, and of course you wouldn't understand theirs, either, as it's completely different. Because their technology is highly developed now, they can tell quite well what you wish to communicate. They know it. So that's how they are. (Li Hongzhi 2015)

Aliens are also referred to once during a speech given in 2016 in Brooklyn. Here, a disciple asks: "Many young disciples in mainland China now play with their cellphones, and watch WeChat and videos on the Web; they especially like to watch videos of small animals. We reminded them but they wouldn't listen, so we are really worried." To this, Master Li answers:

> Everything in this world is attracting you, not letting you obtain the Fa. Not just you, all parents and governments in the world know about this situation, but no one can do anything! This involves not just the issue of people obtaining the Fa. People have also been so affected that they cannot work well, cannot focus on their studies, and they spend a large amount of time on the computer and electronic games – these things tempt you to watch and play them. This is no longer a human state. From antiquity till today humans have not had this state. This is aliens' technology, and demons are utilizing it to get you hooked, get you to abandon everything you have, and have you devote yourself to it. It's wasting your life, yet you are loath to put it down! Even from the perspective of being human you are not right, let alone in cultivation. (Li Hongzhi 2016)

It should also be noted that references to other planets, flying saucers, the idea that our planet has been exploited by technologically advanced beings, and the presence of (allegedly) anachronistic artifacts that demonstrate the existence of ancient civilizations more advanced than the present one can all be found in works by Master Li that predate the earliest mentions of aliens/extraterrestrials recalled here. In the translation of *Zhuan Falun* (Li Hongzhi 1998a), for instance, the following is stated: "However advanced people's means of exploring space and probing life may be, the knowledge gained is limited to certain parts of this one dimension, where human beings reside, at a low plane of the universe. Other planets were explored before by humans during civilizations predating history." In addition, it is argued that: "the standard of our human science and technology is quite low. … However, flying saucers from other planets come and go directly in another space in which there are different concepts of spacetime. Therefore, they come and go so quickly and mysteriously that the human mind finds it difficult to accept it as a fact."

Li Hongzhi, Aliens, and Science   183

In *Falun Gong*, Master Li expands on the concept of (allegedly) anachronistic artifacts:

> The planet we dwell on has been destroyed many times. Each time the planet was remade, humankind again began to multiply. At present, we have already discovered that there are many things on the earth that surpass our present civilization. According to Darwin's theory of evolution, humans evolved from apes, and civilization is no more than ten thousand years old. Yet archaeological findings have revealed that in the caves of the European Alps there exist 250-thousand-year-old frescoes that exhibit a very high level of artistry – one far beyond the abilities of modern people. In the museum of the National University of Peru, there is a large rock on which is an engraved figure who holds a telescope and is observing the stars. This figure is more than thirty thousand years old. As we know, Galileo invented a 30X astronomical telescope in 1609, just over three hundred years ago. How could there have been a telescope thirty thousand years ago? There is an iron pillar in India whose iron content is over ninety-nine percent. Even modern smelting technology cannot produce iron with such high purity; it had already surpassed the level of modern technology. (Li Hongzhi 1993)

In *Zhuan Falun*, volume II, Master Li claims that:

> Earth is but the garbage dump of the universe. There are countless galaxies and planets within countless vast universes, and on each planet there are beings. Human beings deny the existence of other dimensions, so they are unable to see those beings. They exist in other dimensions of the same planets [as the ones that we see], not our dimension, and thus ordinary people cannot see them. It's similar to how human beings say that the Mars of this dimension is hot, but if one were to break through this dimension, it would prove to be somewhat cold over on the other side. Many people with supernatural abilities gaze at the Sun, and after doing so for a while find it no longer to be hot. (Li Hongzhi 1996a)

Furthermore, in a lecture given in Sydney in 1996, Master Li argues the following:

> Some people think, "Our mankind is progressive, and it is already quite magnificent to have evolved to this day from apes." However, let me tell you that historically, during prehistoric times, a hundred thousand years ago or even much, much earlier than that, up to over a hundred million years ago, highly advanced civilizations had always existed on this planet, only that they were destroyed in different time periods. Why were they destroyed? It was because they developed very fast materially and technologically while their morality could not keep pace or was destroyed. They were then no longer allowed to continue to exist and were destroyed. To put it with the understanding of modern science, the motion of matter follows the law. When its motion reaches a certain form, it will inevitably take on another form. For instance, during its motion in this universe, the earth may have been impaired when being hit by some planets. Regardless of what reasons there may be, scientists have now indeed discovered that there have been numerous remains of ancient civilizations on our planet. (Li Hongzhi 1996b)

Analysis and Interpretation

The attentive reader is sure to have noted that what I initially defined as Li Hongzhi's "alien narrative" or "alien theory" is, in fact, a *cluster of narratives*, all entangled with one another and with other teachings in Falun Gong. These narratives, as well as the connections between them, have emerged gradually over time. Master Li gave them particular attention at the end of the 1990s, expanding upon his ideas extensively, and they received public visibility via the aforementioned 1999 *Time* magazine interview. Over the years, Master Li continued to make reference to the alien narratives, reiterating and elaborating upon many earlier points in response to his students' apparent curiosity, as well as the derision with which his ideas were treated in the press. These theories also became a useful element in the dark, apocalyptic vision that Master Li concocted in response to the public persecution faced by Falun Gong. Ultimately, however, these narratives faded away; by the 2000s, they were mentioned quite sporadically, and without further detail being added to existing ideas. Master Li's alien narratives have been neither rejected nor substantially reformulated since that time, and although they are connected to other core teachings in Falun Dafa, it cannot be claimed that they form a *central* element of Falun Dafa itself.

As a preliminary move, in order to understand the conceptual role of these narratives within Falun Gong doctrines, let us break them down into minimal element/sub-narratives. According to Master Li:

1. Aliens exist and have more advanced technology than human beings.
    1.1. This is proved by flying-saucer sightings (and aliens have been observed, for instance, by US authorities).
2. The Earth has been populated several times over the millennia, and certain earlier civilizations developed technology that was far more advanced than present-day technology.
    2.1. This is proved by "out-of-place" objects.
    2.2. Such civilizations can be defined as "human" (*lato sensu*).
    2.3. Regardless of their level of technological advancement, such civilizations degenerated and were thus destroyed.
    2.4. Destruction was decided on, and brought about, by gods.
3. Present-day aliens are "humans" from "past Earths," who, by virtue of their moral excellence, were spared by the gods and placed on other planets when these "past Earths" were destroyed.
    3.1. Aliens belonged to different civilizations, which explains why there are different "races" of alien, each one with a distinct appearance.
4. These aliens were more advanced beings than present-day humans (see point 2), and they continued to develop their technology in "diaspora."
5. Eventually, such aliens also degenerated, in a moral sense.

6. Aliens covet the human body because it is "perfect."
7. Aliens have always intervened in human history, but they started to come to Earth *en masse* during the scientific revolution in the West (which the aliens themselves actually brought about – science and technology were, in fact, initiated by them through their "inspiration" of human beings).
    7.1. This is demonstrated by the incredibly rapid development of science and technology over the past two centuries.
8. Science and technology allow the aliens to manipulate human beings and to keep them under control.
    8.1 Science is limited *per se* because it only allows certain aspects of reality to be studied; other dimensions are excluded. Thus, people who focus solely on science tend to view teachings about elements such as the existence of gods, heavens, and aliens as superstitions.
    8.2. One instrument used by the aliens to keep human beings under control is the special "layer of cells" (or "particles") created in human bodies and/or brains, through which human beings' thoughts are manipulated.
    8.3. Whenever a human being uses a computer, it is recorded.
    8.4. However, the main way in which aliens take possession of human bodies is through *cloning technology*. A cloned body is not provided with a soul by the gods, so it can be entered by an alien.
9. The possibility exists that the aliens could take over Earth. If they manage to control enough human beings and/or enter enough cloned bodies, they will have access to higher institutions, thus being able to implement laws that will accelerate the production of clones, for instance.
10. Individuals who have attained superior powers and levels of knowledge, like Master Li, are working in opposition to the aliens, in alliance with the gods.
11. Master Li (and similar individuals) is able to see the aliens, to erase the "computer catalogues" about human beings, and to destroy the "alien cells" in bodies. Master Li states that he

has already erased computer records for, and deleted alien cells from, his students.
12. Due to feeling under threat, some aliens try to hide among human beings (even marrying humans, for example).
13. Science should not be given up, in Master Li's mind; in fact, there is no alternative to it. However, one should be aware of its origins and limits.
    13.1 Master Li claims that even the aliens have challenged him (during personal meetings) concerning this point – they have asked him why he endorses the use of science and technology when he knows that they are limited? Master Li replies that there is no alternative, and that well-informed usage is what is required.
14. Another way in which the aliens have manipulated human beings, seeking to weaken them physically and psychologically, is through mixing together different races.

Most of Li Hongzhi's alien-related narratives bear a strong resemblance to narratives employed by other authors who seek to challenge traditional religions, as well as those employed by figures who lead or inspire new religious movements by reformulating the teachings of major world religions. For example, the concept that present-day humanity is derived from ancestral aliens forms part of the doctrine of Scientology, being revealed, apparently, to high-ranking members as part of a narrative sketched by the organization's founder, Lafayette Ronald Hubbard (1911–86) (see Rothstein 2009). The idea of aliens endowed with superior technology intervening in human history has been put forth by Claude Vorilhon (Raël), the leader of Raëlism, born in 1946 (see Palmer 2004), and the writers Jean Sendy (1910–78) and Mauro Biglino (born 1950) (see Bigliardi 2017 and 2015a respectively). Likewise, the author David Icke (born 1952) perpetuates the narrative of an alien presence existing in disguise in present-day society (Introvigne 2010; Dyrendal 2014),

I have emphasized that aliens were first mentioned by Li Hongzhi in connection with UFOs, which were cited as an example of the superior technology possessed by other civilizations and/or present

188 *Enlightened Martyrdom*

in other dimensions. Similar ideas and narratives circulate (e.g., the characterization of aliens as "body-snatchers" and the idea of an alien invasion) in innumerable tales, novels, and motion pictures. One could well subscribe to the idea that Li Hongzhi's narratives are not a result of his superior knowledge, but are derived from other sources of inspiration to which he has been exposed. It is difficult to guess which sources exactly might have inspired him; Benjamin Penny suggests, however, that the New Age Western literature that was translated and circulated in China in the 1990s might have had an influence, as might TV series like *The X-Files* (Penny 2012, 90–2, 132, 136–8). At the same time, narratives about the "cell layer," computer recordings, cloning as a method of human control, and the alien-induced mixing of human races might have been Li Hongzhi's own conceptions – or his variations on extant "grand narratives," at least.

What is interesting is that the earliest mentions of cloning as an instrument of human manipulation date back to the 1990s, when such a technique came to prominence in both academic and public debates. The concept was also used aesthetically at this time – as a narrative motif in science-fiction movies, for example. Notably, *Jurassic Park*, Steven Spielberg's blockbuster motion picture depicting the consequences of cloning prehistoric animals (based on Michael Crichton's 1990 novel), was released in June 1993. The birth of the first mammal cloned from an adult somatic cell, Dolly the Sheep (at Roslin Institute, University of Edinburgh), occurred on July 5, 1997. In these ways, cloning-related narratives were in the limelight in the 1990s in academia, where they were discussed by both natural scientists and ethics specialists, and in popular culture, with books and movies exploring the potential of cloning and warning of its consequences.

On a related note, it should be stated that the aforementioned new religious group leader Raël enthusiastically embraced human cloning as a technology that would facilitate eternal life for human beings, like that enjoyed by the extraterrestrials who, according to him, created humanity (Raël 2001). If we reject the idea that the specific narratives discussed by Li Hongzhi were received by him exclusively by means of revelation, narratives of human cloning in Falun Gong in the 1990s (which can be compared with similar discourses in other religious movements) can be seen simply as theological reflections upon a topic that was enjoying particular visibility in popular culture and academic circles at that time (Bigliardi 2015b).

At the outset of this chapter, I remarked that I would not seek to challenge any of Li Hongzhi's narratives by appealing to empirical data; as stated above, my sphere of interest does not include the overall "debunking" of his theories here. It should be made clear, however, that there are some subtle tensions within the sub-narratives listed above. In particular, it is unclear whether or not the alien menace should be considered an *actual threat* to society, or whether it is completely *under control*. In fact, Master Li's stance on this point seems to have shifted over time. Generally speaking, scholars agree that Li Hongzhi has not been very consistent or lucid where the meaning of his teachings is concerned. See, for instance, Ownby (2008, 89–90, 211–12) and Penny (2012, 97). Sometimes, his narratives seem to be geared toward encouraging students to engage with a particular viewpoint, e.g., to take a critical stance toward science. At other times, however, Master Li's rhetoric appears to be a tool through which to reassure his students that their "master" is protecting them by siding with the gods.

The dialectic here can be compared with the one that characterizes Li Hongzhi's views on science. As David Ownby explains (2008, 98–102) and as the extensive quotations provided in the first section of this chapter demonstrate, Li Hongzhi manages both to capitalize on science, where it carries an aura of prestige and modernity, and to express mistrust of science's alleged shortcomings and limitations – especially vis-à-vis "superior teachings," such as those found in Falun Gong (and, even more specifically, the "superior knowledge" with which Li Hongzhi himself is supposedly endowed, but the nature of which he does not completely disclose). An analogous interpretation is given by Penny (2012, 22–3, 130, 192–3).

Certain other sub-narratives and ideas in Li Hongzhi's teachings function as a rhetorical *cordon sanitaire* that protects Falun Gong in relation to claims that are more problematic, empirically speaking – such as the suggestion that some devices and entities are placed in dimensions that can be accessed (and, indeed, acted upon) by Master Li only,[6] or the idea that both the appearance and language of the aliens cannot be recognized or interpreted by those who are not endowed with the knowledge and faculties possessed by Master Li (Ownby 2008, 91).

The alien narratives are part of, and embody, all of these kinds of tensions. The aliens are simultaneously visible *and* invisible, they are a (or even *the*) major threat to humanity *and* are under control, they are human *and* non-human (as well as *inhumane*!), they are human-like but they also come in many forms, their actions are explained by Master Li to his audiences but, at the same time, they *cannot be completely understood* by those who have not reached the master's level. The aliens have been created by the gods, but the gods are also Li Hongzhi's allies in the fight against aliens. The aliens are simultaneously criticized *and* pitied. They are even credited with asking the same kinds of questions (e.g., why Master Li uses science and technology if he also criticizes them) that human opponents of Falun Gong may advance. The ambiguities in the alien narratives are analogous with the ambiguities that characterize descriptions of science in Falun Dafa. The contradictory stance of Master Li is perhaps encapsulated best by his statement in the 1999 *Time* magazine interview, "You do not want to have that kind of thought in your mind," which is followed by a rather detailed description of that which he claims not to want to depict (i.e., an image of the aliens).

The importance of alien narratives in Falun Gong should not be overstated, yet it is definitely an interesting and significant aspect of the group's teachings. Aliens, stripped down to their most basic conceptual function, may well appear to be a postmodern version of demons. However, there is more to the story than that. A close inspection of Falun Gong's "alien theory" reveals a complex game of "Chinese boxes." Aliens clearly fit into the general apocalyptic

---

6. This is the case with the idea of "wheels" being placed in practitioners' abdomens. See, for instance, Penny (2012, 96 and 188–9).

narrative advanced by Master Li, but they are also related to the ambiguous image of science and technology put forth in Falun Gong. By naming the aliens the inventors of science and technology, Li Hongzhi prevents these fields from belonging to any terrestrial civilization. Thus, they become an enemy or a threat, used both to warn Falun Gong students of the consequences of moral degeneration and to reassure them about their master's abilities to save them. Overall, then, Li Hongzhi's aliens are a multifaceted and ambiguous concept that function to assist him with the construction of his own charisma.

References

All web pages were accessed for a final check on September 24, 2016.

Bigliardi, Stefano. 2015a. "I nuovi antichi alieni di Mauro Biglino. Analisi di un fenomeno editoriale e culturale." *CESNUR.*
http://www.cesnur.org/2015/Bigliardi_Biglino.pdf

Bigliardi, Stefano. 2015b. "New Religious Movements and Science: 2Raël's Progressive Patronizing Parasitism," *Zygon: Journal of Religion and Science*, 50 (1): 64–83.

Bigliardi, Stefano. 2017. "A Gentleman's Joyous Esotericism: Jean Sendy Above and Beyond the 'Ancient Aliens,'" *Alternative Spirituality and Religion Review*, 8(1), 1–35.

Dowell, William. 1999. "Interview with Li Hongzhi," *Time* magazine, May 10. Available at
http://content.time.com/time/world/article/0,8599,2053761,00.html

Dyrendal, Asbjørn. 2014. "Hidden Knowledge, Hidden Powers. Esotericism and Conspiracy Culture," in Egil Asprem and Kennet Granholm (eds.), *Contemporary Esotericism.* London and New York: Routledge, pp. 200–25.

Farley, Helen. 2014. "Falun Gong: A Narrative of Pending Apocalypse, Shape-shifting Aliens and Relentless Persecution," in James R. Lewis and Jesper A. Petersen (eds.), *Controversial New Religions*, 2nd ed. New York: Oxford University Press, pp. 241–56.

Introvigne, Massimo. 2010. "Ufo, monarchie europee e complotti massonici. Torna David Icke." *CESNUR*, http://www.cesnur.org/2010/mi-icke.html

Li Hongzhi. *Books & Recent Writings of Mr Li Hongzhi*. Available at: http://en.falundafa.org/falun-dafa-books.html and http://en.falundafa.org/falun-da-recent-writings.html

Li Hongzhi. 1993 [revised translation 2001]. *Falun Gong*. http://en.falundafa.org/eng/pdf/flg_2001.pdf

Li Hongzhi. 1995. "Teaching the Fa in Beijing at the Zhuan Falun Publication Ceremony," January 4. http://en.falundafa.org/eng/pdf/zfl_fajie.pdf

Li Hongzhi. 1996a. *Zhuan Falun*, Vol. II. http://en.falundafa.org/eng/pdf/zfl2.pdf

Li Hongzhi. 1996b. Lecture in Sydney. http://en.falundafa.org/eng/lectures/1996L.html

Li Hongzhi. 1997. "Fa Teaching Given in San Francisco." http://en.falundafa.org/eng/pdf/mgjf.pdf

Li Hongzhi. 1998a. *Zhuan Falun* (translation: http://en.falundafa.org/eng/pdf/zfl_en.pdf)

Li Hongzhi. 1998b. Conference Proceedings, March 29–30, New York. http://en.falundafa.org/eng/lectures/19980329L.html

Li Hongzhi. 1998c. Conference Proceedings, May 30–31, Frankfurt. http://en.falundafa.org/eng/lectures/19980530L.html

Li Hongzhi. 1998d. Conference Proceedings, September 4–5, Geneva. http://en.falundafa.org/eng/lectures/19980904L.html

Li Hongzhi. 1998e. Conference Proceedings, August 22–23, Singapore. http://en.falundafa.org/eng/lectures/19980822L.html

Li Hongzhi. 1999a. Conference Proceedings, February, Los Angeles. http://en.falundafa.org/eng/lectures/19990221L.html

Li Hongzhi. 1999b. Conference Proceedings, March 27–28, New York. http://en.falundafa.org/eng/lectures/19990327L.html

Li Hongzhi. 1999c. Conference Proceedings, May 2–3, Sydney. http://en.falundafa.org/eng/lectures/19990502L.html

Li Hongzhi. 1999d. Conference Proceedings, May 23, Toronto. http://en.falundafa.org/eng/lectures/19990523L.html

Li Hongzhi. 2000. Conference Proceedings, December 9, Ann Arbor. http://en.falundafa.org/eng/pdf/daohang.pdf

Li Hongzhi. 2001. Conference Proceedings, July 21, Washington, DC. http://en.falundafa.org/eng/pdf/daohang.pdf

Li Hongzhi. 2002. "Touring North America to Teach the Fa," March. http://en.falundafa.org/eng/lectures/200203L.html

Li Hongzhi. 2003a. "Fa-Lecture During the 2003 Lantern Festival at the U.S. West Fa Conference," February 15.
http://en.falundafa.org/eng/lectures/20030215L-full.html

Li Hongzhi. 2003b. "Teaching and Explaining the Fa at the Metropolitan New York Fa Conference", April 20.
http://en.falundafa.org/eng/lectures/20030420L.html

Li Hongzhi. 2003c. November 29, Atlanta.
http://en.falundafa.org/eng/lectures/20031129L.html

Li Hongzhi. 2004. Lecture at the International Conference in New York, November 1. http://en.falundafa.org/eng/lectures/20041121L.html

Li Honghzi. 2006. Speech in Toronto, May 28.
http://en.falundafa.org/eng/lectures/20060528L.html

Li Hongzhi. 2011. "What Is a Dafa Disciple?" August 29, New York.
http://en.falundafa.org/eng/lectures/20110829L.html

Li Hongzhi. 2013. Lecture, October 19, Los Angeles.
http://en.minghui.org/html/articles/2013/10/30/142936.html

Li Hongzhi. 2014. Conference Proceedings, May 13, New York.
http://en.minghui.org/html/articles/2014/5/31/1450.html

Li Hongzhi. 2015. Teaching in Los Angeles, October 16.
http://en.minghui.org/html/articles/2015/10/25/153388.html

Li Hongzhi. 2016. Speech in Brooklyn, May 15.
http://en.minghui.org/html/articles/2016/5/31/157233.html

Ownby, David. 2008. *Falun Gong and the Future of China*. New York: Oxford University Press.

Palmer, Susan. 2004. *Aliens Adored*. New Brunswick, NJ: Rutgers University Press.

Penny, Benjamin. 2012. *The Religion of Falun Gong*. Chicago and London: University of Chicago Press.

Raël [Claude Vorilhon]. 2001. "Oui au clonage humain" [Yes to Human Cloning]. Available at: http://fr.rael.org/download.php?view.9

Rothstein, Mikael. 2009. "'His name was Xenu. He used renegades ...': Aspects of Scientology's Founding Myth," in James R. Lewis (ed.), *Scientology*. Oxford: Oxford University Press, p. 365.

Stefano Bigliardi has a PhD in philosophy from the University of Bologna. He has worked as a researcher and a teacher at various academic institutions in Germany, Sweden, Mexico, and Switzerland. He currently serves at Al Akhawayn University in Ifrane (Morocco) as an Assistant Professor of Philosophy. His research encompasses the relationship of

Abrahamic religions and NRMs with contemporary science, as well as with pseudoscience. He has published numerous articles in peer-reviewed journals such as *Zygon, The Muslim World, Nova Religio,* and *Temenos.* He is the author of *Islam and the Quest for Modern Science* (2014) and of a monograph in Italian on contemporary Islam and pseudoscience (*La mezzaluna e la luna dimezzata*, 2017).

9. Falun Gong's Attack on Academic Freedom

Helen Farley

Introduction

For a number of years, I taught Studies in Religion at a major Australian university. I lectured about Eastern religions, taught an introductory course on world religions, and another on meditation in world religions. While teaching these courses, I was approached by a Falun Gong practitioner. She asked if she could come to my classes and speak a little about Falun Gong. I was more than happy to let a practitioner come and talk to my students so that they could get a first-hand account of a movement with which most were unfamiliar. Most people knew little else but that the practice of Falun Gong involved five physical meditations and that there were persistent claims of persecution of practitioners by the government of the People's Republic of China. Somewhere in the back of the collective consciousness was something about the harvesting of organs; maybe that seemed a bit far-fetched. Even so, my students were critical scholars of religion and asked the hard questions that were responded to with respect, albeit a little one-sidedly. The Falun Gong practitioner would hand out flyers to a "Chinese cultural event," which was a thinly veiled propaganda event for Falun Gong. To my knowledge, none of my students ever attended. After one of these classes, a female student came up to tell me she had lived in Hong Kong and there Falun Gong practitioners were considered dangerous. She related that they were scruffy and aggressive and were generally avoided. This was the first time I had heard someone provide a negative narrative of Falun Gong outside of the People's

196 *Enlightened Martyrdom*

Republic of China and my first inkling that there was more to this group than first appeared. Falun Gong had been so successful in portraying itself in the West as an unfairly persecuted minority (for example, see Pan 2017). I did briefly search for some record that could corroborate what the student had told me about Falun Gong in Hong Kong, but I could unearth very little. I could see they were active there, but there was scant negative press (see Law 2002). This was an anomaly that I put to the back of my mind.

I hesitate to say that this chapter forms a narrative of my experiences with Falun Gong because I do not necessarily think that it is. This is a reflection of my experiences with one individual who has taken exception to what I have written about Falun Gong. I cannot confidently say that he represents anyone or anything other than himself. He claimed he was a Falun Gong practitioner, correcting the misinformation that I had allegedly spread. Parts of this story have been told elsewhere by other actors in this tale (Lewis 2016). This chapter details the systematic attack on my academic freedom by a Falun Gong practitioner who was offended by my academic, peer-reviewed writings about Falun Gong, and his sustained campaign to discredit me among my peers and to have me removed from my employment.

Academic Freedom in Higher Education

Tierney and Lanford (2014) defined academic freedom as "the freedom to teach and conduct research without fear or concern of retribution." The belief in its value lies in the understanding that institutions and society benefit from free enquiry and expression; many cite it as necessary for creativity and innovation (ibid.). Academic freedom allows an academic to determine his or her own teaching and research agenda. Researchers are judged on the quality of their work by their peers (ibid.). Hence, academics disseminate their research through peer-reviewed journals, books, and book chapters. Their peers scrutinize their methodologies, the validity of their findings, and the analysis from which they derive their ideas. In the United States, the First Amendment protects the notion of academic freedom. The American judicial philosopher Judge Learned Hand stated: "... there are no orthodoxies, religious, political, economic, or scientific – which are immune from debate or dispute" (quoted in Rubin 2001).

Although this article details the systematic attempt to discredit me by a member of Falun Gong, this sort of persecution of academics by members of new religious movements is not uncommon. In the mid-1990s, the academic Julius H. Rubin was singled out by members of the Bruderhof.[1] A book by him about the Bruderhof was shelved in response to a defamation lawsuit brought against Oxford University Press by the Bruderhof (Rubin 2001). This action was accompanied by a letter-writing campaign that defamed Rubin, and spurious reviews about the upcoming book appeared on Amazon (ibid.). Similarly, an academic writing on the Iraqi religions of Babi and Baha'i, Denis McEoin, was the focus of unwelcome attacks from practitioner academics also working in that field (McEoin 1990). What makes this instance especially troubling is that it occurred within the confines of academia. Practitioner academics masquerading as objective seekers of truth have attacked another who does not wholeheartedly concur with the positive façade put forward by the Babi and Baha'i religions. New Zealand scholar of religion Heather Kavan reported on a Chinese physicist, He Zuoxin, who published a criticism of Falun Gong in an academic journal. In response, 6,000 protesters occupied Zuoxin's university for some 72 hours, seeking a retraction of the article. The retraction was not forthcoming, and the police were eventually called in to dismantle the protest, arresting forty-five people (Kavan 2005). In a bizarre twist, Kavan herself, who wrote about her research into the movement, was to become the focus of adverse attention from Falun Gong members. She received a number of harassing phone calls and was threatened with further "action" (ibid.).

1. The Bruderhof are a controversial Anabaptist Christian movement with communities in several countries including the UK, Australia, the USA, and Germany. They are wary of technology, although they do make use of the internet and smartphones.

198 *Enlightened Martyrdom*

More recently, I learned about a colleague in a nearby city who is now hosting a picket outside of his house by Falun Gong practitioners, who have taken umbrage at his academic writings challenging the widespread belief that Falun Gong practitioners were specifically targeted by the Chinese government for illegal organ removal (Campbell 2016).

Writing about Falun Gong

In 2009, I was asked by Professor James Lewis to write a book chapter about Falun Gong. Another author had withdrawn from a book project, and a fill-in was required. I did not have much knowledge about Falun Gong and even less first-hand experience of either Falun Gong or of its practitioners, but I did have a solid scholarly understanding of both Eastern religions and new religious movements. I accepted the challenge and wrote a chapter based on a growing academic literature (Farley 2010).

I was surprised to learn about a group that had a theology as complex and bizarre as that of the oft-derided Scientology (for example, see Rothstein 2009). Falun Gong practitioners take their lead from a complex theology replete with shape-shifting aliens, multiple planes of existence, and an impending apocalypse brought about by extreme moral degradation from which only a very select few will endure. To a Falun Gong practitioner, karma plays a fundamental role. It is not the abstract karma characteristic of Buddhism, but instead is thought to be a sticky black substance which the practice of the five physically demanding, yet meditative, exercises associated with Falun Gong can at least partially remove (Adams 2011).

I was intrigued by Falun Gong and sought to reconcile the gentle, friendly practitioners that I saw at farmers' markets and other public events with a bizarre doctrinal narrative that would rival Hollywood's latest science-fiction blockbusters. My academic interest in Falun Gong continued to grow and I have authored two more chapters and a journal article about the movement (Farley 2013, 2014a, 2014b).

Academic Freedom under Threat

When the first email arrived from an aggrieved Falun Gong practitioner, I was shocked. I had tried to be very even-handed in my chapters and article about Falun Gong. I did not have anything against that religion but sought to tease out and understand the inconsistencies of their message. I was aware that most people did not know very much about Falun Gong and I wanted to shed some light on their practices and beliefs. Even so, if there was doubt or if information was contentious, I flagged it as being so. I never once expressed doubt about the veracity of Falun Gong's claims of persecution by the government of the People's Republic of China. It is beyond doubt that Falun Gong practitioners are being unjustly targeted (for example, see Noakes and Ford 2015).

I showed the original email to a colleague, who told me just to delete it. I talked with him as to whether I should respond to the email and gently put my case forward. He indicated that he thought that it would do no good and would probably fan the discontent of the practitioner. I took his advice and deleted the email. Very soon, a number of colleagues within the institution where I worked, colleagues from the university where I used to work, senior management at the university where I worked, academics I had written with, and a random assortment of other people, some of whom had no contact with me at all, had also received a very similar email about me. Without exception, these people sided with me and contacted me to alert me to the fact that the email was out there, but they also offered their support. It consoled me that the emails from the practitioner did not have the impact that he had hoped. As a consequence, I decided to do nothing. I only answered the polite enquiries of those who had received the emails and who wished to know the background. Even though I had deleted the email, I still have the original text as he included the full text in his emails to my colleagues.

At the time of this email campaign, I was swamped with work. I had just secured funding for a $AUD4 million project, so I was occupied recruiting personnel, compiling documentation, and planning the project. I did not have a lot of time or energy left over

200 *Enlightened Martyrdom*

to be too concerned about the actions of one unhappy Falun Gong practitioner, and his energies did not seem to be having the desired impact.

The Responses of My Colleagues

The editor of the issue of *Religion and Violence* in which my article was published, Professor James Lewis, was among those contacted by the aggrieved practitioner. He held the same confrontational tone which characterized all of his communications both with myself and with my colleagues and university management (at both my current and my former employers). Patiently, Professor Lewis addressed his concerns and suggested he refute my article in an academic way, rather than personally (Lewis 2016).

Then, a colleague at my current university, a lecturer whom I knew to be a Falun Gong practitioner, contacted me. She asked to meet for a coffee. I reluctantly agreed because I was not sure what was coming but I agreed because she was a colleague wanting to talk; I thought I owed her that professional courtesy. She asked me if I was aware that my articles were being republished in Chinese-language newspapers in Sydney. I replied that I was not aware of this, and I am still not sure whether or not that has happened. She said she wanted to alert me to the fact that my papers were being used without my knowledge. I asked her about the Falun Gong practitioner who was harassing me, and she claimed not to know him, but I thought he was most likely the reason she had asked for us to meet. I had no reason to disbelieve her. I explained how he had been emailing my colleagues. She appeared to sympathize with me and indicated that she thought my articles had been academic, not deliberately critical of Falun Gong. She offered me some Falun Gong materials so I could learn the truth about the organization and undertook to telephone the practitioner who was harassing me and try to set him straight. She said that she believed my position was not adversarial and felt confident that once she explained that to him, he too would understand. I had tried not to think about how the email campaign had impacted me but I found myself crying as I described what had happened to me. As we parted, she embraced me and we both cried. She later left a message saying that she had spoken to him.

The university lawyer first contacted me when members of the university council and several senior members of the executive received letters with content similar to that in the original email but this time suggesting that I be dismissed from my position. The lawyer wanted to reassure me that the university "had my back." Even so, the matter had been referred to the university's audit and risk committee. The chair of that committee also got in touch with me. Both he and the lawyer were supportive and gave me their private cellphone numbers should I need to contact them in an emergency. I forwarded every email about the matter to the university lawyer. In the later stages of the ordeal, the lawyer suggested I engage a private lawyer to take up my case. I declined to do so as I thought it would end up as a battle of the lawyers and whoever had the most resources would win. I could not be sure that it would be me.

The aggrieved practitioner contacted a number of colleagues with whom I had published papers (not about Falun Gong). In these emails, he claimed that my articles had been translated into Chinese by the Chinese government so that the government could demonstrate foreign scholars' condemnation of Falun Gong. He claimed that this strategy was part of a larger initiative which also included the highly controversial Confucius Institute program, to influence Western opinion about Falun Gong. Once more, I was accused of fabricating Falun Gong teachings. He went on to espouse the health benefits of Falun Gong and provided an account of the alleged persecution of adherents by the Chinese government. He implied that my position as a Senior Research Fellow at the University of Queensland was the result of collusion between the University of Queensland, Professor James Lewis, and the Chinese government. As he said:

> I am wondering that the title Honorary Senior Religion Researcher is used solely to promote the articles defaming

> Falun Gong on the Chinese website. I am also wondering that she is not the real author of the articles but just offered her name as the author. (private communication, 2014)

Disturbingly, he tracked down my Linked In account and directly contacted many of my "connections" through that means. I have no idea how many people he reached. At least two people contacted me to say that he had made contact with them. The content of those messages was substantially the same as the earlier emails he had written. I made a complaint to Linked In about him but I am unsure as to whether or not they took any action.

Though the Vice Chancellor of USQ did not contact me directly, I do have a copy of the letter that she wrote in response to the aggrieved adherent's email, as he attached it to the emails he sent to some of my colleagues. Dated 9 June 2015, the letter affirms that the university acts in accordance with the Australian Code for the Responsible Conduct of Research and that I did not have a case to answer. The Vice Chancellor suggested that the practitioner write an academic article and air his views in that way.

Writing for the Right

On May 21, 2016, an article written by Jianguo Wu, the practitioner who was targeting me and my associates, was published in *News Weekly*. Titled, "Honorary fellow means to dishonourable end (sic)," the article rolled out the same claims about me: that I was a tool of the Chinese government, that I had made unsubstantiated claims about Falun Gong, and that I misrepresented Falun Gong's teachings. What I find most interesting is that Jianguo claimed he fled from China in 1992, a year after the immolations at Tiananmen Square, in order to embrace academic freedom, among other things (Wu 2016). Yet he felt comfortable compromising *my* academic freedom in response to something I had written with which he did not agree. Though he was at complete liberty to refute what I had written in an academic way, through publishing an academic journal article, he chose not to.

In this article, it appeared that what Jianguo found most contentious in what I had written was about the alleged self-immolations by Falun Gong members at Tiananmen Square (see Farley 2014b). In the abstract of that book chapter, I wrote:

> The teachings of Falun Gong explicitly forbid suicide, yet in 2001, five protesters set themselves ablaze in Tiananmen Square resulting in the death of two. Allegedly, their stated aim was to bring the world's focus onto the repression of the movement by the Chinese government. Falun Gong spokespeople were quick to speak out in defence of founder Li Hongzhi, saying that the movement strictly forbids suicide in line with the traditional Chinese belief that says that suicide is an affront to the ancestors. They further claimed that the Chinese government had staged the suicides in order to stir up public opinion against the movement and indeed the tide of public opinion did turn against Falun Gong and its founder.

In writing that abstract, I intended to convey an unbiased view of the story. Further, I added a note which read: "Some commentators deny that this massacre took place. See (Munro 2002, 267)." Again, the intention was to demonstrate that this information was contentious. In both the abstract and note reproduced above, I kept in the original references to indicate that this information came from other, reputable, academic sources. These were not my own ideas. I readily admit that I was not an eyewitness to the event and I had not spoken to an eyewitness.

The choice of publication in which Jianguo chose to publish was interesting, and I am a little surprised even that they published this article. *News Weekly* is published by an organization called the National Civic Council (*News Weekly* 2016). It is a conservative Christian lobby group which believes in the family as the basic unit of society (and opposes lifestyles that undermine that), the family farm, the integrity of the individual (from fertilization onwards), patriotism, and Judeo-Christian values (National Civic Council, n.d.). Their website also documents their opposition to same-sex marriage, the promotion of Australian law over Aboriginal law, and rejects the idea that all cultures are equal. It is baffling that *News Weekly* published this article in light of their very conservative views. When the article was published, I was invited by *News Weekly* to respond. I did not reply as I thought that any response would only escalate matters.

China in Perspective

Jianguo Wu published another article about me on a web page called *China in Perspective*. This article was certainly a lot more inflammatory than anything that he has published in English, probably because such an article would not be published in the West due to the risk of litigation. Jianguo probably thought that his article would remain undiscovered as it was written in Chinese.

I have no knowledge about the intended audience or the purpose of the page. In his article, Jianguo claimed that the Chinese government was trying to corrupt Western academic freedom. There has been much controversy about the infiltration of Confucius Institutes into Western universities. Claims have been made that these are merely listening organs and propaganda tools of the Chinese government (see Pan, 2017). Even so, Jianguo claimed that these attempts are minor compared to the direct influence that the Chinese government directly exerts over Western academics. He considered me to be a prime example (Wu 2016).

The article quotes a Canadian academic, a long-time, high-profile supporter of Falun Gong, who allegedly said of my work: "Dr. Farley can at least be accused of profanity of academic rigor. Many of the claims are lacking evidence" (Terence Russell in Wu 2015). I cannot verify that he actually said this. I had decided not to contact him to enquire so as not to bring him into this debacle. The one thing I am sure of is the academic rigor of my articles. Every statement was referenced and I indicated where there was doubt about the veracity of the information provided. All of the information I provided comes from the academic literature, except where it comes directly from the Falun Gong literature, and every article

I have written has gone through rigorous peer review. In a similar way, Jianguo claimed that another academic based in Sydney agreed with the Canadian academic's claims. Interestingly, she did try to obtain my contact details through some mutual colleagues (who declined to provide them), though she could easily have found them on the internet. Upon investigation, I found that she was actually a medical academic at a Sydney university, whose name is often seen in association with writings about Falun Gong. I am not sure her medical expertise would stretch to a valid and critical appraisal of the literature about an eastern religion.

Not content to besmear my reputation, Wu also attacked the reputation of Professor James Lewis, who had originally asked me to write about Falun Gong. He went on to imply that Professor Lewis and myself are actually in receipt of monies from the Chinese government in return for our articles. I can categorically confirm that we are not. Towards the end of the page, he contradicted himself by claiming that Professor James Lewis is the likely author of my articles. Again, I absolutely refute these claims.

Elsewhere in this article, Jianguo made erroneous reports about my career. He called me an Associate Professor of Philosophy, Religion and Classics. In fact, when I was employed at my former place of work, I was a lecturer in studies in religion. I currently hold an honorary role there as a Senior Research Fellow, though Jianguo cast doubt over my association with that institution. He used my Linked In profile as evidence, even though that profile details my work as a studies in religion academic and my current role as a Senior Research Fellow. He further claimed that I had not been an active researcher in religion despite my sustained publishing in the area over this period (for example, Cusack and Farley 2016; Farley 2011, 2013, 2014a, b, c and d, 2015, among many others). Jianguo also claimed that the honorary title with my former employer was due to a secret deal being done with the Chinese government. I would like to think it was because of my publishing and supervision record!

Jianguo also accused me of being fraudulent and of making things up, saying that I had fabricated some of the information that

I claimed as being Falun Gong information. This is not a new technique. Heather Kavan (2005) claimed that this was a tactic used by Falun Gong practitioners. When journalists asked for translations of Master Li's speeches in Chinese, they were told that it was impossible to summarize his words (Stavinros, 1999).

Why Speak out Now?

I received information that a colleague of mine at another Queensland university was similarly being harassed by members of Falun Gong. I chose not to speak out previously because I believed that I was being targeted by a single individual who, I thought, felt he had a sacred duty to try and correct the "wrong" information I had written about his beliefs. Though I did not agree with him, I thought I could understand his motives with which I, at least in part, sympathized. When it became evident that this was part of a wider strategy by Falun Gong adherents, I became more concerned. I could no longer write off the practitioner who had targeted me as a single fanatic. I also learned of the difficulties faced by a colleague in New Zealand who had been targeted by Falun Gong members. I have decided to tell my story as a warning to other academics who will speak against Falun Gong. I cannot imagine that this will stop them writing. What I hope it does achieve is to show them that this is part of a wider strategy employed by Falun Gong. Most of all, I want to stand in solidarity with my colleagues and let them know that they are not alone. I stand for academic freedom and I will stand with them to ensure that they can exercise it. These are just two examples, but there are many more.

What Makes Falun Gong Practitioners So Sensitive to Perceived Criticism?

Those who speak for Falun Gong have long claimed that the government of the People's Republic of China is responsible for the torture, systematic detention, illegal execution and organ harvesting from Falun Gong practitioners (for example, see Greenlee 2006; Falun Dafa 2017; Phillips, 2017). This persecution is portrayed as a human rights abuse to a Western audience that is inclined to demonize the Chinese government and believe them capable of such brutalities (Aldrich *et al.* 2015). For its part, the Chinese government makes counterclaims, stating that Falun Gong is an invidious and evil cult and comparing it to other notorious cults such as Aum Shinrikyo (Embassy of the People's Republic of China in the United States of America, n.d.b). It also asserts that the Falun Gong leadership coerces its members into instigating illegal activities (Ross 2009). They call out Li Hongzhi as a pathological liar who actively deceives those who follow him as well as the general public (Embassy of the People's Republic of China in the United States of America, n.d.a). Those in the West are already very wary of cults (Pfeifer 2016), and it is this attitude which the Chinese government is seeking to leverage by demonizing Falun Gong. This portrayal is reinforced by the unearthly theology that characterizes Falun Gong (Farley 2010).

The Western media have played into the hands of the highly developed Falun Gong publicity apparatus and have ensured that thoughtful citizens are appropriately outraged by the persecution of Falun Gong practitioners in China. The aim of this strategy is to focus international pressure on China and force the government to ease the persecution of Falun Gong members (Greenlee 2006). The government of China has at least partly countered these attempts through the pressures applied via its Confucius Institute project, active in prestigious universities in the West (Tin-yau Lo and Pan 2016). Most recently, in Australia, investigative journalists have uncovered a systematic approach by the government of China to exert "soft power" over that country's government in order to counter dissent and influence political opinion (McKenzie *et al.* 2017). Falun Gong practitioners are most likely correct in their suspicions that the government of the People's Republic of China is trying to exert soft power in order to soften opposition in the West to the continued persecution of Falun Gong practitioners, or at the very least to undermine support for the beleaguered movement outside of China. However, they are too ready to vilify specific academics writing in this area. All that Jianguo has achieved in trying to demonize me is to discredit Falun Gong in the eyes of the Academy.

Conclusion

I reluctantly agreed to take part in this project. I was concerned that I would only stir things up again, just as they had settled down. At least I did not have Falun Gong practitioners picketing my residence, as was happening to my colleague. Even now, I have not told my partner that I am writing this chapter. He would be angry with me, as would be some of my colleagues, concerned for my welfare. No doubt, even my supporters within my university's administration would question my decision to speak out. Writing this has been an intensely painful experience for me. I had pushed all of those concerns and fears just out of consciousness. I busied myself with other projects and activities. I am only now understanding the impact this whole episode has had on me. I have shed many tears writing this account. I am ashamed to say that I did not even reach out to my close colleague in Brisbane who was undergoing his own persecution. It was too painful for me to confront.

Falun Gong adherents perceive that their very survival is at stake, and in many ways, it probably is. Their generalized alertness to transgressions against them by the Chinese government has made them hyper-vigilant, sometimes seeing conspiracies where none exist. Even though a single Falun Gong practitioner has tried to discredit me, I believe he was only doing what he believed he must. Falun Gong doctrine asserts that if there is misinformation disseminated about Falun Gong, then it must be corrected. I believe that is what he believed he was doing. Believing that has stopped me retaliating. I have declined to engage a lawyer to defend my reputation. I have not responded to any of his emails. Until now, I have not sought a public arena in which to defend myself against his claims.

There can be no denying that the government of the People's Republic of China has staged a relentless campaign against Falun

Gong. Its motivation for doing so can only be speculated about, but Noakes and Ford (2015) conclude that the Chinese government would lose too much face if it were to reverse its campaign of persecution and suppression before claiming a decisive victory. What is not as clear is exactly how far it was and is prepared to go. The belief that the Chinese government is actively sponsoring Western academics to discredit Falun Gong cannot be substantiated. I am one of the more active researchers of Falun Gong, and while I am prepared to concede that those articles that can be viewed as being critical of Falun Gong may have been taken and reused (without my permission) in various fora, no approach has been made to me either directly or indirectly.

References

All web pages were accessed for a final check on May 22, 2017.

Adams, R. J. T. 2011. "Falun Gong," in M. Juergensmeyer and W. C. Roof (eds.), *Encyclopedia of Global Religion*. Thousand Oaks, CA: SAGE Publications, p. 389. https://doi.org/10.4135/9781412997898

Aldrich, J., Lu, J., and Kang, L. 2015. "How Do Americans View the Rising China?" *Journal of Contemporary China*, 24(92), 203–21. https://doi.org/10.1080/10670564.2014.932148

Campbell, F. 2016. "An Analysis of the Emerging Role of Social Media in Human Trafficking: Examples from Labour and Human Organ Trading," *International Journal of Development Issues*, 15(2), 98–112. https://doi.org/10.1108/IJDI-12-2015-0076

Cusack, C. M., and Farley, H. (eds.). 2016. *Religion, the Occult, and the Paranormal*. Abingdon, UK: Routledge.

Embassy of the People's Republic of China in the United States of America. n.d.(a). "Exposing the Lies of 'Falun Gong' Cult." Retrieved from http://www.china-embassy.org/eng/zt/ppflg/t263446.htm

Embassy of the People's Republic of China in the United States of America. n.d.(b). "Falun Gong: An Evil Cult." Retrieved from http://www.china-embassy.org/eng/zt/ppflg/t36582.htm

Falun Dafa. 2017. "Stop Organ Harvesting in China." Retrieved from http://www.stoporganharvesting.org/

Farley, H. 2010. "Falun Gong and Science: Origins, Pseudoscience and China's Scientific Establishment," in J. R. Lewis and O. Hammer (eds.), *Handbook of Religion and the Authority of Science*. Leiden: Brill, pp. 141–64.

Farley, H. 2011. "Out of Africa: Tarot's Fascination with Egypt," *Literature & Aesthetics*, 21(1), 175–95.

Farley, H. 2013. "Self-Harm and Falun Gong: Karmic Release, Martyrdom or Suicide," *Journal of Religion and Violence*, 1(3), 259–75.

Farley, H. 2014a. "Falun Gong: A Narrative of Pending Apocalypse, Shape-shifting Aliens and Relentless Persecution," in J. R. Lewis and J. A. Petersen (eds.), *Controversial New Religions.* 2nd edn. Oxford: Oxford University Press, pp. 241–56.

Farley, H. 2014b. "Death by Whose Hand? Falun Gong and Suicide," in J. R. Lewis and C. Cusack (eds.), *Sacred Suicide.* Farnham, UK: Ashgate, pp. 215–32.

Farley, H. 2014c. "Tarot and Egyptomania," in E. E. Auger (ed.), *Tarot in Culture*, Vol. 1. Clifford, ON: Valleyhome Books. Retrieved from http://emilyeauger.weebly.com/tarot-in-culture.html.

Farley, H. 2014d. "The Tower and the Devil in the Visconti–Sforza Deck," in E. E. Auger (ed.), *Tarot in Culture*, Vol. 2. Clifford, ON: Valleyhome Books. Retrieved from http://emilyeauger.weebly.com/tarot-in-culture.html.

Farley, H. 2015. "Tarot," in C. Partridge (ed.), *The Occult World*. Abingdon, UK: Routledge, pp. 571–9.

Greenlee, M. J. 2006. "A King Who Devours His People: Jiang Zemin and the Falun Gong Crackdown: A Bibliography," *International Journal of Legal Information*, 34(3), 556–84.

Kavan, H. 2005. "Print Media Coverage of Falun Gong in Australia and New Zealand", in Peter Horsfield (ed.), *Papers from the Trans-Tasman Research Symposium, "Emerging Research in Media, Religion and Culture."* Melbourne: RMIT Publishing, pp. 74–85.

Law, L. 2002. "Defying Disappearance: Cosmopolitan Public Spaces in Hong Kong," *Urban Studies*, 39(9), 1625–45.

Lewis, J. R. 2016. "Sucking the 'De' Out of Me: How an Esoteric Theory of Persecution and Martyrdom Fuels Falun Gong's Assault on Intellectual Freedom," *Alternative Religion and Spirituality Review*, 7(1), 93–109.

McEoin, D. 1990. "The Crisis in Babi and Baha'i Studies: Part of a Wider Crisis in Academic Freedom? *British Society for Middle Eastern Studies*, 117(1), 55–61. https://doi.org/10.1080/13530199008705506

McKenzie, N., Koloff, S., and Davies, A. (writers). 2017. "Power and Influence," *Four Corners*, June 5. ABC Television. Sydney, Australia.

Munro, Robin. 2002. "On the Psychiatric Abuse of Falun Gong and Other Dissenters in China: A Reply to Stone, Hickling, Kleinman, and Lee," *Journal of the American Academy of Psychiatry and the Law*, 30: 266–74.

National Civic Council. n.d. "About Us." Retrieved from https://national-civic-council.org.au/about-us/

News Weekly. 2016. "*News Weekly* and the National Civic Council," December 16. Retrieved from http://newsweekly.com.au/about.php

Noakes, S., and Ford, C. 2015. "Managing Political Opposition Groups in China: Explaining the Continuing Anti-Falun Gong Campaign," *China Quarterly*, 223 (September), 658–79. https://doi.org/10.1017/S0305741015000788

Pan, D. 2017. "'Shen Yun' Offers a Glimpse into Chinese Persecution of Falun Dafa," *Post and Courier* (Charleston, SC). January 17. Retrieved from http://www.postandcourier.com/features/shen-yun-offers-a-glimpse-into-chinese-persecution-of-falun/article_31532772-d830-11e6-8b20-973527e9c0ce.html

Pfeifer, J. E. 2016. "Cults in Court: Jury Decision-making and New Religious Movements," in J. T. Richardson and F. Bellanger (eds.), *Legal Cases, New Religious Movements, and Minority Faiths*. London: Routledge, pp. 205–26.

Phillips, J. 2017. "Falun Gong Persists After 17 Years of Chinese Communist Persecution: Rights Group," *Epoch Times*, March 1. Retrieved from http://www.theepochtimes.com/n3/2228713-falun-gong-persists-after-17-years-of-chinese-communist-persecution-rights-group/

Ross, R. 2009. "Is Falun Gong a Cult?" Retrieved from https://www.culteducation.com/group/1254-falun-gong/6922-is-falun-gong-a-cult.html

Rothstein, M. 2009. "His Name Was Xenu. He Used Renegades …": Aspects of Scientology's Founding Myth," in J. R. Lewis (ed.), *Scientology*. Oxford: Oxford University Press, pp. 365–87.

Rubin, J. H. 2001. "Contested Narratives: A Case Study of a Conflict Between a New Religious Movement and Its Critics," in B. Zablocki and T. Robbins (eds.), *Misunderstanding Cults: Searching for Objectivity in a Controversial Field*. Toronto: University of Toronto Press, pp. 452–77.

Stavrinos, A. 1999. "Head of Spiritual Movement Addresses Sydney Faithful." Australian Associated Press, May 1.

Tierney, W. G., and Lanford, M. 2014. "The Question of Academic Freedom: Universal Right or Relative Term," *Frontiers of Education in China*, 9(1), 4–23. https://doi.org/10.3868/S110-003-014-0002-X

Tin-yau Lo, J., and Pan, S. 2016. "Confucius Institutes and China's Soft Power Practices and Paradoxes," *Compare: A Journal of Comparative and International Education*, 46(4), 512–32.
https://doi.org/10.1080/03057925.2014.916185

Wu, J. 2016. "Honorary fellow means to dishonourable end [sic]," *News Weekly* (2972).

Helen Farley has taught and researched across a broad range of areas at the University of Queensland, including eastern religions, meditative traditions, the history of esotericism, religion in immersive virtual environments, and the history of divination. She was the convenor of the Alternative Expressions of the Numinous conference and the founding editor of *Khthónios: A Journal for the Study of Religion*. Helen is also an Adjunct Associate Professor and former Director of the Digital Life Lab at the University of Southern Queensland.

10. Friendly Fire
How Falun Gong Mistook Me for an Enemy[1]

Heather Kavan

> Even when we are silenced we must continue to write – to assert freedom, to find meaning.
>
> Richard Flanagan (2016)

It was 2012 – the year of the Hunger Games, London Summer Olympics, and Vladimir Putin's election victory – and I was sitting at my university desk in New Zealand when I opened an email from an unfamiliar source. The sender, who had a Chinese surname, told me that Falun Gong practitioners were increasing their efforts to vilify me. I got up from my desk and went outside, inviting the rush of cold air to disentangle my thoughts. Was the sender aware of other puzzling messages I had received? Might the email be related to the car that had been following me at night? And how had a peaceful meditation exercise ended in a haze of paranoia, accusations, and mistrust?

This is an account of my research on Falun Gong and the events that ensued when members of the spiritual movement mistook me for their enemy.

When I was invited to tell my story for this volume I knew there would be challenges. The first is the risk of writing at a time when

---

1. This article was originally published in *Alternative Spirituality and Religion Review* (2017), 8(2), 249–61 and is reprinted with permission of the editor.

practitioners and advocates are campaigning to get scholars dismissed from their jobs and to get articles that do not support them withdrawn from journals. The second is the bewildering nature of the events that occurred in the aftermath of my research. Many of them felt like a mixture of Plato's cave and Sartre's *No Exit* – Plato's cave in the sense that Falun Gong and the Chinese Communist Party are shadowy, and *No Exit* in the sense that it was futile for any of us to hope others would see us through our own eyes. It was only when I came across a manual on how to overthrow dictators that the events began to make sense.

A Chance Encounter

I first came across Falun Gong in 2001, at a time when I was researching other spiritual groups. As biologist Lois Isenman observes, when people spend a great deal of time working in a specialist field, they often develop an intuitive sense in that area of knowledge (Isenman 2013). On this day, I was walking along Bowen Street in Wellington when I sensed that a spiritual gathering was taking place. I looked around to see whether the sensation was coming from the nearby cathedral. To my surprise, the source was the Parliament buildings. As I approached, I saw eight Chinese protesters wearing yellow T-shirts standing outside Parliament, their hands above their heads, and their faces emanating strength and tranquillity. Later, I identified them as Falun Gong practitioners and read a story in the local newspaper about how they were persecuted in China.

I did not give the encounter much thought until 2003 when I learned that practitioners had sent hundreds of letters to academic institutions inviting scholars to research them. At the same time, a Falun Gong group advertised in my local newspaper, inviting the public to a demonstration of the exercises. I was keen to meet the group to see if I could do research that might help them. Although I am a European New Zealander, I felt I could relate to Chinese practitioners as I enjoy meditation and had practiced *qigong*, of which Falun Gong is an offshoot.

The Meetings

When I arrived at the hall at the advertised time, a woman I will call Jia welcomed me. The first thing I learned was that answering an invitation to watch a demonstration of Falun Gong exercises means that one is expected to do the exercises. Jia taught me the exercises that were soon to become my daily activity.

On the second week, we were sitting in a circle on the floor when I heard the sound of a car pulling up and footsteps. A police officer walked in. He just watched for an hour, said nothing, and left. What was going on in Falun Gong that was so worthy of police attention? I mentioned the officer's presence to Jia after he left, but she did not think it was unusual. Another practitioner had told me they were used to outsiders because spies often attended their sessions in China before Falun Gong was banned.

After a month of weekly meetings, Jia invited me to do the exercises outdoors with the group at 6 a.m. every morning. For almost all of the meetings, I did the exercises with my eyes closed, and we did not speak. We were communicating at a deeper level than words, united in the physical challenges as we held postures, inhaling the early-morning air, hearing the birds sing over the sound of the exercise audiotape, and smiling empathetically at each other when we left.

But it was not all harmony and light. As I delved into leader Li Hongzhi's books and speeches, something felt amiss. The tone was aggressive and demanding, compared with the beauty of other Chinese scriptures such as the *Tao Te Ching*, and even of the meditative experience itself. Li's ideas, claims, and speech style reminded me of my experiences researching other spiritual paths when occasionally a person would lose touch with reality after excessive spiritual activities. The person would go into a temporary psychosis, jumbling spiritual truths with fragmented subconscious memories of supernatural material from film and print media. He or she would claim to be a supreme being who was saving the world from destruction and would often attempt to dominate others. Transpersonal psychologists recognize these experiences as spiritual emergencies (based on the pioneering research of Grof and Grof, 1989).

I wondered about exploring the controversial research on *qigong* psychosis, but there was a more pressing issue. Practitioners had relatives in China who were at risk of imprisonment and they hoped Western media would help them by exposing the persecution. I asked Jia how she would feel if I researched media portrayals of Falun Gong, and to this day I feel sad when I think about how happy she was. She brought me books, magazines, papers, and videos. She never asked for money and only accepted it if I wanted to buy the products.

As summer ended, the physical demands increased and I found the practice less enjoyable. The sky poured with rain and the consequent flooding brought mosquitoes to the practice site. Temperatures dropped below zero. At the same time, my university workload seemed to double. Once during the standing exercises, I dropped my arms, faint from insufficient sleep, and I struggled to hold the seated lotus position for a full hour. "Strengthen your mind," Jia would tell me.

The Unnamed Refugee

One day as I was getting ready to leave a meeting, Jia told me about a practitioner who belonged to another Falun Gong group. The woman had been imprisoned and tortured in China several times but had escaped to New Zealand after her daughter bribed an airport official to get her mother on a plane out of China. She arrived in New Zealand unable to speak English and located other Falun Gong members who took her in.

Jia explained that recently the woman had applied for refugee status, but the Immigration Service declined her application, purportedly because the interpreter's translation understated the danger to her life. Jia said the woman had told her that, although as a practitioner she should be able to face adversity, she did not want to be tortured again. Jia added that the woman was old and her body weak from previous torture, and she would be unlikely to survive.

During the week, I phoned the Immigration Service and asked how I could help. The advisor told me applicants could appeal within ten working days of the decision. I phoned Jia and asked her to pass this message on to the woman urgently, and offered to help by getting a university interpreter. Jia was uncharacteristically evasive, but said she would contact another member.

When I next saw Jia, the woman would have had less than 24 hours to appeal, so I asked if she had passed on my message. She hesitated and said the woman needed to purify more (in Falun Gong beliefs one is purified by suffering), therefore they had not passed on my message. I urged her to reconsider, offering to do anything to help. But Jia was resolute, saying she herself had stood next to the woman and noticed she had not been meditating properly.

At this moment I realized there was a side of Falun Gong that I did not fully understand. Jia looked at me sympathetically and – appearing to be quoting from one of Li's speeches – said she felt sorry for me because I worked hard to do the exercises but had never experienced the persecution, and therefore would never be able to reach the higher stages of Li's heaven. "But it's all predetermined," she sighed.

My fears for the woman's safety lingered for months, so I checked the Immigration and Protection Tribunal decisions, now publicly available from the Ministry of Justice (2017). To my relief, I learned that the woman had successfully appealed the decision, with support from two witnesses who are likely to have been practitioners (Refugee Status Appeal Authority 2005). This experience highlighted for me how, on emotional issues, conflicting views about Falun Gong can arise from the varying experiences of different groups.

The End of the Research and Its Aftermath

After over a year of daily meetings, the group had a break, and I knew it would be the last time we met. I worked on the research, and, after it was finished, I was quoted in a press release about new religious movements. In the release I said the FBI's definition of a potentially violent religion was so broad that several groups in New

218 *Enlightened Martyrdom*

Zealand would fall into it, and cited Falun Gong as one of several examples. Here is my record of the events that followed:

> Falun Gong members monitor the media daily, and discovered the press release even before I did. They were offended that they were classified with other religions that they perceived to be "totally evil", and I received a phone call warning me that I would be deluged by a hundred callers from a Falun Gong email list. Several emotionally charged phone calls followed, in which the callers demanded the press release be removed from the Internet. A member contacted me at home and relayed accusations that I was being paid large amounts of money by the Chinese government, and repeatedly said that the situation was "extremely dangerous". Each time I asked exactly what the danger was, she did not explain. (Kavan 2008, 16)

I have some empathy for practitioners in this situation because when the Chinese government banned Falun Gong, officials likened it to extreme religious groups. Therefore the media release could have stirred up memories of collective trauma and yearnings for healing and justice.

The situation blew over and I published two conference papers in Australian and New Zealand anthologies (Kavan 2005, 2008). In the latter, I included the account of how I had inadvertently upset practitioners. That, I thought, was the end of the conflict.

But it was only the end of the beginning. Practitioners read my articles and emailed me. One of the first messages was from the Falun Dafa Association. The author apologized for members harassing me and said he thought my paper was "well-researched." However, most emails from practitioners were not as kind-hearted, and the authors seemed unable to resist inserting slurs, for example: "Your saddest folly ...," "Darwin and Newton deceived you," "You have played right into the hands of the Communist Party." I replied amiably to the thoughtful emails and ignored the others.

Next came the emails to my colleagues across three campuses. They arrived in spates every couple of months. I thought they were from Falun Gong impersonators, as they seemed to be caricatures of Li's inflated style ("the earth is a garbage dump," "human society suffers like a rotten apple") and two writers alluded to elements of his teachings that most practitioners do not share with outsiders ("aliens are controlling the human mind," "dirty people, such as mixed-blood"). I imagined Falun Gong detractors composing them between sniggers and told colleagues the emails were black propaganda, in which senders deliberately misattribute the source. None of us took them seriously. In the context of pressures to publish, funding cuts, teaching loads, and administrative demands, the writers' exhortations to "stop your stupid work and become a deciple" [sic] were more risible than threatening.

Even so, there was something about the emails that was unnerving, and that was their timing. Sometimes I would receive positive messages from readers saying my article resonated with their challenging experiences of Falun Gong. Although I would have heard nothing from Falun Gong members for months, within forty-eight hours a practitioner would send me an email, usually criticizing me. I wondered if the article had been circulated on a shared list as this could explain the timing; however, this explanation proved incorrect when I checked with the first senders. One expert suggested there could be a single person playing several roles, using different email addresses, but that seemed unlikely as the positive emails were from identifiable people such as academics and therapists. A second expert suggested my emails were on a firewall and being intercepted – but by whom? It was the Chinese government, not Falun Gong, that had a firewall, and they would be unlikely to disagree with readers who had experienced challenges with the spiritual movement.

Wikipedia Manipulation

The email timing was one of several disconcerting events. Between 2009 and 2012 potentially defamatory comments about me appeared on the Wikipedia Talk pages under the guise of content discussion. Pro-Falun Gong editors repeatedly misquoted my articles to make them sound uninformed, and made several inaccurate

220 *Enlightened Martyrdom*

statements, for example, that I had no peer-reviewed research on Falun Gong (Archives 28 and 31, 2009a and d; User Talk 2009 and 2012). Echoing Li Hongzhi's (1999) sexism, they depicted me as "this woman," whose research – along with that of another female researcher – was inferior to the real experts like David Ownby and Benjamin Penny (Archive 28, 2009a, para. 6; Archives 30 and 31, 2009c and d). The comments were laced with innuendoes such as "people get away with very sloppy stuff in conference papers" and insinuations that my work was a tool for the Communist Party (Archive 28, 2009a, para. 4; User Talk, 2012).

As political scientist Patricia Thornton (2008) has observed, Falun Gong tactics sometimes backfire. The Wikipedia discussion sparked interest in my papers that, having been published in local conference proceedings, were not indexed on influential databases and might otherwise have been unread. Other editors defended me (for example, Archive 29, 2009b, and Archive 32, 2010) and several pro-Falun Gong editors were banned from the site for using it for ideological purposes and harassing perceived opponents (Wikipedia 2011). Readership increased and my Academia.edu page rose to a position in the top 2 to 5 percent of pages, measured by number of article downloads. Subsequently, international media quoted the articles, giving them even more attention (Bagnoli 2016; Griffiths 2014).

Strange Occurrences

In late 2011 the tension escalated. Several times I noticed I was being followed when driving home at night. One evening there was a Chinese woman in my garden flashing an electric torch. Then my house was broken into, and the burglars left valuable electronic goods untouched, but took spiritual objects including crystals and my meditation blanket.

I knew I was experiencing a phenomenon that practitioners talk about: a series of events that, if mentioned to outsiders, could make the person experiencing them sound paranoid. They believe these events are orchestrated by the Chinese Communist Party (Kavan, 2008). I now understand how practitioners feel. As it turned out, in my case the events had a rational explanation. The burglars had been high on drugs when choosing the items to steal and were drawn by visually appealing objects. The woman in my garden turned out to be a neighbor looking for a lost cat. Another female driver had similar experiences and knew the man to be a traffic officer who drove an unmarked car.

While this was going on, my university was engaged in discussions with Chinese officials about export education, and the embassy was also inviting scholars to attend conferences on religious "cults." I attended only two meetings, along with colleagues. The day after I received the invitation to the second meeting, I received an email warning me of "sinister" plans in which practitioners intended to vilify me by linking me to the Chinese state. I went to the meeting regardless and (like the other meeting I attended) it was unrelated to Falun Gong.

In 2015 the New Zealand government passed the Harmful Digital Communications Act which made internet and email harassment illegal. The emails decreased, and, at the same time, other academics were attracting practitioners' ire.

Two Australian scholars were targeted using similar tactics, along with James Lewis, the former editor of the *Journal of Religion and Violence*, who declined a practitioner's request that he retract a scholar's article on Falun Gong (Lewis 2016). Additionally, supporters of Falun Gong's organ-harvesting claims contacted the editor of the *Journal of Medical Ethics* requesting the retraction of a paper that did not concur with Falun Gong assertions that China is harvesting organs from prisoners (Retraction Watch 2016). More recently, following pressure from the same supporters, the editors of *Liver Journal* retracted an article that contained data referring to the use of organs, which advocates claim could have been retrieved from prisoners (Mondelli, Younossi and Negro 2017). The authors face a lifelong embargo on submitting their work to the journal. The calls for retraction have been accompanied by articles from practitioners denigrating the scholars (for example, Ong 2017; Wu 2016).

222 *Enlightened Martyrdom*

One of the disparaging articles gave me a clue to the mystery of the emails to my colleagues. An Australian practitioner mentioned that he and other members sent emails to colleagues of a scholar who published an article that did not concur with Falun Gong claims (Wu 2016). Given the similar modus operandi and proximity of Australia and New Zealand, it now seems likely that some of the emails sent to my colleagues were from genuine practitioners. An alternative explanation is that opponents imitated a Falun Gong tactic or vice versa.

The Hard Question

By this stage it was clear that I and other researchers would benefit from understanding practitioner and advocate tactics. We had explored their explicit actions like marches, rallies, demonstrations, public exercises, and media releases, but had relatively little knowledge of how they used covert, psychological techniques to achieve their goals. For me, this was the hard question of scholarship because these processes were often gradual, anonymous, indirect, and ambiguous, and they co-existed with an ironic rhetoric of human rights and truth-telling.

Searching the internet, I came across references to a 2001 intelligence report published by India's foreign intelligence agency, Research and Analysis Wing (R&AW or RAW). The report stated that former United States Army Colonel Robert Helvey was believed to be acting as an adviser to Falun Gong (Kampmark 2015; Mowat 2005).

Helvey's name sparked my interest because I had come across it before – in the work of the late Mark Palmer, founder and former director of Friends of Falun Gong, an organization that partially funds Falun Gong media (Kavan 2017). In his book *Breaking the Real Axis of Evil: How to Oust the World's Last Dictators by 2025*, Palmer recommends Helvey's training in how to use nonviolent force to topple despots (Palmer 2005). After this, he devotes a chapter to bringing down China and suggests Li Hongzhi might be the "best hope" for breaking the "geriatric repressive regime" (Palmer 2005, 245, 249).

Although it is impossible to verify whether Helvey advised practitioners (as this would be confidential) two observations can be made. First, Helvey does not advise dissidents in the sense of directing them and choosing their targets; rather he shares nonviolent techniques they can use to oust tyrants and seize political power (Helvey 2004). In this context, "nonviolent" means "non-physically violent to others." Psychological aggression is part of the tactical repertoire and there is also scope for violence to oneself through martyrdom.

Second, Helvey's techniques are no secret and his manual *On Strategic Nonviolent Conflict* is available on the internet, in both English and Mandarin Chinese (Helvey 2004). Predictably, the publication is not in China's bookshops, and in 2016 three activists caught studying the manual and related books received jail sentences of between two-and-a-half and five years (*The Guardian* 2016). While it may seem strange that Chinese dissidents use a U.S. book on tactics when their own country is renowned for military classics like *The Art of War*, *The Thirty-six Stratagems* and *The Six Secret Teachings*, Helvey offers specific suggestions for current political situations.

On Strategic Nonviolent Conflict reads like a checklist of Falun Gong tactics. Here are several suggestions from it, to which I have added examples of Falun Gong activities in parentheses:

1. Disseminating black propaganda (publishing a purported announcement from official Meng Weizai that he was resigning from the Communist Party).
2. Declaring a victory before one has fully got it (Tuidang announcements that over 200 million Chinese have quit the Communist Party).
3. Airing exposure through congressional hearings (the 2012 United States Congressional Executive Commission on China).
4. Circulating propaganda that attempts to appear authoritative (the reports of the World Organization to Investigate the Persecution of Falun Gong).

5. Provoking opponents to negatively react for the purpose of igniting outrage at their reaction (inviting political leaders to the Shen Yun Performing Arts Show seemingly to goad China).
6. Blaming one's opponent for all the facts (attributing practitioner misbehavior to Party culture [Li Hongzhi 2016]).
7. Attacking a multi-national corporation that supports the regime whose headquarters are based in another country (Falun Gong's lawsuit against Cisco).

Curiously, given the disputed self-immolations, Helvey also discusses the tactic of self-immolation accompanied by invitations to "international news agencies to cover and to photograph the event" (Helvey 2004, 35).

Additionally, Helvey explains the importance of rumor-spreading, and his advice on how to create the stories may be helpful to researchers analyzing organ-theft narratives:

> It is important that the rumor be based upon at least a slim, factual basis, or at least could be perceived as being based upon known or suspected facts. The subject of rumor should be of importance to the target and it should be interesting so that others will repeat it. Rumors can be used to raise or lower the morale of the target audience, or engender emotions such as hate, disgust or admiration. (ibid., 84)

A further, unmentioned step is to characterize those who question the rumors as agents of the regime.

How do scholars fit into the plan? Although there is no explicit reference to academics, Helvey suggests dissidents use "teachers" and "others who are respected in their own communities" to spread their propaganda (ibid., 8). Falun Gong invitations to academics to conduct research on them seem to dovetail with this strategy. However, as researchers tend to critique knowledge claims, rather than broadcast them, the stage is set for conflict.

Although Helvey signals that the methods are to be directed at tyrants, the manual contains several tactics Falun Gong activists have used on scholars. These tactics are similar to ones used in psychological warfare by both China and the United States (described by Cheng 2013 and Thomas 2003). They include: isolating opponents by attempting to pull away their pillars of support, looking for opportunities to place them in situations where the only outcomes are unfavorable, and generating distrust and confusion to lower their morale and divert attention from one's own vulnerabilities or intention (Helvey 2004).

Challenges and Possible Responses

These tactics, with their impressive lineage in psychological warfare and international successes in ousting tyrants, seemed a little wasted on me. That is because I like practitioners and have goodwill towards them. Further, the tactics backfire, damaging the reputations of innocent members who genuinely embrace "truth, compassion and forbearance."

As well as being inappropriately aimed at academics, the tactics are not well suited to spiritual movements. Since Bondurant's (1958) research on Gandhi, nonviolent resistance is divided into two categories: principled and tactical (coercive). Principled non-violence prohibits both physical and psychological violence and seeks mutually beneficial solutions, while tactical non-violence prohibits only physical violence and seeks to win by antagonizing, manipulating, and coercing opponents. As a spiritual movement (especially one that has the law of karma as a key tenet), Falun Gong would benefit from switching to principled non-violence. While its current tactics do not cause direct physical damage, its psychological attacks have the same harmful intent as physical attacks and can be equally injurious. As philosopher Barry Gan says, "The heart of violence is in the mind of the perpetrator, not in the means by which the intention is carried out" (Gan 2013, 22).

I believe it is vital that scholars publish their experiences so future researchers are aware of the risks. In this vein, I offer six suggestions for academics researching Falun Gong: (1) check every story, as situations may not be as they seem; (2) familiarize oneself with the tactics of psychological warfare and tactical nonviolent resistance; (3) connect with scholars who have transversed the minefield; (4) if practical, respond to media enquiries in writing so statements can be worded to avoid emotional triggers; (5) forewarn journal editors that activists have previously called for retractions of articles; and (6) ensure witnesses are present in any discussions with Chinese officials so there is evidence against accusations of collusion.

Final Thoughts

My experiences of Falun Gong and those of several other researchers show what happens when members of a spiritual movement use harmful tactics on misidentified enemies. The irony of the conflict is that scholars and practitioners have much in common. Both engage in mental challenges that require intense focus – practitioners in meditation and scholars in academic discovery. Both seek knowledge – for practitioners, spiritual revelations, and for academics, nuggets of information. Most important, both aim to be loyal to their values regardless of political influences, with practitioners upholding their right to religious freedom and scholars upholding their right to academic freedom.

For Jia and me, there was another similarity, and I became aware of it when our paths crossed unexpectedly during the conflict. Without hesitation, we hugged each other and then moved on. We did not speak because that would have tainted our rapport, and beneath our different worldviews, neither of us wanted to be the other's enemy. Our freedom to choose harmony over conflict was a glimpse of light in the research equivalent of Plato's cave.

References

All websites listed in the references were accessed on October 8, 2017.

Archive 28. 2009a. Wikipedia Talk: Falun Gong. Available from: https://en.wikipedia.org/wiki/Talk:Falun_Gong/Archive_28

Archive 29. 2009b. Wikipedia Talk: Falun Gong. Available from: https://en.wikipedia.org/wiki/Talk%3AFalun_Gong%2FArchive_29

Archive 30. 2009c. Wikipedia Talk: Falun Gong. Available from: https://en.wikipedia.org/wiki/Talk%3AFalun_Gong%2FArchive_30

Archive 31. 2009d. Wikipedia Talk: Falun Gong. Available from: https://en.wikipedia.org/wiki/Talk:Falun_Gong/Archive_31

Archive 32. 2010. Wikipedia Talk: Falun Gong. Available from: https://en.wikipedia.org/wiki/Talk%3AFalun_Gong%2FArchive_32

Bagnoli, L. 2016. "Genocidi, alieni e proteste in Italia: dentro il controverso mondo del Falun Gong cinese," *Vice News*, September 28 Available from: https://news.vice.com/it/article/falun-gong-cina-italia

Bondurant, J. V. 1958. *Conquest of Violence: The Gandhian Philosophy of Conflict*. Princeton, NJ: Princeton University Press.

Cheng, D. 2013. *Winning Without Fighting: The Chinese Psychological Warfare Challenge.* Washington, DC: The Heritage Foundation. Available from: http://www.heritage.org/global-politics/report/winning-without-fighting-the-chinese-psychological-warfare-challenge

Flanagan, R. 2016. *Because Writing Matters.* Inaugural Boisbouvier lecture at the 2016 Melbourne Writers Festival. Available from: http://speakola.com/arts/richard-flanagan-boisbouvier-lecture-mwf-2016

Gan, B. L. 2013. *Violence and Nonviolence: An Introduction.* Studies in Social, Political, and Legal Philosophy. Lanham, MD: Rowman & Littlefield.

Griffiths, J. 2014. "Why China Fears the Falun Gong," *Los Angeles Daily Times*, July 14. Available from: http://www.dailynews.com/2014/07/14/why-china-fears-the-falun-gong/

Grof, S. and C. Grof. 1989. *Spiritual Emergency: When Personal Transformation Becomes a Crisis*. New York: St. Martin's Press.

Guardian, The. 2016. "China Jails Three Activists for Trying to Start Civil Disobedience Movement," January 29. Available from: https://www.theguardian.com/world/2016/jan/29/china-jails-three-activists-for-trying-to-start-civil-disobedience-movement

Helvey, R. 2004. *On Strategic Nonviolent Conflict: Thinking About the Fundamentals.* Boston: The Albert Einstein Institution.

Isenman, L. 2013. "Understanding Unconscious Intelligence and Intuition: 'Blink' and Beyond," *Perspectives in Biology and Medicine*, 56(1), 148–66.

Kampmark, B. 2015. "To Find or Be Forgotten: Global Tensions on the Right to Erasure and Internet Governance," *Journal of Global Faultlines*, 2(2), 1–18.

Kavan, H. 2005. "Print Media Coverage of Falun Gong in Australia and New Zealand," in Peter Horsfield (ed.), *Papers from the Trans-Tasman Research Symposium, "Emerging Research in Media, Religion and Culture."* Melbourne: RMIT Publishing, pp. 74–85.

Kavan, H. 2008. "Falun Gong in the Media: What Can We Believe?" in E. Tilley (ed.), *Power and Place: Refereed Proceedings of the Australian and New Zealand Communication Association Conference, Wellington*. Available from: https://www.anzca.net/documents/2008-conf-papers/112-falun-gong-in-the-media-what-can-we-believe-1/file.html

Kavan, H. 2017. "Victims, Martyrs, Crusaders: Archetypal Figures in News Stories about Falun Gong," *Alternative Spirituality and Religion Review*, 8(2), 273–96.

Lewis, J. 2016. "Sucking the 'De' Out of Me: How an Esoteric Theory of Persecution and Martyrdom Fuels Falun Gong's Assault on Intellectual Freedom," *Alternative Spirituality and Religion Review*, 7(1), 93–109. https://doi.org/10.5840/asrr20166921

Li Hongzhi. 1999. "Teaching the Fa at the Eastern U.S. Fa Conference," New York, March 27–28. Available from: http://en.falundafa.org/eng/lectures/19990327L.html

Li Hongzhi. 2016. "Fa Teaching at the 2016 New York Fa Conference," Brooklyn, May 15. Available from: http://en.minghui.org/html/articles/2016/5/31/157233.html

Ministry of Justice (New Zealand). 2017. Refugee/Protection Decisions. Available from: https://forms.justice.govt.nz/search/IPT/RefugeeProtection/

Mondelli, M., Younossi, Z. and Negro, F. 2017. "Editor's Note," *Liver International*, 37(5), 768. https://doi.org/10.1111/liv.13400

Mowat, J. 2005. "Coup d'État in Disguise: Washington's New World Order 'Democratization' Template." Montreal: Centre for Research on Globalisation. Available from: https://www.globalresearch.ca/articles/MOW502A.html

Ong, L. 2017. "Top Chinese Transplant Surgeon Involved in Anti-Falun Gong Campaign Has Study Retracted," *Epoch Times*, February 7. Available from: https://www.theepochtimes.com/top-chinese-transplant-surgeon-involved-in-anti-falun-gong-campaign-has-study-retracted_2220541.html

Palmer, M. 2005. *Breaking the Real Axis of Evil: How to Oust the World's Last Dictators by 2025*. Lanham, MD: Rowman & Littlefield.

Refugee Status Appeal Authority (New Zealand). 2005. Refugee Appeal NO 75330, January 25. Available from: https://forms.justice.govt.nz/search/Documents/IPTV2/RefugeeProtection/ref_20050125_75330.pdf

Retraction Watch. 2016. "Is China Using Organs from Executed Prisoners? Researchers Debate Issue in the Literature." Available from: http://retractionwatch.com/2016/07/25/is-china-using-organs-from-executed-prisoners-researchers-debate-issue-in-the-literature/

Thomas, T. L. 2003. "New Developments in Chinese Strategic Psychological Warfare," *Special Warfare*, 16(1), 2–11.

Thornton, P. 2008. "Manufacturing Dissent in Transnational China: Boomerang, Backfire or Spectacle?" in Kevin J. O'Brien (ed.), *Popular Protest in China.* Cambridge, MA: Harvard University Press, pp. 179–204.

User Talk: Colipon. Archive 5. 2009. Available from: http://www.like2do.com/learn?s=User_talk:Colipon/archive5

User Talk: Colipon. Archive. 2012. Available from: https://en.wikipedia.org/w/index.php?title=User_talk:Colipon&oldid=499472667#I.27m_a_Falun_Goner

Wikipedia. 2011. "Arbitration/Requests/Enforcement." Available from: https://en.wikipedia.org/w/index.php?title=Wikipedia:Arbitration/Requests/Enforcement&oldid=459818930#PCPP

Wu, J. 2016. "Human Rights: Honorary Fellow Means to Dishonourable End," *News Weekly*, May 21. Available from: http://newsweekly.com.au/article.php?id=57305

Heather Kavan is a senior lecturer at Massey University in New Zealand, where she specializes in teaching Speech Writing. On the research front, she is fascinated by unconventional spiritual paths. Her PhD is in Religious Studies, and her publications have focused on phenomena associated with transcendent states of consciousness, including visions, glossolalia, and spiritual channeling. She has helped film-makers, lawyers, scholars, and ordinary people who need specialist information about unconventional religions.

11. The Falun Gong Political Narrative
Creating the Illusion of So-called "Forced Organ Harvesting"

Campbell Fraser

Introduction

The Falun Gong (FLG) organization have for the last several years placed stories of so-called forced organ harvesting as central to their sustained and concerted effort to stand in opposition to the Chinese government and, specifically, the Communist Party of China.

These claims have been comprehensively investigated by a team of internationally renowned experts in human organ transplantation. This team was formed following the Vatican Summit on Human Organ Trafficking in 2017, and has undertaken several trips to various provinces in China to meet with doctors, hospital administrators, and government officials. While I have been part of this group, the views expressed in this chapter are entirely my own. As such, I believe that the FLG claims are substantively without merit, and in 2019 I found no compelling evidence of any FLG members being involved in any way in so-called forced organ harvesting. I have additionally been involved in collaborating with Chinese transplantation professionals as the country transitions from using the organs of executed prisoners to an international-standard organ donation system.

There is a major difference between the use of executed prisoners' organs for transplantation and the illusion of "forced organ harvesting." While China has openly admitted that organs used for transplantation in the past have originated from executed prisoners, I have not found any evidence that the executions were incentivized in any way by the fact that the organs of these prisoners were used to save the lives of several other people.

Despite this conclusion, based on several trips to China, the FLG continue to lobby governments and international organizations with what they claim to be evidence of ongoing mass murder of their members in China. There is a clear reason for this; the FLG have invested so much time and effort into promoting so-called forced organ harvesting as their central battleground theme, they must find ways to perpetuate these rumors lest they lose face in the international community.

Likewise, the so-called organ-harvesting theme has provided a useful vehicle for other individuals and groups who actively seek to undermine and destabilize the communist-led government, and has been used by several Western politicians as a platform for an anti-China agenda. Therefore, it seems likely for the foreseeable future that the FLG will continue to lobby for sympathy by screening to selected audiences in political and academic venues propaganda "documentaries" and movies which focus on the so-called forced organ harvesting. The FLG believe that organ harvesting is the most bankable approach to gaining public support. For this reason, it is essential to FLG strategy that they give the false impression to the world that so-called organ harvesting exists in China.

The FLG have been careful to position themselves as victims, and have used this mentality throughout in order to present their case as an underdog against the might of China. The FLG literature is full of "David and Goliath" type political statements. Such positioning by the FLG is indeed ironic. On one hand the organization claims to have millions of active members, yet it enjoys the advantages of positioning itself as a small, feeble underdog. In this paper we explore the manifestations of this victim mentality, through an analysis of the FLG organization and its supporters.

An Overview of the FLG Organization

The origins and beliefs of the FLG organization have been detailed in a multitude of other works and it is not the intention to repeat these here. I have, however, developed a classification system for different levels or tiers of membership, which are not reported elsewhere and are introduced below. Note that these classifications are not recognized, accepted, or approved by the FLG organization.

While the FLG label all followers as practitioners, for the purpose of this paper we classify FLG membership into three distinct tiers. At the base of the FLG are Tier 1 *Practitioners*, members with casual affiliation and limited commitment to the organization. These are principally individuals attracted to the organization's exercise and meditation programs. Tier 1 practitioners have little interest in FLG politics and experience few barriers to entering or exiting the organization. These individuals, however, do provide a vital cover for the political wing of the FLG.

Tier 2 *Cultivators* of the FLG have made a commitment to work towards the end goal of *Consummation* and follow FLG doctrine faithfully. They are actively involved in the political operations of the organization. They are committed to cultivation, a key concept of FLG belief and as such are required to make personal sacrifices for the political benefit of the organization. They are actively involved in activities specifically designed to inflict maximum damage to the reputation of China on the global stage.

Finally, at the highest level are the Tier 3 *Leaders*. They control the information on the FLG websites and media, and provide political guidance to the FLG organization. Tier 3 Leaders do not necessarily follow FLG doctrine, but are all revered by the Tier 2 Cultivators for their leadership and guidance. They flourish in the FLG inner circle and comprise university faculty, politicians, and other educated individuals. While Li Hongzhi is the designated spiritual leader, this group of intellectuals appears to constitute the executive responsible for political strategy. These individuals are widely promoted by *The Epoch Times* newspaper, the principal media outlet of the FLG. A series of professionally produced propaganda materials, presented as documentaries, have been widely distributed internationally on behalf of this executive.

The Tier 3 leaders have developed an effective method of communication with practitioners using online technologies which provide the capability to update key political documents in real time. FLG practitioners are, where possible, directed to the online rather than printed version of doctrine. This has given those in control of the FLG media the power to change specific beliefs and communicate expected political behaviors of their members. The leadership additionally manages the multitude of subsidiary groups responsible for propaganda dissemination. In 2019, DAFOH (Doctors Against Forced Organ Harvesting) is perhaps the most vocal of these quasi-organizations.

The overarching theme, however, regardless of the tier of membership, is that FLG present themselves as victims, and, as such, the organization appears to believe that it is excused from normal societal expectations of true representation of facts and transparency. As victim and underdog, the FLG executive believes it can justify harassing any individual or organization thought to stand in the way of its political objectives.

FLG Claims of So-called Organ Harvesting – Situation in January 2019

International FLG activism is often directed towards medical specialists involved in organ transplantation, as part of a coordinated campaign to attract worldwide sympathy by making claims of so-called organ harvesting. This has now apparently become the *raison d'être* of the organization.

In January 2015, China officially outlawed the use of executed prisoner organs for transplantation. In its place, the government began to develop a deceased organ donation system. By September 2016, there was a marked reduction in foreigners who successfully obtained organ transplantation in China. Indeed, I met Chinese nationals who had travelled to other countries for transplantation, given the shortage of organs now existing in China. As of January 2019, there are only isolated cases of foreigners travelling to China for the purpose of organ transplantation, and this is occurring in "rogue" hospitals operating in a clandestine manner without government approval. This compares with the literally hundreds of foreigners who were travelling to China for transplantation prior to the reforms being established. Despite this, the FLG leadership have continued to perpetuate their claims. If the so-called "organ harvesting" claim loses credibility, then the FLG will lose the principal persecution argument they have been presenting to the world.

As mentioned above, I have been a member of an international team with expertise in a range of different aspects of organ transplantation who are regularly in China working with transplant professionals there. The group engages with Chinese doctors who provide treatment to patients waiting for organ transplants, prepare patients for transplantation surgery, and provide lifelong aftercare for patients after they receive a replacement organ. The group also engages with the surgeons who recover organs from donors and transplant them into recipients. They additionally work with Chinese organ-procurement organizations (OPOs), who are responsible for locating and recovering organs, and are also the institutions responsible for organ allocation, and they decide who receives recovered organs, using an algorithm based on both clinical need and time on a waiting list. Finally, the team works with hospital administrators, Ministry of Health representatives, and patient advocacy groups.

I have not found credible evidence of systemic organ harvesting in China in 2019, and I continue to support and encourage the ongoing reforms. I have only found historical evidence of executed prisoners being used as a major source of organs for transplantation, a practice that the Chinese government openly admits to. However, we must remain vigilant to ensure that organs from executed prisoners do not once again become the dominant source of organs for transplantation. At a practical level this involves investigating Chinese hospitals that engage in organ trafficking. Major improvements have taken place, although the new system is still very much a work in progress.

The Falun Gong Political Narrative 235

Despite the evidence presented, the FLG continue to insist that they have been victims of forced organ harvesting, both historically and currently. The campaign that they operate is well documented elsewhere, but it is worthwhile to explore why the FLG have chosen forced organ harvesting as their central theme.

Firstly, FLG doctrine appears to be very suspicious of the medical profession in general. This been used to great advantage by the FLG Tier 3 leaders. FLG cultivators are taught to be extremely sceptical of the whole concept of transplantation. The author was told by individuals purporting to be FLG practitioners in Hong Kong, protesting outside a transplantation conference, that people with organ failure should be left to die. Organ failure, the author was told, is the result of karma, and any attempt to rectify this through using another's organ merely overwhelms and destroys the transplanted organ. It is possible that the reason FLG leaders have targeted organ transplant surgeons in their political propaganda is that the story will easily be understood and accepted by Tier 2 cultivators. It has high impact in the internal environment of FLG life, and fits into its ongoing narrative.

Looking at the external environment of the FLG, the fact that China has historically utilized organs of executed prisoners to save the lives of people in need of transplants provided the basis for a prima facie victim claim. The FLG executive thought they had a watertight story, in the mistaken belief that nobody outside China would check the veracity of the claims. The FLG believed they had such a perfect victim story that they developed it into the central theme of their campaign against the Chinese Communist Party.

However, the welcoming of Chinese transplant professionals into the international community led to close and high-level engagement between China and several other countries with highly developed transplantation systems. This engagement during 2016 and 2017 led to a collaborative approach to developing transplantation in China according to international standards, leading to a significantly better understanding of what really happens in relation to organ donation and transplantation in China. It is through this engagement that we can confidently state that the FLG claims are without basis.

236 *Enlightened Martyrdom*

This international engagement has been a public relations disaster for the FLG. They have fought hard against this interaction, organizing desperate protests at the Hong Kong Transplantation Congress in September 2016, the Vatican Organ Trafficking Summit in February 2017, and the Organ Donation Congress in Geneva in September 2017.

In late 2017, in apparent reaction to the expert visits to China, the FLG appeared to be attempting to win support from wider constituencies. For example, when Western politicians or journalists wish to make an anti-China comment, they may make reference to so-called organ harvesting as a way to build their case. The perpetuation of the rumor in such circles is now an important strategy of the FLG. However, this strategy is not without risks. In October 2017, media sympathetic to the FLG ran a story suggesting that the MH370 airplane tragedy had links to so-called organ harvesting. Such an outlandish theory is unlikely to further the FLG cause, especially in relation to the suffering such claims will cause to families of MH370 victims, desperate to find some closure on the loss of their loved ones.

Truth versus "Truth"

While so-called "Truth" is known for being one of the key foundations of FLG doctrine, the concept of "Clarifying the Truth" appears to relate principally to a carefully orchestrated release of propaganda to a global audience for political purposes, rather than for consideration as a core internal value.

With the FLG positioning themselves as victims, their "research" and "evidence" are often not subjected to anything close to the level of scrutiny that regular university researchers are required to achieve. Indeed, several Western journalists and academics have reported to me that they have not challenged the FLG "research" findings because they consider the FLG to be "victims." There is also a reluctance amongst Western journalists and university faculty to challenge FLG "truth" for fear of retaliation and revenge attacks.

I personally have first-hand experience of such attacks, as have several other independent scholars of FLG. In addition, FLG "research" is not subjected to the ethical approval processes required in most research organizations. The research methodologies purported to be used by the FLG lack all accepted standards of rigor, and the data presented at international conferences have not been collected in accordance with internationally acceptable standards.

Building on this notion of FLG "truth," I talked with several people identifying with the FLG while they were distributing copies of *The Epoch Times* outside an international transplantation conference in Hong Kong in August 2016. On each occasion, a claim was made by the distributor that *The Epoch Times* represented the "truth." The overall objective of "truth" in 2019 appears concerned primarily with attempting to mobilize large numbers of political activists. It is also an attempt to recruit influential people and organizations outside China to support their cause. The so-called "organ harvesting" claims provide a convenient, high-impact and hard-hitting vehicle to carry the FLG's cause forward.

A final important aspect is the assumption that anyone who dares challenge so-called "organ harvesting" is automatically an enemy of all human rights activists and a collaborator with the Chinese government. This is a complete logical fallacy. To the best of my knowledge, none of the transplantation experts who have challenged the FLG organ claims, or religious studies scholars who have criticized FLG doctrine, have any specific political affiliation with the Chinese government or the Communist Party of China. The claims are rejected because they appear to be false and fabricated, not because they conflict with any political ideology or system of national governance.

The Victims of the FLG

While the FLG have intentionally positioned themselves as being the "victims," it is worthwhile to explore the fact that the FLG Tier 3 leadership has in many respects been responsible for creating its own victims. In September 2017 I met former FLG members who had been incarcerated at a "re-education" facility. In my conversations with these individuals, I learned of the pressure they felt to conform with the requirements of the FLG leadership, even if it meant potentially breaking the law in China and being subjected to legal sanctions. This does not mean, however, that I in any way condone the use of these "re-education" facilities, the existence of which has been widely criticized by those outside of China.

Regardless of any individual opinion about the outlawing of FLG in China, it is an indisputable fact that the FLG leadership, now based in the USA, specifically pressured members inside China to break the law. This is clearly not in the best interests of the individual. The individual FLG member is placed at risk of legal sanctions and can be claimed by the FLG as their own "victim," which they can then use for their own propaganda purposes. These Tier 2 cultivators, in an act of loyalty and devotion to the FLG, took up the political cause, believing it would accelerate their own cultivation. The Tier 3 leaders, however, left China with great haste when FLG transitioned into politics, and resettled in the USA, where other Tier 3 leaders were recruited to lead strategic transformation into a politically active organization. Most troubling of all is the fact that the FLG leadership does not appear to put itself in physical danger, yet enjoys the political advantage it can leverage internationally by claiming its members are persecuted. To put it simply, the FLG Tier 3 leaders are directly responsible for placing their members in situations which inevitably lead to them breaking the criminal law in China.

Perhaps the most concerning group of victims are the family members of FLG. Following informal conversations with the families of FLG members in both New York and Taipei in 2016, I discovered that in many cases the grown-up children of Tier 2 cultivators have lost a parent, usually a mother, to the FLG. They claim that their mothers' first love is to the FLG, not to their own children. The doctrine of abandonment of attachments has been interpreted by some FLG members as an abandonment of family – with love, affection, and sense of belonging being primarily directed to FLG life instead.

The New York group widely reported that family un-attachment is not necessarily a sudden event and, unlike other cults, it does not involve the open denouncement of family. Instead, adult children report a gradual and consistent withdrawal of their mothers from family life, and a distinct lack of physical affection. Bizarrely, there also appears to be a lack of any attempt to include family members in their FLG cultivation. This can perhaps be explained by the fact that family members are perceived as being attachments, therefore un-attachment has more efficacy in the quest for cultivation than would be found by merely recruiting family members. One adult child additionally reported that his FLG mother refused to speak to him because she suspected he was homosexual (homosexuality appears to be forbidden in FLG doctrine). Another adult child reported that her FLG mother had denounced her because she had married a man of another race. Interracial relationships also appear to be problematic to some devout FLG cultivators.

The Taipei group of FLG family members revealed a particularly concerning set of issues, which focused on FLG cultivators refusing medical treatment from doctors, not only for themselves, but also for their children. While the ambivalence of the FLG towards conventional medicine is well documented elsewhere, the withholding of medical care for children represents unacceptable behavior which has to be condemned. These innocent victims not only lost the normal love and safety of the family unit, but also were placed in possible direct harm from lack of access to medical care.

FLG as a Political Organization

This chapter has evaluated the FLG in terms of their strategic positioning as a victimized organization. This has remained a consistent theme throughout the transition from a quasi-spiritual to a political organization. When FLG entered the political arena, many thousands of Tier 1 practitioners left the organization, having no interest in political activism. The hard core of Tier 2 cultivators remained with the FLG, with a smaller but more intensely devoted level of membership. In 2019, little remains of the original organization, other than the brand and a series of teachings which have now been manipulated to have different meanings for this new political organization.

The growing influence of China on the political and economic landscape of several regions of the world has given rise to significant debate and discussion in Western political parties, governments, and media organizations. This has proved lucrative for the FLG claims of so-called forced organ harvesting, which have provided a foundation for favorable coverage of FLG as part of an overall reaction to the rise of China. This is happening in an era when Western media organizations routinely have their budgets slashed, and no longer have the resources and capabilities to carry out long-term investigative journalism. Several FLG documents can be found "cut-and-pasted" into Western media stories without any serious attempt at verification. This is convenient and inexpensive copy for media campaigns lamenting the growth of China and its impact on domestic affairs and has been a significant windfall for the FLG propaganda machine.

The FLG have additionally recruited sympathizers who provide pro bono political, propaganda, and doctrine consultancy. These consultants receive favorable exposure in *The Epoch Times* ad nauseam, and become heroes of the FLG. There are a number of older politicians, lawyers, and academics who have positioned themselves to take advantage of the fame offered by *The Epoch Times*, and use this to create a legacy for themselves as anti-China activists. While they are not necessarily salaried as such, they gain a loyal following from cultivators, which raises their international profile. This allows them to amass popularity on social media. The inertia of this popularity leads to paid speaking engagements around the world, which, cumulatively, equates to potentially significant remuneration.

Is the FLG a Cult?

I have stated on numerous occasions in public forums that in my opinion the FLG is a cult. There are a number of reasons for this position, but the overarching factor that defines FLG as a cult can be found in the organization's reaction to any party who dares criticize them. The FLG have made several formal complaints to my employer, and also made attempts to have my work withdrawn from international human organ transplantation conferences. Rather than attempt to debate me on issues with which they disagree, in the normal and accepted academic way, the FLG choose the cowardly approach and attempt to block me from speaking. This behavior has been recognized as diagnostic of the existence of a cult.

Moreover, the FLG leadership uses *The Epoch Times* as an additional medium of retaliation. A common approach appears to be publishing an op-ed piece in either *The Epoch Times* or one of several other online FLG media which attempt to discredit those who oppose them. A typical retaliation will state that the academic does not have the qualifications to understand FLG, and therefore what they have written is wrong. Academics have reported being heckled at conferences with general insults and have been told, in public, that they are "stupid" and "nobody takes you seriously" while trying to give a public presentation. This vitriolic response from the FLG is, once again, the epitome of cult response. These attacks are typically backed up by an email-writing campaign. I myself receive daily emails from the FLG and its sympathizers.

Having positioned itself as a victim, the FLG can make repeated claims against any party, with no consequences whatsoever if its claim fails. For most professional scholars, a formal complaint about another scholar's conduct would have far-reaching consequences if it was determined to be without merit. It could potentially be very damaging to the professional reputation of the scholar and could possibly result in legal action. However, there are no such consequences for the FLG. For this reason, scholars critical of the FLG know that they will receive constant and repeated complaints, to each of which they will be required to make a full and comprehensive response. These repeating cycles have now become commonplace for all authors who criticize the FLG, and have just become part of their routine work.

Conclusion

In this chapter I have explored how the FLG have used a strategy of victimization in order to pursue their political agenda against the Chinese government or any party which dares to speak out against them. Despite the fact that a group of international experts have made repeated trips to China and found no evidence of so-called forced organ harvesting, the FLG continue to make claims to the contrary. Their so-called "research" appears to have avoided any serious scrutiny by a research ethics body, and, as such, would be unpublishable according to protocols followed by practically all research establishments throughout the world. The FLG have built an expansive media network to disseminate this "research," and to broadcast their agenda. They have additionally found support among Western journalists and scholars who oppose China's growing role in the global political and economic environment. Any scholar who challenges the "research findings" of the FLG is subjected to ongoing and relentless revenge attacks, both professional and personal.

Organ transplant professionals throughout the world will continue to establish collaborative partnerships with their colleagues in China, regardless of any attempts by the FLG to frustrate this process. Although dealing with the repeated complaints and protests does take some time and can be a nuisance, it merely motivates those who believe in the real truth, not FLG "truth," to continue to make progress and develop closer links with transplantation professionals in China.

The support for the FLG in Western media and academia appears to be primarily a reaction to China's growing influence in world affairs, rather than being specifically related to the FLG claims. For this reason, as the world adjusts to this new global order, it is likely that such support will wane. The FLG have not presented any new compelling evidence for several years. Indeed, while they celebrate ten years since the publication of their organ-harvesting propaganda material, they demonstrate that they have nothing new to offer other than recycled myths from a decade ago.

In addition, as organ transplantation in China becomes more integrated with the international transplant community, it will become harder for the FLG to perpetuate their unfounded claims. It is therefore essential that the international transplant community continues in partnership with China to work towards solving the global shortage of organs for transplantation and to develop solutions that will benefit all patients who need access to timely transplantation services.

The long-term viability of FLG will be dependent on its being able to attract young people to the organization, especially those of Chinese origin. However, it is unlikely that it will be able to attract new, younger recruits in sufficient numbers. I have had widespread engagement with members of the Chinese diaspora around the world, and on the whole they appear to be dismissive of the FLG. For this reason, the FLG cannot become a sustainable political force. Youth in the Chinese diaspora appear to be particularly suspicious of the FLG, mainly in relation to the impact the organization has on traditional family values. It is therefore most probable that over time the FLG will reduce in size and eventually, like so many cults before it, cease to exist within a few years.

Campbell Fraser is a senior lecturer in the Department of Business Strategy and Innovation at Griffith University in Brisbane, Australia, and an international authority on human organ trafficking. He serves on the advisory boards of both organ-procurement organizations and kidney disease advocacy groups, and is an active member of The Transplantation Society and the International Society of Organ Donation and Procurement. He has developed protocols for proactively combating human organ trafficking, and has implemented investigative and reporting mechanisms to verify claims of such activity. He has a specific interest in the link between human organ trafficking and terrorist funding, and the emerging problem of political special-interest groups fabricating stories of so-called forced organ harvesting. His work regularly appears on television, radio, newspaper, and online media in several countries and in multiple languages.

12. "Clarifying the Truth"
Falun Gong's Media Strategies

James R. Lewis

The Falun Gong (FLG) organization has been mostly successful at promoting itself to the world outside of mainland China as a peaceful spiritual exercise group that is being unfairly persecuted by the Chinese government. This is partly the result of denying or downplaying the aspects of Li Hongzhi's teachings that are vengeful, belligerent, and violent. However, this is also the result of a conscious media strategy which involves, on the one hand, creating its own media outlets that focus on persecution and human rights themes and, on the other hand, deploying a sophisticated media strategy that takes advantage of anti-PRC sentiments in Western media.

Factors in Falun Gong's Media Success

More than ten years ago, Heather Kavan (a contributor to the present volume) read all of the stories with more than a minimum mention of FLG that had been published in Australian and New Zealand newspapers from the time it was first mentioned in May 1999 until the end of June 2005 (excluding Chinese media and FLG's own newspaper, *The Epoch Times*). Her findings remain broadly representative of overall trends and can be extended to the present period and to the Anglophone media world more generally:

> Although studies of the Australian media found that the press tend to discredit new religious movements and magnify their deviance (Richardson, 1996; Selway, 1992), reporters seem to be receptive to Falun Gong, minimising the religion's unusual

"Clarifying the Truth" 245

> beliefs and presenting the movement as compatible with mainstream activities. ... I found that journalists have been supportive of Falun Gong. 61% of reports were favourable, 33% were neutral, and only 6% were negative. (Kavan 2005)

Given these rather remarkable statistics and the sharp contrast between media treatments of FLG and of other new religious movements (the latter being mostly negative), the question becomes: Why is FLG treated differently? I believe this arises from a combination of different factors.

In the first place, as other chapters in the present collection point out, Li Hongzhi (LHZ) explicitly discourages followers from telling outsiders about the group's inner teachings, some of which are quite strange, not to mention racist, sexist, and homophobic. Instead, he instructs them to present FLG as an innocent spiritual movement being persecuted by the People's Republic of China (Li Hongzhi 2002, 2003).

A second important factor that plays into Falun Gong's media success is that by shifting conversations about FLG away from the group's inner teachings to a discourse about human rights, FLG is able to situate itself in a popular interpretive framework which views the People's Republic of China through the lens of political repression. In an article originally published in 1999, James Mann argues that stories about China in the American media (and, by extension, Western media more generally) "tend to be governed at any given time by a single story, image or concept":

> In the 1950s and the 1960s, the "frame" was of China as little blue ants or automatons. In the 1970s, following the Nixon administration's opening, the frame was of the virtuous (entertaining, cute) Chinese, displaying their timeless qualities even under communism. In the 1980s, the frame was that China was "going capitalist." And for most of the 1990s, the frame was of a repressive China. ... since the American frame of the 1990s says that China is a repressive regime, then virtually every story about China seems obliged at some point to mention the theme of political repression. (Mann 1999)

246 *Enlightened Martyrdom*

In other words, the storyline that LHZ encourages his followers to present to outsiders fits nicely into a narrative that Westerners are prepared to hear – it reinforces what they already think they know about China.¹

Over and above this narrative frame, it is, of course, objectively the case that China is and has been repressing FLG – a factor that should be analytically separated from the larger generic interpretive frame that observers bring to media reports about the PRC. However, this factor is not as simple as it first appears. To repeat a point made in other chapters in this book, "by their provocative acts," it is clear that followers "deliberately seek" and provoke brutalization at the hands of authorities (David Palmer, this volume). In the early days following the banning of the movement, individual practitioners could avoid jail terms simply by signing a statement renouncing Falun Gong. LHZ, however, preached the spiritual benefits of being persecuted (Lewis 2016) – even going so far as promising full "Consummation" to those who made the ultimate sacrifice (Susan Palmer, this volume). I would not normally include facts on the ground such as these as being part of a larger media *strategy*. In this case, however, Li Hongzhi's conscious intention behind encouraging protest and resistance in China seems to have been that he expected the media spectacle of practitioners being brutalized by police would evoke international outrage, thereby bringing pressure to bear on the PRC to lift the ban on FLG.

Yet another factor is FLG's various media enterprises and sophisticated use of the internet. The group was already effectively using email in China for the purpose of organizing demonstrations (e.g., the Zhongnanhai demonstration) before being banned (Bell and Boas 2003, 283). Four years later, practitioners were maintaining "hundreds of sites around the world" (ibid., 278). This number has undoubtedly multiplied in the intervening dozen years, due, in part,

---

1. It should also be noted that the stereotype of "oriental despotism" has a long history, antedating the formation of the People's Republic of China by centuries (Mackerras 1999, 186).

to the fact that "most overseas members are Chinese students and scholars who have both easy access to the Internet and the requisite cultural capital and technical capabilities" (Zhao 2003, 214).

> At the global level, [this] has ensured that [FLG's] interpretation of events prevails over that of the PRC government. Western press coverage has been overwhelmingly supportive of Falun Gong and critical of PRC authorities, and negative assessments of the movement outside of the PRC are few and far between. Undoubtedly, the extensive information which practitioners have posted on their websites provides a ready resource for sympathetic journalists with tight deadlines. (Bell and Boas 2003, 287)

Additionally, by May 2000 – shortly following the ban – members had set up their own newspaper (*The Epoch Times*) outside of China and were publishing it on the web by August. In 2001 they established New Tang Dynasty TV (initially in New York), a channel directed particularly to the Chinese diaspora. Sound of Hope radio was initiated in 2003. Beginning in 1999, Western media outlets who lacked their own reporters on the ground in China have received "most of their international information about Falun Gong from press releases from the Rachlin media group. What we are not told is that this group is essentially a public relations firm for Falun Gong, managed by Gail Rachlin – one of Li's most avid disciples who is also spokesperson of the Falun Dafa Information Centre" (Kavan 2005).

FLG has thus been able to influence other media via its extensive presence on the web, through its direct press releases, and through its own media. Falun Gong has also been able to propagate its point of view indirectly, through other, non-FLG sources, which creates the impression of multiple sources for the same narrative. Thus, for example, "The press often quote Amnesty International, but Amnesty's reports are not independently verified, and mainly come from Falun Gong sources" (ibid.). Additionally, Falun Gong followers and/or sympathizers de facto control the relevant webpages

248 *Enlightened Martyrdom*

in Wikipedia.[2] FLG's domination of their Wikipedia pages is especially important,

> because Wikipedia's articles are the first- or second-ranked results for most Internet searches. ... This means that the content of these articles really matters. Wikipedia's standards of inclusion – what's in and what's not – affect the work of journalists, who routinely read Wikipedia articles and then repeat the wikiclaims as "background" without bothering to cite them. (Garfinkel 2008)[3]

Journalists often work under tight deadlines (Kavan 2005). As a consequence, Wikipedia seems to offer an attractive option as a seemingly independent, neutral source of information. However, like Amnesty International reports, relevant Wikipedia entries turn out to be little more than mouthpieces for the FLG point of view.

Yet another factor for understanding FLG's media dominance is that the PRC seems to have mostly abandoned the media field outside of China. The People's Republic of China's point of view on FLG is sometimes represented to the outside world by such periodicals as the *People's Daily* and on Chinese Embassy websites in other countries, but the only sustained counter-voice from China is the "Facts" website (http://www.facts.org.cn/).

"Rectifying the Truth": The Development of Falun Gong's Attack Strategies

One final but highly significant factor in Falun Gong's overall media strategy has been its attacks on critical media, which later expanded to include demands to be given fora for expressing their messages. This media warfare emerged as a core tactic some years before the

2. E.g., in this regard refer to Sheng Jiang (2015) and Colipon (2014).
3. For some academics, Wikipedia "seems to represent the worst of how the Internet has dumbed down the research process, with its easily accessible but unsubstantiated (if not downright false) information" (Crovitz and Smoot 2009, 91).

"Clarifying the Truth" 249

group was banned. More specifically, after FLG had grown into a large enough movement in China to attract media attention, "Falun Gong's consistent response to any negative media story [was to relentlessly] counterattack against the responsible outlets [using] strategies ranging from exercising in front of news organizations to harassing individual editors and reporters" (Zhao Yuezhi 2003, 214–15).

> Between 1996 and mid-1999, practitioners initiated over 300 protests against negative media reports, forcing dismissals of reporters and receiving public apologies. In China the media are free only as far as they facilitate social stability, so when Falun Gong threatened civil unrest, media managers were quick to capitulate to their demands. For example, when 2,000 protestors surrounded Beijing Television after the station broadcast a segment about a doctoral candidate who became psychotic while practising Falun Gong, the station fired the reporter, aired an immediate sympathetic portrayal, and – to show extra goodwill – handed out 2,000 boxed lunches to the protestors. [Then, h]aving learnt that such protests were fruitful, Falun Gong members [became] unstoppable. To prevent social unrest, Beijing authorities introduced a blackout against any negative media reports on the movement. (Kavan 2008, 3)

One should also understand that FLG demanded more than simply "the right to reply to media criticism: It demanded the censorship of opponents' views in the first place. ... [In fact,] the movement actually urged the Chinese government to use its powers of censorship to muzzle the opponents of Falun Gong" (Zhao Yuezhi 2003, 215).

FLG seems to have been unique among *qigong* groups (most of which were experiencing criticism in the late 1990s) in vigorously counterattacking its critics. This almost certainly means that followers were ultimately receiving their marching orders from LHZ himself – though he disingenuously attributed such actions to the independent initiative of others in the movement. Thus, for example, in "Digging Out the Roots," an essay published a year before FLG was banned, LHZ refers to defending the "Dafa" – a complex term

250 *Enlightened Martyrdom*

comparable to the Buddhist "Dharma" and the Taoist "Tao" (though, in Falun Gong circles, equivalent to Li Hongzhi's teachings):

> Recently, a few scoundrels from literary, scientific, and *qigong* circles, who have been hoping to become famous through opposing *qigong*, have been constantly causing trouble, as though the last thing they want to see is a peaceful world. Some newspapers, radio stations and TV stations in various parts of the country have directly resorted to these propaganda tools to harm our Dafa, having a very bad impact on the public. This was deliberately harming Dafa and cannot be ignored. Under these very special circumstances, Dafa disciples in Beijing adopted a special approach to ask those people to stop harming Dafa – this actually was not wrong. This was done when there was no other way … when students voluntarily approach those uninformed and irresponsible media agencies and explain to them our true situation, this should not be considered wrong. (Li Hongzhi 1998)

At the time, LHZ was insisting that FLG was not a political movement, an identification that would have immediately provoked government suppression. Thus, in the same essay, he tries to describe these essentially political actions as non-political: "I have said that Dafa absolutely should not get involved in politics. The purpose of this event itself was to help the media understand our actual situation and learn about us positively so that they would not drag us into politics" (ibid.).

After being banned in the PRC, Falun Gong continued aggressively seeking to silence critics. As an example of the movement's efforts to suppress contrary voices, in 2001 the Canadian *La Presse Chinoise* [*Chinese Press*] published a critical piece based around the testimony of a former practitioner. In that case, the newspaper was sued for libel. Four years later, Quebec's Supreme Court decided against the plaintiff. The ruling included the statement that "Falun Gong is a controversial movement which does not accept criticism." Similarly, in response to a condemnatory statement published in the *Chinese Daily* newspaper in Australia, Falun Gong filed a

"Clarifying the Truth" 251

defamation lawsuit in 2004. Two years later, the Supreme Court of New South Wales ruled in favor of the *Chinese Daily* (Lewis 2016).

There have been a number of other lawsuits, but in most cases practitioners rely upon different tactics – though often using the implied *threat* of lawsuits as part of their overall strategy. Thus, for example, in response to an AP piece in 2005, "Chinese Show off Repentant Falun Gong" (Associated Press 2005), practitioners staged a protest at AP headquarters and demanded that the report be withdrawn. And to refer to one more example, in 2008 the *New York Times* published an article, "A Glimpse of Chinese Culture That Some Find Hard to Watch" (Konigsberg 2008), critical of a Shen Yun program that had been promoted as a Chinese cultural event, but which included a heavily politicized attack on the PRC by the FLG. Movement websites responded with dozens of pieces attacking both the newspaper and the article's author.

According to incomplete statistics, FLG practitioners have filed over 100 lawsuits since 2001 in countries as diverse as the United States, Canada, Sweden, Germany, Belgium, Spain, South Korea, Greece, Australia, Bolivia, and the Netherlands, but have seldom won; perhaps like the Church of Scientology, FLG values lawsuits as more of a harassment tactic than as actions they actually hope to win (China Association for Cultic Studies 2009). In more recent years, FLG news outlets have tried to reignite international media interest by featuring such stories as the supposed mass renunciation of the Communist Party by members within China (which most other media recognize as implausible) and the supposed mass harvesting of organs from imprisoned FLG members. Before concluding this chapter, it will repay our efforts if we examine this last claim in a little more detail.

Falun Gong's Promotion of the Organ-harvesting Controversy

The People's Republic of China has acknowledged that it formerly took organs from executed prisoners for the purpose of organ transplants. China officially stopped extracting organs from prisoners in 2015 (Li Ruohan 2017). This practice, which was formally authorized by the PRC in 1984, came to be referred to as "the 1984 policy." Originally an internal government document, a copy of this policy was made public in 1995 by the prominent China critic, Harry Wu (Junker 2016, 23). The organ-harvesting controversy refers to the specific accusation that the PRC was systematically using political prisoners – especially living Falun Gong prisoners (who were regarded as political prisoners) – for this purpose. Furthermore, practitioners insist that FLG prisoners continue to be executed for transplant purposes, and thus they dispute claims that this practice has ceased. The Chinese authorities, on the other hand, assert that political prisoners were never killed solely for their organs. As of this writing, Falun Gong followers continue to mount vigorous protests against this practice, despite convincing evidence that executed prisoners are no longer used as sources of transplanted organs (e.g., Associated Press 2017; *China Daily* 2017).

The controversy began in 2006, when Falun Gong started promoting the accusation that China was "harvesting" organs from, and then murdering, imprisoned practitioners for the purpose of selling them on the international organ market. The central point of reference for this accusation was the 2006 report by David Kilgour and David Matas, "An Independent Investigation into Allegations of Organ Harvesting of Falun Gong Practitioners in China." On the positive side, the authors were both credible voices: Kilgour was a former Canadian MP, while Matas was a human rights lawyer. Negatively, however, the report was sponsored by the Coalition to Investigate the Persecution of Falun Gong, a FLG-affiliated organization. Additionally, the "investigators" never conducted any original research of their own in China, but rather relied upon questionable sources, mostly provided by Falun Gong, and inferences from available transplant data. Three years later, Kilgour and Matas had an expanded, updated version of their report published under the title *Bloody Harvest: The Killing of Falun Gong for Their Organs* (2009). More recently, Ethan Gutmann has written a related book that was published as *The Slaughter: Mass Killings, Organ*

Harvesting, and China's Secret Solution to Its Dissident Problem (2014).

The initial claims of involuntary mass organ extractions from FLG prisoners emerged in March of 2006. Two anonymous individuals stepped forward who claimed to have direct knowledge of an organ-harvesting operation at the Sujiatun Thrombosis Hospital in Shenyang in Liaoning province. These accusations were subsequently reported by the *Epoch Times*, the Falun Gong-affiliated newspaper to which I have already referred. Shortly after the allegations appeared in *Epoch Times*, non-affiliated investigators, which included official representatives of the U.S. Department of State, visited Sujiatun and concluded that there was insufficient evidence to support the allegations.

Additionally, in September of the same year, Harry Wu – the same person who had originally exposed China's practice of transplanting organs from executed prisoners – began very publicly to express the opinion that the scope of Falun Gong's claim of the large number of people killed at Sujiatun was simply not possible. Additionally, Wu also pointed out that:

> Falun Gong's claims are not corroborated by photos, documents or detailed information, but are based on the testimony of [a] few witnesses, neither of whom had first-hand information. "I tried several times to see the witnesses, but they said no," he explained. "Even today, I don't know their names." The two witnesses, who are now in the West, have refused to meet international agencies to provide more detailed information. Since they claim to have knowledge about thousands of people whose lives may be in danger it would be essential they be more open. Mr. Wu said he sent his own investigators but they failed to find the concentration camp or corroborate the claims of forced organ removals. According to Mr Wu, ... Falun Gong's claim that they are victims of an Auschwitz-like camp runs the risk of being treated as "political propaganda." (*AsiaNews.it* 2006)

However, the story did not end here. Wu subsequently authored an essay in which he described his experiences investigating Falun

Gong's concentration-camp accusations. In that essay, he revealingly described:

> ...being threatened by senior Falun Gong representatives, who counseled him to keep his reservations to himself. Rather than heed this advice, Wu shared his concerns in writing with a member of the US Congress, whose staff leaked the letter to high-ranking Falun Gong representatives in the United States. Shortly thereafter, Falun Gong-related media outlets, including "Secret China" [a Falun Gong-related YouTube activity] and *The Epoch Times* began a coordinated smear campaign against Harry Wu, publishing accusations that he was a "butcher," a "Chinese Communist senior-level spy," and that Wu had "betrayed his conscience and the conscience of the Chinese people." (Thornton 2008, 200)

Conclusion – Theorizing Falun Gong's Media Strategies

There have been several attempts to theorize the conflict between Falun Gong and the Chinese authorities, from Junpeng Li's application of a conflict-amplification model (see Chapter 1 in this collection) to my and Nicole D'Amico's partial application of a moral panic approach (Lewis and D'Amico 2017). To focus more specifically on FLG's media strategies, Andrew Junker used the notion of tactical repertoires developed by social movement theorists (e.g., Tilly 1994; Taylor and Van Dyke 2004) to contrast Falun Gong's approach to protest against PRC authorities with the Chinese democracy movement's approach. The aspect of his analysis that is particularly relevant to my analysis here is his discussion of how "[f]amiliar strategies of action shape what actors attempt to accomplish" (Junker 2014, 333). Junker demonstrates that both movements rely upon strategies they had developed in China as the basis for their continued demonstrations in other countries. Thus, for example, both movements used the tactic of posting petitions or open letters in China, and continue to use this tactic overseas. FLG utilized public displays of Falun Gong exercises to attract attention in China and continues to deploy the same tactic outside of China (which has no parallel in the democracy movement). And the Chinese democracy movement fund-raised in China and continues to fund-raise overseas (which has no direct parallel in FLG).

However, Junker's reliance on a "tool kit" approach causes him to focus on specific, ground-level tactics and to miss larger strategies such as Falun Gong's attacks on media outlets that broadcast critical stories. For a few years in the late 1990s, FLG enjoyed marked success counter-attacking media critics in the PRC, and seems stuck in this approach as a way of silencing critics outside of China – without considering the ill-will that this tactic potentially evokes.

Using the examples of Suma Ching Hai International, Zhong Gong and Falun Gong/Falun Dafa, the potential for expatriate protest to backfire on protesting groups (which she refers to as "cybersects") is discussed in Patricia M. Thornton's chapter in Kevin J. O'Brien's volume, *Popular Protest in China* (2008). Thornton builds her analysis on what Keck and Sikkink (1998) term "boomerangs" of transnational support, which are attempts to mobilize international networks and international opinion as part of an effort to force change back home. However, she points out that cultivating a boomerang effect

> ... comes, not infrequently, at a cost: the bids of these banned sects for transnational support have resulted in increased domestic and international scrutiny of their internal affairs and public relations tactics, and have occasionally produced a backlash of negative media attention for both the networks and their supporters. In contrast to the transformative backfire generated by repressions, which can produce a "take off" in popular mobilization, backlash undermines the credibility of movement organizers and their capacity to influence established media, politicians, and the public at large. (Thornton 2008, 187–8)

In her section on Falun Gong, she discusses how the group's media outlets – particularly *The Epoch Times* – "manufacture dissent" by promoting an ongoing pseudo-story about supposed mass resignations from the Communist Party of China by high-ranking officials. Though dismissed as "laughable" by other news outlets, *The Epoch Times* and its affiliated organizations continue to maintain a running count of "resignations" on their websites. She also discusses the example of the Falun Gong's attack on the late Harry Wu, the prominent China critic who, as we saw, had challenged Falun Gong's story about the mass harvesting of organs from imprisoned practitioners and the selling of them on the international organ market. Falun Gong viciously attacked Wu, accusing him, among other things, of being on China's payroll – extremely improbable, given Wu's conflicted history with the PRC (ibid., 199–200).

To conclude, Falun Gong's heavy-handed efforts to silence critics are the least palatable of FLG's various strategies aimed at directly influencing the media. This approach even threatens – to use Thorton's term – to "backfire" on FLG, which would thus undermine the movement's PR strategy of painting itself as an innocent spiritual exercise group. FLG could be proactive and save itself from this negative scenario, but LHZ seems to have become progressively more antagonistic toward international media and thus not inclined to call a halt to his followers' belligerent activities in this arena. It thus seems only a matter of time before global media outlets wake up and begin to re-perceive Falun Gong as a negative organization – as a kind of Chinese Church of Scientology – that will likely slowly decline in numbers and influence and gradually fade away.

References

AsiaNews.it. 2006. "Harry Wu Questions Falun Gong's Claims about Organ Transplants."
http://www.asianews.it/news-en/Harry-Wu-questions-Falun-Gong's-claims-about-organ-transplants-6919.html (accessed July 18, 2015).

Associated Press. 2005. "Chinese Show Off Repentant Falun Gong." http://www.washingtonpost.com/wp-dyn/articles/A26902-2005Jan21_2.html (accessed June 5, 2015).

Associated Press. 2017. "U.N. Wary But Sees Progress in China Moves to Stop Taking Executed Inmates' Organs."
http://www.japantimes.co.jp/news/2017/02/10/asia-pacific/u-n-wary-sees-progress-china-moves-stop-taking-executed-inmates-organs/#.WKD7WPkrJPZ (accessed February 12, 2017).

Bell, Mark R., and Taylor C. Boas. 2003. "Falun Gong and the Internet: Evangelism, Community, and Struggle for Survival," *Nova Religio: The Journal of Alternative and Emergent Religions*, 6:2 (online).

China Association for Cultic Studies. 2009. "Lodging False Accusations and Filing Abusive Lawsuits Outside China."
http://www.facts.org.cn/Feature/hand/political/200904/08/t20090408_781013.htm (accessed February 2, 2017).

China Daily. 2017. "Organ Transplant Claims Rejected," February 15. http://www.china.org.cn/china/2017-02/15/content_40289449.htm (accessed February 15, 2017).

Colipon. 2014. User: Colipon/Falun Gong.
https://en.wikipedia.org/wiki/User:Colipon/Falun_Gong (accessed June 20, 2016).

Crovitz, Darren, and W. Scott Smoot. 2009. "Wikipedia: Friend, Not Foe," *The English Journal*, 98:3, 91–7.

Garfinkel, Simson L. 2008. "Wikipedia and the Meaning of Truth: Why the Online Encyclopedia's Epistemology Should Worry Those Who Care about Traditional Notions of Accuracy," *MIT Technology Review* (online). https://www.technologyreview.com/s/411041/wikipedia-and-the-meaning-of-truth/ (accessed July 9, 2016).

Gutmann, Ethan. 2014. *The Slaughter: Mass Killings, Organ Harvesting, and China's Secret Solution to Its Dissident Problem*. Amherst, NY: Prometheus.

Junker, Andrew. 2014. "The Transnational Flow of Tactical Dispositions: The Chinese Democracy Movement and Falun Gong," *Mobilization: An International Quarterly*, 19:3, 329–50.

Junker, Andrew. 2016. "Live Organ Harvesting in China: Falun Gong and Unsettled Rumor," *American Journal of Cultural Sociology*, 6:1, 1–29.

Kavan, Heather. 2005. "Print Media Coverage of Falun Gong in Australia and New Zealand," in Peter Horsfield (ed.), *Papers from the Trans-Tasman Research Symposium, "Emerging Research in Media, Religion and Culture."* Melbourne: RMIT Publishing, pp. 74–85.

Kavan, Heather. 2008. "Falun Gong in the Media: What Can We Believe?" ANZCA08 Conference, *Power and Place*, Wellington, NZ (July). https://www.massey.ac.nz/massey/fms/Colleges/College%20of%20Business/Communication%20and%20Journalism/ANZCA%202008/Refereed%20Papers/Kavan_ANZCA08.pdf (accessed May 27, 2015).

Keck, Margaret E., and Karen Sikkink. 1998. *Activists Beyond Borders: Advocacy Networks in International Politics.* Ithaca, NY: Cornell University Press.

Kilgour, David, and David Matas. 2006. "An Independent Investigation into Allegations of Organ Harvesting of Falun Gong Practitioners in China." http://www.david-kilgour.com/2006/Kilgour-Matas-organ-harvesting-rpt-July6-eng.pdf (accessed February 12, 2017).

Kilgour, David, and David Matas. 2009. *Bloody Harvest: The Killing of Falun Gong for Their Organs*. Niagara Falls, ON: Seraphim Editions.

Konigsberg, Eric. 2008. "A Glimpse of Chinese Culture That Some Find Hard to Watch," *New York Times*, February 26.
http://www.nytimes.com/2008/02/06/nyregion/06splendor.html?scp=1&sq=A+Glimpse+of+Chinese+Culture+That+Some+Find-+Hard+to+Watch&st=nyt (accessed June 5, 2015).

Lewis, James R. 2016. "Sucking the '*De*' out of Me: How an Esoteric Theory of Persecution and Martyrdom Fuels Falun Gong's Assault on Intellectual Freedom," *Alternative Spirituality and Religion Review*, 7:1, 93–109.
https://www.academia.edu/12926903/Sucking_the_De_Out_of_Me (accessed January 13, 2017).

Lewis, James R., and Nicole D'Amico. 2017. "Innocent Victims of Chinese Oppression, or Media Bullies? Falun Gong's In-Your-Face Media Strategies," *Alternative Spirituality and Religion Review*, 8:2, 219–36.

Li Hongzhi. 1998. "Digging Out the Roots."
http://en.falundafa.org/eng/jjyz72.htm (accessed June 20, 2016).

Li Hongzhi. 2002. "Touring North America to Teach the Fa." (March). http://www.falundafa.org/book/eng/na_lecture_tour.htm (accessed June 13, 2002).

Li Hongzhi. 2003. "Explaining the Fa during the 2003 Lantern Festival at the U.S. West Fa Conference," February 15.
http://en.minghui.org/html/articles/2003/3/21/33575.html
(accessed June 14, 2015).

Li Ruohan. 2017. "After Prisoner Organ Ban, Efforts Recognized Internationally But Challenges Remain," *Global Times*, February 14. http://www.globaltimes.cn/content/1032930.shtml (accessed February 25, 2017).

Mann, James. 1999. "Framing China," *Media Studies Journal: Covering China*, 13:1 (online).

Mackerras, Colin. 1999. *Western Images of China*. Rev. edition. New York: Oxford University Press.

Richardson, James T. 1996. "Journalistic Bias Towards New Religious Movements in Australia." *Journal of Contemporary Religion*, 11:3, 289–302.

Selway, Deborah. 1992. "Religion in the Mainstream Press: The Challenge for the Future," *Australian Religious Studies Review*, 5:2, 18–24.

Sheng Jiang. 2015. "Is Falun Gong's Wikipedia Page Objective?" https://www.quora.com/is-Falun-Gongs-Weikipedia-page-objective (accessed June 19, 2016).

Taylor, Verta, and Nella Van Dyke. 2004. "'Get up, Stand up': Tactical Repertoires of Social Movements," in David A. Snow, Sarah A. Soule, and Hanspeter Kriesi (eds.), *The Blackwell Companion to Social Movements*. Maden, MA: Blackwell Publishing, pp. 262–93.

Thornton, Patricia M. 2008. "Manufacturing Dissent in Transnational China," in Kevin J. O'Brien (ed.), *Popular Protest in China*. Cambridge, MA: Harvard University Press, pp. 179–204.

Tilly, Charles. 1994. "Contentious Repertoires in Great Britain," in Mark Traugott (ed.), *Repertoires and Cycles of Collective Action*. Durham, NC: Duke University Press, pp. 15–42.

Zhao Yuezhi. 2003. "Falun Gong, Identity, and the Struggle over Meaning Inside and Outside China," in Nick Couldry and James Curran (eds.), *Contesting Media Power: Alternative Media in a Networked World*. Lanham, MD: Rowman & Littlefield Publishers, pp. 209–26.

James R. Lewis is a much-published researcher in the field of new religious movements, and is Professor of Philosophy at the School of Philosophy, Wuhan University, China. At present, he edits or co-edits four academic book series, and is the general editor for the *Alternative Spirituality and Religion Review*, and Associate Editor of the *Journal of Religion and Violence*. Recent publications include *New Age in Norway* (Equinox, 2017), *Cambridge Companion to Religion and Terrorism* (Cambridge University Press, 2017), and *Oxford Handbook of New Religious Movements* (Oxford University Press, 2016).

Index

1.23 Incident 1, 4, 72, 85–104, 203
  CNN reports 91–2
  False Fire 88, 92
  Falung Gong's analysis 91–2, 93–5, 203
  government response 88–9, 92
  media campaign 92
  motivation 93, 95, 98–100
  as propaganda 89, 92
  survivors' accounts 86, 87, 88, 98
  see also martyrdom; self-immolation

Abhidharma 131
abjuration 131–3
academic freedom
  attacks on 6–7, 195–209, 218–19, 221–2, 241
  definition of 196
  in higher education 196–8
accommodation strategy 27
activism 22–6, 239–40
  apocalyptic ideology and 2, 62, 63, 70–1, 78, 97, 98–9
  directions in the protest movement 76–80
  letter-writing campaign 22, 197
  Li Hongzhi and 22, 23, 25–6, 61
  mobilization capacity 3, 24, 27, 35, 97
  as necessary for salvation 26
  philosophy of protest 76
  sit-in protests 23–4
  see also civil disobedience; demonstrations
aliens 3, 6, 138, 160–91
  alien cell layer in human body 42, 168, 171, 172–3, 175–6, 177–8, 186, 188
  anachronistic artifacts and 183–4, 185
  cloning of humans 165, 173, 174, 175–6, 186, 188–9
  communication with 168
  computers and 42, 164, 168, 173, 182
  conference lectures 166–84
  fa-rectification and 77, 179–80
  in FLG literature 165–6, 183
  as humans from past Earths 138, 169, 177, 185
  Industrial Revolution and 172–3, 186
  Li's 1999 *Time* interview 162–5, 184
  mixing of races and 170–1, 188
  science and 37, 41–2, 151, 160, 164, 167, 168, 172, 174–5, 178, 186, 187

technology and 164, 169–70, 181–3
UFOs/flying saucers 138, 143–4, 166, 170, 182, 185, 187–8
"Almighty God" group 110
altered states of consciousness 54
Amnesty International 90n., 247, 248
ancestor worship 44, 51
animal demons 44, 51
apocalyptic ideology 16, 77
   civil disobedience and 2, 62, 63, 70–1, 78, 97, 98
   emergence of 71–6
   moral corruption and 40–4
   universal cycles (*kalpas*) 3, 37, 40–1
Aum Shinrikyo 19–20, 207
authoritarianism 19, 28, 29

Baconianism 144n.
banning of Falun Gong 20, 21, 25, 27, 100, 142
Beijing Television (BTV) 22, 23, 249
Bell, Mark R. 247
Biglino, Mauro 187
black matter 45, 67, 198
Boas, Taylor C. 247
Bondurant, J. V. 225
Branch Davidians 80
broadcast media 255
   Beijing Television (BTV) 22, 23, 249
   New Tang Dynasty TV 88, 92, 247
   Sound of Hope radio 247
Bruderhof, the 197
Buddha 17, 131, 132–3

Maitreya 40n.
Sakyamuni 40, 48, 72n., 102
Buddha dharma (*fo-fa*) 136, 140
Buddha-nature 45, 116, 147
Buddhism 16, 48, 50, 51, 120, 123, 198
   Abhidharma text 131
   on abjuration 131–2
   on attainment/gaining 131
   choice and 132–3
   Jataka Tales 102
   Lotus Sutra 102
   Mahayana Buddhism 102
   self-immolations 102–3
   universal cycles 3, 37, 40–1, 72
Buddhist Association of China 21

censorship 249
Chen Guo 87, 94, 98, 99
Chen Zhao 77–8
Chen Zixiu 77–8
China in Perspective webpage 204–6
Chinese Daily 250–1
Christianity 48, 50, 144n., 156, 197
civil disobedience
   apocalyptic ideology and 2, 62, 63, 70–1, 78, 97, 98–9
   deaths due to 4
   see also activism; demonstrations
clarifying the truth 3, 27, 29, 236
cloning of humans 165, 173, 174, 175–6, 186, 188–9
commitment 4, 63, 64, 232
common people
   devils and 4, 5, 115–23, 124, 157
   eradication of 116

FLG practitioners compared with 116–18
medicine and 51
scientists as 150
value of 122, 123
worthlessness of 121–2
Communist Party of China (CCP) 19
alleged mass renunciations of 251, 256
FLG as anti-CCP movement 8, 26, 28, 36, 230, 235
FLG as ideological challenge 3, 24, 27
Guangming Daily 20
Li's criticism of 25–6
United Front Work Department 21–2
computers, aliens and 42, 164, 168, 173, 182
Confucius/Confucianism 42, 143
Confucius Institute 201, 204, 207
consummation 1, 69–70, 232
individual 61, 65, 72, 77
martyrdom and 72–3, 77, 79, 98, 100, 101, 246
conversion 4, 64
apocalyptic vision 70–1
fa-rectification 70–1
four-phase process 64, 65–71
healing 66–8
moral reform 65, 67, 68
ritual testimonial 64
seven-step model 64
spiritual salvation 69–70
cosmic battle 4, 73, 74
cosmology 19, 66, 79, 139
crackdown on Falun Gong 1, 19, 24–5, 27–9, 60, 62n., 72, 85
banning 20, 21, 25, 27, 100, 142

see also persecution of Falun Gong
Crichton, Michael 188
crime 43, 151n.
cult, FLG as 36, 134n., 207, 241–2
cultivation 1, 14, 15, 17, 73, 123–4, 232, 238
aim of 61, 75, 78
aliens and 181
common people and 121
devils and 114–15, 117–20
family members and 239
karma/sickness and 66, 117, 126–7
man-woman dual cultivation 101, 138
practices 63, 66, 81, 126
sickness and 127–8
steadfast cultivation 22–3
Cultural Revolution 11, 38, 42

Dai Nan 112
D'Amico, Nicole 254
Daoism 16, 46, 48, 50
Darwin, Charles 136, 183
see also evolution theory
deaths
civil disobedience and 4
in custody 72
refusal of medical treatment 56
see also martyrdom
demons 44, 50, 51, 56, 73, 74, 81, 182
see also devils
demonstrations 20, 22, 23, 80
mobilization capacity 3, 24, 27, 35, 97
sit-in protests 23–4
Tiananmen Square 56, 62, 73

Zhongnanhai (1999) 16, 23–4, 27, 35, 97, 246
  see also activism; civil disobedience; self-immolation
devil-killing 4–5, 110–24
  categories of victims 110–13
  Li's justification of 123
devils
  characteristics of 113–15
  common people and 4, 5, 115–23, 124, 157
  creation of 118–19
  cultivation and 114–15, 117–20
  definition of 115–20
  possession by 112, 113, 119–20
  transformation into 120
  see also demons
disease, *see* illness
Dolly the Sheep 188
Dowell, William Thatcher, 1999 *Time* interview 162–5

enlightenment, *see* consummation
Epoch Times, The 232, 241, 244, 247, 255, 256
  favorable exposure in 240
  organ harvesting claims 253, 254
  the "truth" in 237
Ethnic Affairs Committee (China) 21
evolution theory 136, 137, 149–50, 183
exclusivity/exclusivism 3, 7, 38, 50, 157
Experience Sharing Conferences 60, 64, 70, 75, 78, 81–2
extraterrestrials, *see* aliens
eyes 139, 141

fa 7–8, 12, 72, 74, 140

fa-rectification 4, 61, 63, 70–1, 82
  aliens and 177, 179–80
  meaning of 79
  as path to salvation 73
  Facts on Falun Gong website 90–1, 248
False Fire (Falun Gong video) 88, 92
falun 69
Falun Gong Research Society (FGRS) 11, 12
  assistant centers 18
  withdrawal from QSRAC 15
family life 68, 203, 238–9
Farley, Helen 88–9, 96, 97, 99, 139, 154n.
Flanagan, Richard 213
flying saucers, *see* UFOs/flying saucers
fo-fa (Buddha dharma) 48, 136, 140
forbearance 20
forbidden practices 3, 38, 50–1, 52, 153, 155, 239
forced organ harvesting, *see* organ harvesting
Ford, C. 209
Friends of Falun Gong 222
Fu Yibin 122

Galileo 183
Gan, Barry 225
Gandhi 62, 78, 225
  Li compared to 7
  satyagraha 62, 73, 82
Garfinkel, Simson L. 248
Gould, Steven Jay 157
Great Dharma 46, 48, 51
Great Law of the universe 3, 25, 36, 38, 48, 56, 77

Guan Shuyun 112
guanding (purification of karma) 65, 67, 69–70
Guangming Daily 20–1, 22
gymnastic forms 49–50, 54

Hammer, Olav 144n.
Hand, Judge Learned 197
Hangzhou 20
Hao Huijun 87
He Zuoxin 197
He Zuoxiu 20, 22, 23
healing 11, 12, 66–8
heavenly eyes 139, 141
Heaven's Gate 80
Helvey, Robert 222–5
homophobia in Falun Gong 239, 245
Huang Daisheng 111, 112
Hubbard, Lafayette Ronald 187
human rights 7, 25, 62, 78, 89, 130–3, 207, 245

Icke, David 187
illness 6, 44, 51–2, 56
  elimination of bad karma 5, 47, 52, 127–8
  karma and 5, 47, 51, 52, 67, 125–8
  Li's statements about 5, 67, 125–30
    as abuse of human rights 130–3
    contradictions in 128–30
  medicine and 5, 44, 51–2, 56
  restoration of bad karma 5, 128–30
Inborn Mother 40n.
International Federation of Qigong Sciences 19

internet 76n., 81, 221
  China in Perspective webpage 204–6
  Facts on Falun Gong website 90–1, 248
  FLG websites 98, 203, 232, 246–7, 251
  Wikipedia manipulation 90n., 219–20, 247–8
Isenman, Lois 214

Jesus 51
Jian Xiaojun 100
Jiang Zemin 25, 61, 63, 72, 74, 75, 81
Jianguo Wu 202–6, 208
Johnson, Ian 26
Junker, Andrew 254–5
Jurassic Park (film) 188

kalpas, see universal cycles
karma 20, 89, 225
  black matter 45, 67, 198
  cultivation and 127
  elimination of bad karma 5, 47, 52, 127–8
  illness and 5, 47, 51, 52, 67, 125–8
  karmic debts 20, 44, 45, 47, 51
  martyrdom and 75, 100
  organ failure and 235
  purification of (*guanding*) 44–5, 65, 67, 69–70
  restoration of bad karma 5, 128–30
  white matter 45, 55
Kavan, Heather 197, 206, 244–5, 249
Kilgour, David 252

Index 265

Lanford, M. 196
Laozi 48
Law of the universe, *see* Great Law of the universe
Law Wheel 11
Lei Feng 42
letter-writing campaign 22, 197
Lewis, James 144n., 198, 200, 201, 205, 221
Li Hongzhi 60–1, 66
  1.23 Incident and 7, 100
  birth 11, 17
  career in China 11–12
  control of followers 130–1
  doctrine of 35–57
  early life 46
  emigration to USA 1, 21
  martyrs and 1, 72–3, 74, 75, 100
  as messiah/savior 3, 17, 38, 46–9
  supernatural powers 3, 17, 38, 46, 154
  writings, *see* writings of Li Hongzhi
Li Yuandong 112
Liu Baorong 87
Liu Chunling 87
Liu Siying 87, 93, 95
Liu Yunfang 86, 87, 97
local governments 24
Lofland, John 64
Lotus Sutra 102
Luo Guili 96

McEoin, Denis 197
Mahayana Buddhism 102
Maitreya 40n.
Mann, James 245
martyrdom 1–2, 3, 99–100, 223

consummation and 72–3, 77, 79, 98, 100, 101, 246
karma and 75, 100
Li and 1, 72–3, 74, 75, 100
as mass suicide 81
see also 1.23 Incident; suicide
Matas, David 252
media
  1.23 Incident 91–2
  attacks on critical media 248–51
  boomerang effect 255
  censorship 249
  defamation actions 250–1
  FLG strategy 8, 207, 232, 233, 242, 246–55
  lawsuits 250–1
  manufacturing dissent 255–6
  monitoring of 218
  radio/television, *see* broadcast media
  state-controlled 12, 19, 20–1
  threat of lawsuits 251
  Western media 216, 236, 240, 242, 245–6, 247
  see also internet; newspapers
medicine 5, 44, 51–2, 56, 126
  refusal of treatment 239
  see also illness
meditation 38, 49, 50, 54, 73, 215
messiah/savior, Li Hongzhi as 3, 17, 38, 46–9
MH370 airplane tragedy 236
Milky Way 48
Ministry of Civil Affairs (MCA) 19
Ministry of Public Security (MPS) 12, 19, 21
mixing of races 51, 170–1, 188
mixing of traditions 40n., 50

mobilization capacity 3, 24, 27, 35, 97
moral reform (*xinxing*) 65, 67, 68, 79, 81
mothers 238, 239

National People's Congress 21
New Age Western literature 188
New Tang Dynasty TV 88, 92, 247
newspapers
  apologies from 23
  articles 19, 20, 21
  Chinese Daily 250–1
  defamation actions 250–1
  Guangming Daily 20–1, 22
  letter-writing campaign 22
  New York Times 251
  News Weekly 202, 203–4
  People's Daily 98, 248
  Presse Chinoise, La 250
  threat of lawsuits 251
  see also Epoch Times, The
Ngo Dinh Diem 102
Noakes, S. 209
nonviolent resistance 20, 62, 225
  principled 225
  tactical 225, 226
Nostradamus 25, 72, 81
number of FLG practitioners/followers 18, 35

oral tradition 76
organ harvesting 8, 195, 198, 221, 230–43
  anti-China comments 231, 236
  FLG promotion of controversy 251–4
  FLG "research" 236–7, 242, 252–3
  investigation of claims 230, 234, 252–3
  MH370 airplane tragedy 236
organ transplantation
  donation system 233
  from executed prisoners 230, 231, 233, 251–2
  international engagement 235–6, 242, 243
organization of Falun Gong 232–3
  cultivators 232, 235, 238, 240
  leaders 232–3, 235, 237–8
  mobilization capacity 3, 24, 27, 35, 97
  political activism 239–40
  practitioners 232, 235, 239–40
  tiers 232–3
Oriental Health Exposition 12
Ownby, David 60, 61, 63, 64, 66, 189, 220
ozone layer 172

Palmer, David 13, 18n.
Palmer, Mark 222
Palmer, Susan 100
Pan Guoyan 21
paranormal powers 11, 39, 47
Penny, Benjamin 188, 189, 220
People's Temple 80
persecution of Falun Gong 1, 8, 56, 61, 207
  spiritual benefits of 75, 246
  see also activism; crackdown on Falun Gong; demonstrations
pets 51
pineal gland 139, 141
Plato 214, 226
political activism, see activism
political movement, Falun Gong as 2–3, 19–27, 28, 29, 250

Porter, Noah 52n.
possession by devils 112, 113, 119–20
Presse Chinoise, La (*Chinese Press*) 250
protest, *see* activism
pseudoscience 19, 20, 29, 39
psychological warfare 225, 226
psychosis 19, 22, 215, 216

qi 11, 13, 14, 52
qigong 38–9, 55
   crackdown on 19–20, 24–5
   FLG differentiated from 13–15, 56
   as healing practice 11–12, 66–7
   as pseudoscience 20, 29, 39
   qigong fever 57, 141–2, 143
   as science 11, 13, 21, 39, 55, 142–3
   as social event 142
   as spiritual practice 13–14
   state approval 2, 11, 14, 28, 38
Qigong Science Research Society of China (QSRAC) 12, 14, 15, 21, 56
Qing dynasty 57

Rachlin, Gail 247
Rachlin media group 247
racism 239, 245
   see also mixing of races
radio, *see* broadcast media
Raël (Claude Vorilhon) 187, 188
Rapport, Jeremy 144n., 145–6
re-education facilities 238
repression of Falun Gong 37, 56, 246
   steadfastness in the face of 42–3, 53, 56

Rubin, Julius H. 197
rumor-spreading 224
Russell, Terence 204

Sakyamuni Buddha 40, 48, 102
sarin gas attack 20
Sartre, Jean-Paul 214
satyagraha 62, 73, 82
science 5–6, 51
   aliens and 37, 41–2, 151, 160, 164, 167, 168, 172, 174–5, 178, 186, 187
   Baconianism 144n.
   ban on scientific discussions 153
   empirical proofs 137–8, 189
   as enemy of morality 3, 42, 135
   evolution theory 136, 137, 149–50, 183
   FLG scientific discourse 6, 136–8
   origins of 141–5
   para-scientific discourse 139–40
   sci-fi discourse 138, 143–4
   "super-science" 135, 136, 139, 140, 144, 145, 148–9, 152–3
   types of 135–41
   moral degeneration and 42, 151, 167
   pseudoscience 19, 20, 29, 39
   qigong and 11, 13, 21, 39, 55, 142–3
   as religion 151–2
   as source of legitimation 134–5, 145–55
   status in Chinese culture 144
   as truth 144–5
science fiction 138, 143–4, 188
scientific socialism 145

Scientology 80–1, 198, 251
sectarian practice 3, 38, 49–53
self-defence 62, 74, 82
self-immolation 95–6, 100–3
  Buddhists 102–3
  see also 1.23 Incident
Sendy, Jean 187
sexism 43, 220, 245
Shen Yuzhen 111
Sima Nan 20
singers 43
sit-in protests 23–4
Solar Temple 80
Sound of Hope radio 247
Spielberg, Steven 188
spiritual discipline 3, 37–8, 44–6, 47, 50
spiritual emergencies 215
spiritual group, FLG as 13–19, 28–9
spiritual salvation, see consummation
Stark, Rodney 64
suicide 80–1, 89, 95–7, 100–1
  in labor camps/reeducation centers 96
  mass suicide 80–1, 96
  as political protest 101–2, 103
  religious suicide 102–3
  self-immolation 95–6, 101–3
  as a sin 92
  see also 1.23 Incident; martyrdom
suicide cults 80
Sujiatun Thrombosis Hospital 253
supernatural powers 3, 38, 46, 142, 154, 183
superstition 21, 29, 42, 140, 152, 167

Taiping Rebellion 24, 57
Tan Yihui 96
Tang dynasty 40
Tang Shuling 112
technology
  aliens and 164, 169–70, 181–3
  ban on use of 153–4
television, see broadcast media
Thich Quang Duc 102
Thornton, Patricia M. 220, 255, 256
Tiananmen Square
  1989 incident 14
  demonstrations 56, 62, 73
  self-immolation incidents (2001), see 1.23 Incident
Tianjin demonstrations (1999) 16
Tierney, W. G. 196
torture 75, 77–8, 96, 216
truth, benevolence, forbearance (*zhen-shan-ren*) 16, 45, 53, 68, 146–7
truth clarification campaign 3, 27, 29, 236

UFOs/flying saucers 138, 143–4, 166, 170, 182, 185, 187–8
  see also aliens
ugliness 43
United Front Work Department 21–2
universal cycles (*kalpas*) 3, 37, 40–1, 72

victim status 8, 233, 236, 237, 241
Vietnam 102
Vorilhon, Claude (Raël) 187, 188

Wang Anshou 111

Wang Jindong 87, 93–4, 97, 98
Wang Lun 40
websites, *see* internet
Wei Zhihua 112
Weller, Robert P. 28
White Lotus rebellion 24
white matter 45, 55
Wikipedia manipulation 90n., 219–20, 247–8
Williams, Philip F. 62n.
women's liberation 43
writings of Li Hongzhi 36–7
  apocalyptic theme 3, 37, 40–4, 72
  exegesis 76
  Falun Dafa: Essentials for Further Advancement 146–7, 150n.
  Falun Gong – Essentials of Diligence 129–30
  messianic theme 3, 38, 46–9
  reading of 16, 36, 48
  as sacred scriptures 36
  sectarian practice 3, 38, 49–53
  spiritual discipline 3, 37–8, 44–6, 47, 50
  textual analysis 76
  Zhuan Falun, *see Zhuan Falun*
Wu Deqiao 110–11
Wu, Harry (Wu Hongda) 252, 253–4, 256

Wu, Yenna 62n.

X-Files, The 188
xinxing (moral reform) 65, 67, 68, 79, 81
Xu Hongru 40

Yan Xin 66
Yiguandao 40n.
yin and *yang* 43
Yuan Runtian 111–12

Zhang Kunlun 61–2
Zhao Yuezhi 249
zhen-shan-ren (truth, benevolence, forbearance) 16, 45, 53, 68, 146–7
Zhongnanhai demonstrations (1999) 16, 23–4, 27, 35, 97, 246
Zhuan Falun 15–19, 48, 65, 66
  aliens 138, 182, 183
  described as pseudoscience 20–1
  on hardship 20
  number of copies sold 18
  as primary scripture 15–16, 36, 65
  reading of 16, 48, 49, 67
  science and 134, 136, 137, 140
  theological system 16

www.ingramcontent.com/pod-product-compliance
Lightning Source LLC
Chambersburg PA
CBHW050843230426
43667CB00012B/2124